The Tropic of Baseball
Baseball in the Dominican Republic

Rob Ruck

with a new afterword by the author

UNIVERSITY OF NEBRASKA PRESS
LINCOLN AND LONDON

Library of Congress Cataloging-in-Publication Data
Ruck, Rob, 1950–
The tropic of baseball: baseball in the Dominican Republic / Rob Ruck.
p.   cm.
Originally published: Westport, Ct.: Meckler, c1990, in series: Baseball and American society.
Includes index.
ISBN 0-8032-8978-2 (pbk.: alk. paper)
1. Baseball—Dominican Republic—History.   I. Title.
GV863.29.A1D657   1999
796.357′097293—dc21
98-45479   CIP

The author gratefully acknowledges the permission of the following publishers to republish parts of articles originally written for them. These include: Warner Books for "Baseball in the Caribbean," from *Total Baseball* (1989); *Baseball America* for "Winter Ball in Crisis," from the February 25, 1990, issue; *Pittsburgh Magazine* for a story on Tony Peña, from the April 1986 issue; *Américas* (the bimonthly magazine published by the General Secretariat of the Organization of American States) for "*El Beisbol en el Caribe*," from the September/October 1986 issue; *Urban Resources* for "A Celebration of Sport: Baseball, Race, and Community in San Pedro de Macoris," in the Spring 1989 issue; and *Scarboro Missions* for "The Boys of Winter," from the February 1989 issue.

Reprinted from the original 1991 edition by Meckler Publishing, Westport CT.

For Maggie and Alex

Contents

Foreword

I first journeyed south in the summer of 1972 with a traveling companion, Paul Boas, who guided me through this incredibly diverse region with an infectious enthusiasm for its physical splendor and peoples. Since then, I've returned as often as I could. In 1980, while writing about black Pittsburgh sport, I traveled to Cuba and the Dominican Republic to investigate Latin ball's connection to the Negro Leagues. I went back to the Dominican Republic in 1984 and have since spent about six months there and elsewhere in the Caribbean basin.

Branch B. Rickey opened the gates to winter baseball for me in 1984, and Winston Llenas and Tony Peña showed me what was inside. Critical support came in the form of a Research Grant from the Latin American and Caribbean Division of the Social Science Research Council and a Summer Stipend from the National Endowment for the Humanities. Richard Smethurst, Reid Andrews, James Barrett, Laird Bergad, Richard Blackett, Preston Covey, John Modell, David Montgomery, Mitchell Seligson, and Jules Tygiel provided indispensable guidance in obtaining these grants. The Center for Latin American Studies and the Pittsburgh Social History Center offered a scholarly haven.

Jenny and Sean Barrett, David Bear, Bruce Calder, Doron Levin, Peter Levine, Martin Murphy, Michael O'Neal, and Jon Scher critiqued the manuscript or helped in the research. Charles Schwartz and John Krich came along for part of the ride while Jay Reifer and Ken Boas lent me their thoughts on the trails of Frick Park. Faith Hamlin, my agent, steered the project along the way and Miguel Sague translated many of the Spanish-language interviews, uncovering meaning I would have otherwise lost. Mark Cohen dissected the manuscript from his worksite on the coast of Malaysia and shared his thoughts with me later when we toured the peninsula to begin the decade.

To say that I was treated graciously and accorded undeserved respect while in the Dominican Republic would be understating it. I am especially thankful to the Rev. Joseph Ainslie, Manuel Joaquín Báez Vargas, Roberto Caines, Cuqui Cordova, Leonel Fernández, Tito Hernández, Lucretia Mota, Pedro Julio Santana, and Bernardo Vega for their help and friendship while in Canada and the Dominican Republic. They also evaluated a draft of the manuscript and saved me from innumerable cross-cultural blunders. Countless other Dominicans went out of their way to help me in ways that I'll never forget.

Maggie Patterson and Alex Ruck accompanied me on these tropical research excursions and are no worse for the wear. As usual, Maggie subjected my writing to its most rigorous editing, while Alex, our son, kept matters in perspective. I'm counting on many more trips with them in the years ahead.

Fall 1990

Introduction: Los Muchachos of Winter

Ankle deep in the waters off Punta Garza, Cruzibal Bryant hits porous chunks of coral into the Caribbean. Sending his driftwood bat skimming in the direction of the late afternoon sun, the Dominican youth picks a tattered mitt off the beach, shrugs his way into a tee-shirt, and heads for the road leading to San Pedro de Macoris.

Like *muchachos* throughout the United States and the Caribbean basin, Cruzibal Bryant's game is baseball. But his is much more than the summer game. For after the World Series marks season's end in the United States, baseball springs back to life in and around the Caribbean. There, against a backdrop of orange and purple skies and to the rhythms of *salsa* and *merengue,* some of the best baseball in the world is played each winter. From its southernmost perimeter in Barquisimeto, Venezuela, through Cuba, Puerto Rico, and the Dominican Republic, and into parts of Mexico and Central America, baseball is played with an intensity that goes beyond mere passion. "It's more than a game," Dominican manager Winston Llenas told me during my first visit to winter ball in 1984, "it's a national fever. Here, in the Dominican Republic, it's almost a way of life."

Nowhere is that more evident than on Hispaniola, the island that the Spanish-speaking, baseball-playing Dominican Republic shares with French-speaking, soccer-playing Haiti. This republic of 6,000,000 has spearheaded the Latin infusion of talent into the major leagues since the early 1960s.

And if the Dominican Republic has become the epicenter of Caribbean baseball, San Pedro de Macoris is its Mecca. It is to this port of about 100,000 people on the southeastern end of the island that Cruzibal Bryant now makes his way.

The *café-au-lait*–colored boy walks along a rutted dirt road that parallels the beach. Italian, German, and Canadian tourists, their skin glistening with cocoa-scented oils and their breath heavy with rum, wander the grounds of pastel-painted, stucco-walled hotels and cabanas that sit on both sides of the road. Refugees from winter, they sprawl by pools and amble through the waves.

Another group of refugees labors nearby, completing the hotels that are fast making this beachfront strip into a cosmopolitan tourist center. These ebony-skinned emigrés are from Haiti, whose lowest-per capita income in the Western Hemisphere has been made even worse by the chronic political instability and violence of recent years. A few of the Haitians glance at the tourists from time to time, before returning to the dawn-to-dusk work which brings them about three dollars a day. These Haitians are the lucky ones. Their less fortunate brethren cut cane for wages they often never collect and live in squalid barracks in the canefields.

Cruzibal ducks through a fence into one of the construction sites and grins at a young Haitian girl tending a fire alongside the plywood shed where the workers sleep at night. The girl speaks to him in a patois before halting in embarrassment when she realizes that Cruzibal does not understand her. She then giggles at the boy, who waves and exits through the gate on the backside of the site.

Reaching the highway that leads into San Pedro, Cruzibal crouches in the shadow of a billboard advertising *Presidente* beer. Flagging down a slow-moving cane truck that bears the logo of the state-run Santa Fé sugar mill, he climbs onto the truck's bed and stands, precariously balanced, as the driver heads to town. The truck breezes by boys on horse-drawn carts and pink and green wooden shanties with corrugated sheeting roofs. Roadside stands offer *cocos fríos* and young girls shake clusters of slowly writhing crabs at passing motorists.

The smokestacks of the sugar mills encircling San Pedro are visible on the horizon and the vinegarish smell of refining sugar wafts over the boy as the truck crosses the bridge into town. Off to the right stand the late nineteenth century remnants of San Pedro, once the economic and cultural entrepôt of this Caribbean island. To the left, along the banks of the *Río Higuamo,* sits an array of ramshackle habitations.

The truckdriver taps his horn to scatter a crowd of pedicabs and circles the rotary as he heads toward *Ingenio* Santa Fé, a sugar mill on the other side of the town. Cruzibal jumps off the back of the truck as it pauses by the traffic light next to the stadium, yells his thanks to the driver, and strides toward the park.

Outside the state-built and -supported *Estadio Tetelo Vargas,* women barbecue chicken and deep fry pastries on braziers made from fifty gallon barrels. A boy peels oranges with a makeshift device that skins the fruit in a matter of seconds. Another hawks the caps of the six Dominican teams, while still others sell Chiclets, cigarettes, and candies from a display case mounted on the front fender of a battered bicycle.

Cruzibal pauses long enough to buy a few slices of fried plantain before heading toward a nearby soccer field usurped by a dozen young boys playing baseball. Cruzibal watches the game and jokes with a young boy, perhaps three years old, and naked except for a dingy pair of underpants, who stands nearby, swinging a two-foot-long piece of cane at imaginary pitches. His coiled torso with hands held cocked could very well be the Dominican national stance. Insinuating himself into the infield, Cruzibal deftly nabs an erratically-hopping groundball and throws to first in time to retire the barefooted runner. Playing just long enough to get a chance at the plate, Cruzibal bids a few of the other boys farewell and walks to the back of the stadium.

There, he shimmies up a palm tree, from which he lightly jumps to the top of the left field wall. He is not alone. About fifty boys, many equipped with long poles with nets affixed at the end, sit along the fence, shouting to the *peloteros* (ballplayers) below. A few snare errant balls as players from the *Estrellas Orientales* (Eastern Stars) of San Pedro and the *Aguilas Cibaeñas* (Eagles of the Cibao) from Santiago go through their pre-game rituals. Three boys with connections to the *Estrellas* shag flies in the outfield alongside the professionals they hope to one day emulate.

Players take turns darting in and out of the batting cage to get in their swings, while others talk to young girls and boys through the screen behind the backstop. Along one foul line, *Aguilas* pitching coach Juan Jiménez puts a half dozen teenagers through a tryout, patiently offering instructions and a few words of encouragement. Nearby, his pitching staff, a mix of young Dominican and North American minor leaguers, sprints from one foul pole to the other, before jogging back and repeating the process. They are, with the exception of Cecilio Guante, a major leaguer and the *Aguilas'* top reliever, lathered in sweat. The lanky Guante lags behind, listening to a different drummer.

Alfredo Griffin, the graceful All-Star shortstop who plays for the Los Angeles Dodgers during the summer and the *Estrellas* in the winter, stretches in the outfield grass. Tony Peña, the St. Louis Cardinals' catcher, who anchors the *Aguilas,* sneaks up behind him, lifting Griffin off the ground and swinging him in circles before collapsing to the ground and convulsing in laughter. They sit in the grass, the sun down but the sky still a Maxfield Parrish painting, a couple of millionaires in a nation mired in poverty.

Shortly their repose is broken by the demands of the local media, and Peña walks off to answer questions he could by now field in his sleep. The boys on the fence hover above Peña and his interrogator, straining to hear their demigod speak. When asked about the future of Dominican baseball, the solidly built catcher gestures to the boys on the fence. "You see these boys, they are the future. One of them might be in the big leagues some day. *Cabeza,*" he says, referring to Toronto Blue Jays All-Star shortstop Tony Fernández, "lived just behind that wall when he was young and he used to be up there every night just like them. He still climbs over the fence when he comes here to play. Those boys see him and they know it's possible for them, too."

The interview concludes by focusing on the difficulties Peña's Cardinals have encountered since their defeat in the seventh game of the 1987 World Series and the off years a number of prominent Dominicans have experienced recently. Reversing his cap, Peña smiles almost apologetically for such serious talk about the game for which he cares so much, and with a wave to his young compatriots atop the wall, trots off to join a game of flip by the dugout.

A dozen *Aguilas* players and San Pedro's Griffin have formed a loose circle and whack the ball back and forth with their glove hand. A miss or a ball stuck in the glove and you're out.

Moving into the center of the game, Peña quickly goes *mano a mano* with the lone U.S. import playing, Bennie Distefano, a Brooklyn native more than a thousand miles from home. The rapid play highlights the Dominicans' dexterity, and Distefano soon is relegated to the sidelines.

With the *gringo* gone, the players focus on Peña, and the agile Griffin sends him toppling onto his rump. Peña's teammates whoop in delight and Peña's protestations belie his happiness at being here in his baseball haven, playing for the team he listened to on the radio as he fell asleep as a boy.

The game breaks up as the managers bring their lineups to home plate and confer with the umpires. Griffin and his San Pedro teammates take their positions on the field and remove their caps as a scratchy rendition of the Dominican national anthem momentarily brings the otherwise frenetic crowd to a pause. Even the boys on the fence stand, their poles held aloft like lances. When the tune comes to its triumphant conclusion, the boys jump off the wall and disappear into the streets behind. Most will insinuate themselves into the ballpark by one means or another before the night is through. Cruzibal retreats to the palm tree by the right field foul pole, draping himself over a convenient hump in the trunk from which he will not budge until game's end.

Firecrackers explode behind the bleachers and a *merengue* band snakes its way through the stands. Women sell rum and an array of delicacies while bettors wager on every conceivable aspect of the game. A little boy in a torn Mickey Mouse tee-shirt shuffles through the dugouts, offering *negritos,* thimble-sized cups of strong, sweetened coffee, to the players. Despite these diversions, the *fanáticos* follow their baseball closely. Generally more knowledgeable about the game than their counterparts in the States, they are quick to let the players know it, especially if they detect a lack of hustle.

The dugout reflects the multiracial, bilingual melange that has long made winter ball a proving grounds for interracial sport. During the decades when major league ball in the United States was segregated by race, many Negro Leaguers as well as white major leaguers came south to compete with and against each other in the Latin leagues. Nowadays, the flow is both ways.

In the third inning, Griffin does a reasonable imitation of Michael Jordan, soaring to take a hit away from Miguel Diloné, the Charlie Hustle of winter ball.

"He was the first to start the running game here," *Aguilas* manager Winston Llenas says of Diloné. Now in his mid-thirties, Diloné broke the Dominican record for stolen bases in each of his first three years and led the league in stolen bases ten of his first twelve years.

"Once he gets on first," coach Luis Silverio adds, "he's hungry to get to the next base. He loves to get dirty."

Perhaps it's the strut with which he leads off first, or maybe it's that scraggly mustache he has. Whatever the reason, the fans love to ride him. The night before in Santiago, Diloné cracked his 800th and 801st career hits, passing Manny Mota for third place overall in the Dominican League. Only San Pedro coach Rafael Batista and Jesús Alou are left for Diloné to overtake and he will catch up with both by the final game of the next season.

In the stands behind the San Pedro dugout, Rico Carty, a tall, muscular man with shiny black and thick curly hair makes his way to his seat, his progress repeatedly halted by fans who insist on shaking his hand and exchanging *"Felicidades,"* the customary Dominican New Year's greeting. In the 1950s, after baseball's color line ended and the Cuban Revolution removed that island from orbit around the major leagues, the Dominican Republic emerged as the chief source of Latin talent. Carty, the child of mill workers in Consuelo, a sugar mill town ten kilometers north of San Pedro, was part of that current. The grandson of St. Martin islanders, Carty's play at the 1959 Pan American Games dazzled major league clubs. When nine of them offered him a chance to play pro ball, Carty accepted them all. "I just go ahead and sign cause all I want to do is play baseball," he later recounts. "I get the baseball in my blood and I keep on signing."

After Rico, who wound up with the Braves, came a score of major leaguers from Consuelo, and San Pedro's other mill towns, Angelina, Santa Fe, Cristóbal Colón, Quisqueya, and Porvenir.

A tall thin man in his late twenties slides into the seat next to Carty and shakes his hand. Andy Caines is a mechanic at the Consuelo mill as well as a sometimes student in engineering at the *Universidad Central del Este* in San Pedro. He lives in Guachupita, the same *barrio* where Carty was raised, in a small company-owned house in the compound where his father, Roberto, also resides. When Carty was a youth, Roberto Caines and the other sporting elders of Guachupita nurtured baseball with a devoted stewardship. Speaking in a Caribbean-accented English, the language of many of Consuelo's mill workers, Andy Caines relays information about a league his father still runs to Carty, one of its principal sponsors. Business conducted, the two men shake again, and Andy goes to his seat in the bleachers.

In the fifth, San Pedro takes a 2–0 lead and threatens to score more. Peña and Llenas, a coach with the Blue Jays during the summer, go to the mound where Billy Fultz, a class AAA pitcher in the Mets organization, is tiring. Llenas, fighting for a play-off spot, has seen enough and signals for Larry Acker, a minor-league free agent from Meadville, Pennsylvania, while Fultz storms off the mound. He disappears into the locker room. No one says a word to him. Nor does anyone see him again.

Fultz exits the stadium before the end of the game, drives back to Santiago by himself, and with his bride of a few weeks, leaves the island, without saying *adiós* to his teammates. Some North Americans never make their peace with winter ball. Others, like Distefano and Acker, who speaks fluent Spanish, seem to thrive in the different milieu.

Acker allows the runner on third to score via a sacrifice but retires Griffin to end the inning.

Peña paces back and forth in the dugout, exhorting his teammates, "*Vamonos, coños*! Let's go!" A double and a single that even a leaping Griffin cannot reach produce one run. Then, little Leo Garcia, a speedster who has been up and down with the Reds, ties up the game with a dash around the bases for an inside-the-park home run. The dugout rings with cries of "Leito! Leito!"

Peña singles in the eighth and slaps the hand of first base coach Julio Martínez, confirming yet again that he did the right thing taking a young Peña to a tryout with Pittsburgh Pirates' Caribbean scout, Howie

Haak, in 1975. "He had a taste for the game—a real hunger to play," Martínez remembers. Martínez had that hunger once, too, and romped through the years for the team he now coaches. He is one of five Martínez brothers to play professional ball. His oldest brother, Horacio, and Tetelo Vargas, for whom the stadium in San Pedro is named, are the two most famous Dominican players from the epoch before Dominicans made it to the major leagues Stateside.

Distefano follows with a shot up the middle that Griffin snags before his momentum carries him down on the grass. He lies prone but somehow his arm whips the ball to first. The umpire signals out and the *Aguilas* threat is over.

Acker tires in the bottom of the inning and Ceclio Guante relieves. He strikes out former teammate Nelson Norman on three pitches. The enigmatic Guante, traded from the Pirates to the Yankees to the Rangers over the past two seasons, spent the first part of the game sprawled in the bull pen grass. Before the game, he feigned not to understand English when a North American reporter tried to get him to open the clubhouse door. Minutes later, when pitcher José Bautista banged on the door, Guante pretended not to understand Spanish, either.

In the dugout, a boy sells peanuts he wraps in a square of paper, and Rafaelito, the locker room manager, fashions a giant priapus out of a towel, with which he pokes the unsuspecting.

In the tenth inning, Peña pivots atop the dugout steps, thrusts his hands toward the swirling sky of blue and gray clouds, and beseeches the heavens. "*Dios! Por favor,* get this crazy sidewinder out of the game. Bring in another pitcher. Anybody but heeem!"

On the mound, the target of Peña's supplications, right-handed reliever Máximo del Rosario, stares impassively at the catcher as he approaches the plate. Rosario's first pitch almost grazes Peña's head and sends him tumbling.

Returning to the plate, Peña adjusts his batting helmet, tugs his sleeves, and digs in with his back foot. He measures his stance, but when Rosario shakes off the signal Peña steps out and repeats the ritual. As the crowd's impatience mounts, Peña pulls Rosario's next offering into left and soon stands on first base, grinning back at his teammates.

But Griffin's *manos dulces* (sweet hands) confound the *Aguilas* again by turning a hit into a double play. In the bottom of the inning, Peña yells at Guante, his former Pirate batterymate, after each pitch. When Rafael Ramírez, the Houston Astros shortstop during the summer, goes to an 0–2 count, Peña shouts, "Rafaelín, fastball right down the middle," and the San Pedro native stands there dumbfounded when

Guante throws just that for the third strike. Peña smiles all the way back to the dugout.

Distefano doubles down the right field line the next inning and when he scores the go-ahead run, Peña waits until the other players have congratulated him before offering his hand. As Distefano reaches, Tony quickly withdraws it, laughs, and then bear-hugs his teammate.

Llenas brings in Peña's younger brother, Ramón, to close the game. Sixteen years ago, Tony drew a circular strike zone on the adobe wall of a house in Palo Verde, a banana company town where they grew up, and dared Ramón to throw their homemade ball by him. The circle is still there and so, too, as frequently as they can be, are the brothers Peña. Released by the Pirates, Ramón labored for years in the Detroit farm system before making it to the majors in 1989.

He makes quick work of San Pedro, and with the final out, a squadron of boys leaps off the dugouts to congratulate their heros. Ramón tosses the game ball into the stands, while Tony is surrounded by admirers. Alfredo Griffin, on deck when the final out is made, shakes his head and heads into the dugout. Cruzibal, who had fallen asleep during the top half of the inning, only to be awakened by the response to Distefano's hit, climbs down the palm. Rico Carty and Andy Caines stand, stretch, and make their way to the exits.

Griffin showers and joins his friend Ramón Mercedes at a local disco before returning to his pink stucco home in the section of San Pedro which has become something of a ballplayers' ghetto. His next-door neighbor is Joaquín Andújar, the eccentric Houston pitcher, while Carty, who first built a home there, lives an easy throw away.

Many of the fans make their way to the town's central square. There, they join the thousands celebrating Three Kings Night, the epiphany, in a cacophony of noisemakers, *merengue,* and youthful anticipation of the next morning's gift-giving. Many of the children will be up at dawn to stand outside Andújar's house for his annual distribution of sporting largesse. Griffin, who danced nearly to the dawn, will rise considerably later and evade most of the spillover from neighbor Andújar's house to take a car filled with running shoes and gloves to Consuelo where he grew up.

While his players rinse with cold water in a shower room shared with mosquitos, Winston Llenas sits in the dugout of the almost deserted ballpark, tugging on a beer. Although only 45, Llenas has played, coached, and managed in his own country as well as in Mexico, Japan, and the United States. He looks and sounds a bit like Raul Julia, the Argentine actor, as he soliloquizes about Dominican baseball.

"This town, San Pedro, has become the best spot for baseball anywhere in the world." With enough native sons in the majors to field a franchise by itself, this sugar cane center has sent more players to the pros than any town at any time in history. "And you want to know why? It's because of those kids who were sitting on the outfield wall before the game, and their brothers back in the *ingenios,* who play ball every day of the year. They're hungry. They want to make it like Peña and Griffin did. And some of them will make it.

"Tomorrow morning, all over this country, children will receive presents for *Reyes* (Three Kings Day). Most of the boys will get a ball or a bat. The lucky ones will get a glove. And those who are not so fortunate will make their own out of cardboard or canvas. They'll play anywhere—in the streets or a cane field—and they'll play hard. Some of them will have the ability and learn the discipline to be signed."

The youngster who had peddled coffee out of a thermos during the game appears out of the runway shadows and sits next to the *Aguilas* manager. Llenas, father of four girls, ruffles the boy's hair. "This is a poor country, but we have been playing ball for almost a century now. Americans don't realize that, because most Latins were barred by the color line until Jackie Robinson. But we have had a love affair with baseball that goes way back. And that love has evolved and deepened over the years, not only here in San Pedro de Macoris, but in Santo Domingo and the Cibao, too.

"The baseball is best in San Pedro now, but the game has been a long time in the making, not only here in San Pedro de Macoris, but in Santo Domingo and the Cibao. In the United States, you have football and basketball, and hockey, too. Your children have Nintendo and Nickelodeon—so many more options than this *muchacho* and ones like him have. Here we have mainly baseball. I don't know if you can ever comprehend how much this game means to us."

Rafaelito interrupts to tell Llenas that the bus is ready to leave. Handing the young coffee vendor a ball from his jacket pocket, Llenas takes one last look at the diamond and walks back down the runway to the locker room.

Only a few stragglers remain. Outside, Cecilio Guante departs after a few words with his teammates, honking the horn of his BMW as he circumvents pedestrians and roars out of the stadium lot. Tony Peña, Miguel Diloné, and Winston Llenas take seats aboard the bus that will carry them into the night and back to Santiago. Cruzibal Bryant walks to the spot by the road to Consuelo where the *guaguas,* the collective cabs, pass and waits. Andy Caines is soon standing alongside him.

The stadium lights shut off with a click but the crowds do not hurry away from the ballpark. Many continue their dining and drinking at the booths and carts near the stadium entrance, while others seem to cling to the ambience of the game for just a moment longer.

No other aspect of Dominican life, except perhaps for *merengue,* has provided as much *joie de vivre* for this Third World country, as baseball, its highest art form. Like the highway from San Pedro to Santo Domingo and then north to Santiago, baseball connects Dominicans to each other, as well as to the rest of the Caribbean and to *el norte*. And it has done so for almost a century now.

1
The Apostles of Baseball

The next morning, Pedro Julio Santana strides across the plaza outside *La Catedral Primada de America* in what once was the colonial zone of Santo Domingo, the oldest European city in the western hemisphere. Inside the church, bones reputed to belong to Christopher Columbus lie in repose. Outside, the *buscavidas,* the hustlers "looking for the life," congregate in small groups and evaluate the hapless tourists upon whom they will soon descend. Street sweepers push debris from the previous evening's Three Kings revelry into piles by the curb.

A tall man with patrician bearing, Santana passes them by with hardly a glance. With a half dozen newspapers tucked under his arm, the 76-year-old Santana climbs the five flights of stairs to his office. Frequent power outages have rendered riding the elevator an act of faith, one that this fervent member of the church of baseball is not about to make on an early January morning. In the office where he still organizes literary competitions for *Ron Siboney,* Santana sips a *negrito* and stands by the window overlooking the church. Beyond it, on the walk by the sea, stands a monument to Bartolome de las Casas, the *conquistador* who responded to the appalling decimation of this island's natives by becoming their foremost advocate. De las Casas and Columbus represent the two poles of the Spanish conquest, but Santana searches for words to describe a more felicitous invasion—that of the penetration of baseball into the Dominican Republic and the rest of the Caribbean basin.

Glancing below to the hulking walls of the first Catholic cathedral in *el mundo nuevo,* Santana finds his metaphor. "It is much the same as that which happened with Christianity. Jesus could be compared to the North Americans, but the apostles were the ones that spread the faith, and the apostles of baseball were the Cubans. They went out into the

1

world to preach the gospel of baseball. Even though the Dominican Republic and Puerto Rico were occupied by the North Americans, the Cubans brought baseball here first, and to Mexico and Venezuela, too."

Caribbean baseball's headwaters were in Cuba, which lies due west of Hispaniola. Despite colonial ties to Spain which survived the early nineteenth century wars of independence, Cuba shifted its dependency to the United States by the late nineteenth century. Baseball arrived there almost simultaneously, brought by North American sailors, students, and businessmen as well by Cubans who had traveled north and carried the game back as part of their newfound cultural baggage.

The initial setting for the game was Matanzas, a conduit for the extensive trade which developed with the United States as the latter took advantage of Spain's mid-nineteenth century debility to become the island's new metropolis. Dock workers picked up the game first, playing against the crews of North American ships taking on sugar as early as 1865 or 1866, according to Cuban baseball historian Edel Casas. By 1868, *El Club Habana* formed, crushing a team from Matanzas, 51–9, in the first organized contest of two Cuban teams.

Habana's triumph featured two Cuban sporting pioneers, Esteban Bellan and Emilio Sabourín. Catching for the Havana team that day, Bellan hit three home runs, and scored seven runs, while Sabourín played left field and tallied eight before darkness mercifully ended play. Born in Havana in 1850, Bellan became the first *Latino* to break into organized baseball in the United States. The dark-skinned third baseman played parts of three seasons with the Troy Haymakers and the New York Mutuals in the National Association, the first organized pro circuit in the States, during the 1870s.

Sabourín, the A. G. Spalding of Cuban baseball, was the motive force behind the *Liga de Beisbol Profesional Cubana,* whose inaugural tournament was won by the re-constituted *Habana* club in 1878. Baseball, however, did not meet with approval by the colonial authorities, who distrusted Cuban students in general, and mistook their sporting implements for disguised tools of war. Ballplayers resorted to clandestine practice of what they dubbed *pelota americana* (American ball). Sabourín proselytized for his sport as well as for the cause of Cuban independence from Spain until his diversion of baseball revenues to Jose Marti's independence movement incurred the wrath of Spanish officials. They arrested Sabourín and a number of baseball-playing revolutionaries in December 1895 and banned baseball in parts of the colony. Sabourín was soon shipped to *El Castillo del Hacha,* the Spanish prison in Morocco. The soon-to-be former colonial rulers kept this proponent of baseball and independence in detention until his death from pneumonia in 1897. Baseball proved much harder to constrain.

As Spain's colonial cadres retreated to the Iberian Peninsula to lick their wounds and ponder why four and half centuries of sway in the Americas had brought them so little of lasting value, a new flotilla was approaching the Pearl of the Antilles. This armada bore the best of North America's ballplayers, who found in Cuba a chance to continue their trade after the end of the regular season. On the island, these North American ballplayers found that the winter game had already, for the most part, caught up with its summer counterpart.

Initially a game of the more affluent and those with contact with the United States, baseball soon spread to all classes of Cuban society, both urban and rural. As North American companies and the Marines, who earned Frequent Fighter points during three post–Spanish-American war occupations, incorporated the Cuban economy, and with it, Cuban political autonomy, into a United States–defined system, baseball became ubiquitous. Teams from the National and American Leagues, along with squads of black players then barred by organized ball's color line, toured the island. They found a well-developed league structure in place.

And as Cuban baseball blossomed into the game's first truly international and interracial arena, it became the sport's beacon throughout the Caribbean basin. By the time the Good Neighbor Policy supplanted Teddy Roosevelt's Big Stick in the 1930s, baseball was entrenched. Moreover, Cuban baseball had become the focal point of an international network that stretched from the Caribbean basin through the ghettos of North America.

Until Fidel Castro's team from the *Sierra Maestre* mountains came to power in 1959 and the United States responded by blockading the island, Cuba set the standard for Caribbean play. It sent the most players to the major and Negro leagues, while its winter and summer tournaments featured the highest caliber of Latin ball and attracted players from both the States and the basin. Cuban players, radio broadcasts, and emigrés, in turn, became the game's emissaries.

"We listened to the Cuban games on radio," Santana muses. "We listened to them eagerly and followed them in our own newspapers. Cuba had the greatest players in the Caribbean and they began to come here to play—for a tournament and sometimes even a season. Meanwhile, our best players, like Tetelo Vargas and Horacio Martínez, played in the Cuban league. Much of the structure we set up in Dominican baseball was an attempt to follow the efforts of the Cubans. We even copied their metaphors and expressions for the game from the great Cuban radio announcers. And, of course, the Cubans were the first to play baseball here."

During the expansion of their empire, Spaniards passed through Hispaniola to Cuba and then on to the plunder of Aztec Mexico and Incan Peru. But as the empire crumbled in the nineteenth century, the migratory patterns reversed. Several thousand Cubans, fleeing the chaos of the Ten Years' War (1868–1878), the first Cuban War of Independence, went into exile on Hispaniola in the 1870s. These exiles brought the know-how and capital to create a modern sugar industry on the island. And they brought baseball.

Burrowing through his stack of newspapers, Santana finds the morning's edition of *Listín Diario.* "Here is the story of the first Cubans to play ball here—by Cuqui Cordova. He can tell you about the seeds of our game."

And much more, too. Across town in a residential neighborhood of white stuccoed houses with red tiled roofs, not far from former president Antonio Guzmán's enclave, the foremost chronicler of the Dominican passion sits in a study surrounded by the records and memorabilia of the game he has loved since youth. Pictures of Ted Williams, Juan Marichal, Tommy Lasorda, and a score of others from baseball's hagiology peer down at Cordova, who reclines behind the desk at which he has written columns recounting sports history in the Dominican Republic for almost twenty years. "I have liked sports since I was a child," the 59-year-old Cordova explains. "And I have followed baseball here, and in Cuba, and even in the United States, where I studied as a youth." Cordova's stint abroad in the late 1940s was in part his family's response to political difficulties with the Trujillo regime, which jailed both father and son. "I was a *desafecto*—a dissident—and I was jailed in August 1952. I spent a month in *Sans Souci* prison with a thousand other young men waiting to be sent to Korea to fight. But I was lucky. There was an armistice ending the Korean War and they let us go home. I only start to write about sports very late in my life, but I am maybe the only one who writes about the history of baseball here."

Born in La Vega, a city north of Santo Domingo in the Cibao, a fertile expanse from which much of the nation's agricultural produce emanates, Cordova has worked in the capital for most of his adult life. Now the Shell Company's public relations manager, Cordova is a fixture in both the promotion of baseball and in its remembrance. He began writing a weekly column for *El Nacional* in 1968 and later switched to *Listín Diario,* where he has become a twice-a-week institution over the last decade. Making use of the now-tattered and crumbling copies of newspapers in the national archives and tracking down the survivors of baseball's early, 'romantic,' years, Cordova has retrieved the nation's sporting memories.

His pinstriped shirt open to a graying chest, Cordova nods his assent to Santana's explanation of Cuban influence. "They were running from war then and came to the Dominican Republic to live. They wanted to work, not fight, and they established themselves here. And soon, those who stayed wanted to do more than work. They wanted to play."

Two brothers, Ignacio and Ubaldo Alomá, left their home in Cienfuegos, Cuba, and emigrated to Santo Domingo in 1880. As ironworkers, they built balconies and grillworks in Santo Domingo and repaired the bridge over the Ozama River after it was damaged by the hurricane of 1893. In June 1891, they formed the first two clubs to play ball on the island and filled their lineups with Cuban compatriots, a handful of Dominicans, a few North Americans, and a German restaurateur. Dominican baseball would keep such a cosmopolitan cast forever after.

They named one club *El Cauto,* after the river of that name in Cuba. The other was called *Cervecería,* for the beer factory where a number of the players worked. Most fans know them by their colors, as the *Azules* (Blues) and the *Rojos* (Reds). They played their first game at the Alomá brothers' ironworks, not far from Pedro Julio Santana's office in *Ciudad Nueva,* using a ball they got from a sailor aboard a North American brig docked in Santo Domingo.

"In La Vega," Cordova adds to his recounting of baseball's genesis on the island, "there was another Cuban, Dr. Samuel Mendoza y Ponce de León, from Matanzas. He brought baseball to the interior of the country at more or less the same time that the brothers Alomá were starting it in the capital." In 1893, Mendoza began two clubs, also known as the *Azules* and the *Rojos.*

If the Cubans were baseball's apostles, Dominican youth were its ready disciples. As the new century dawned, baseball began to win the hearts and minds of young Dominicans, especially those who had studied in the States. Both the Spanish, who fled the Haitian takeover of the island in 1822, and the United States Marine Corps, which occupied the nation from 1916 to 1924, would have been envious of such a swift and total conquest. One of the first skirmishes in this sporting crusade took place in *Ciudad Nueva,* the original colonial zone of the capital, in the courtyard of the family of one of Pedro Julio Santana's dearest friends, Manuel Joaquín Báez Vargas.

Professor Manuel Joaquín Báez Vargas stands over six feet tall, erect and slim-waisted, projecting a vigor that belies his eighty-two years. Like Santana, Báez Vargas has partaken of both the sporting life and more intellectual pursuits. An educator and sportsman for over half a century, Báez Vargas now contemplates his nation's past from his home in Santo Domingo. A rooster crows incessantly in the courtyard outside and the greenish-blue waves of the Caribbean slapping against the *malecón* can be seen from the window in his study.

"When I was born in 1906, here in Santo Domingo, in *Ciudad Nueva,* there was only one field for baseball in the capital, *La Bombita,* where the Hotel *Jaragua* is now. It was just a savannah, a field, then and it wasn't specifically for baseball; *fútbol*—soccer—was played there, too. But as the game began to pick up interest among the youth, it was played in the city on empty lots."

The sport's first acolytes were boys from better-off families, especially those who had studied in the United States. The Dominican Republic, like the rest of the Caribbean and much of Latin America, was re-orienting itself at the turn of the century. Spanish influence plummeted after defeat in Teddy Roosevelt's "splendid little war." The penalty for defeat was the loss of Cuba and Puerto Rico, the last of her Caribbean possessions, as well as the Philippines. The United States, meanwhile, had become a model of development that most of the Western Hemisphere envied, if with some trepidation. A former colony itself, the North American nation had become the strongest manufacturing power on the globe in a century's time. Its economic and cultural clout was bolstered by frequent military incursions during which the United States landed its Marines in ten different Caribbean basin nations a total of thirty-four times between 1898 and 1933. The Dominican Republic, which had come within a few votes in the United States Senate of annexation by the United States in 1870, joined its immediate neighbors, Cuba to the west and Puerto Rico to the east, in looking northward. It was as if the island's axis had shifted.

Upper-class Dominican boys pursued their studies abroad and U.S. ships docked with increasing frequency, especially as North American capital flooded the rapidly expanding Dominican sugar industry. "These boys were exposed to baseball while they were in school in the United States or Puerto Rico," Báez Vargas explains. "Boys like José Sabino, Lulu Pérez, and Frank Hatton—whose father was North American—were the first to play, but we who were not from such affluent backgrounds were not far behind."

Sketching a grid of streets that made up the neighborhood in *Ciudad Nueva* where he grew up, Báez Vargas adds the houses of each of his boyhood chums. "Those of us who lived inside the city made baseball fields out of any lot. The lots were open then and ran into each other. These *solares,* or lots, were contiguous and created a large open field that we used for baseball. My family's yard—*el patio de los Báez*—had home plate and the pitcher's mound. And from that field, great players emerged."

Báez Vargas hardly exaggerates. One of these *patio de los Báez* compatriots, his cousin Tetelo Vargas, ranks as one of the two greatest Dominican players from the first half of the century, while others, Miguel Pinales (a.k.a. *Turco Prieto*), Vicente Pichardo (a.k.a. *Memphis*), and Tetelo's brother, Eduardo, also made their baseball debuts on the lot rimmed by their families' homes.

Most of them were the sons of artesans. "My father was a carpenter. My uncle, Isias Vargas, the father of Tetelo, was a shoemaker. The fathers of the other boys were all working people—tradesmen with crafts. They were the descendents of the skilled workers that Spain sent to build the churches and the dwellings after Cristóbal Colón [Christopher Columbus] arrived and conquered."

From their backyard field, this cohort matriculated to the *Gimnasio Escolar,* a sporting academy by the sea, where they developed their bodies and sporting passions under the guidance of *Don* Federico Ramírez Guerra. Putting up backboards, *Don* Federico introduced basketball to the capital, and Báez Vargas, already towering over most of his friends, was a star pupil. These boys from the capital did not yet specialize in baseball. At the *gimnasio,* they tried gymnastics and played handball, basketball, and soccer.

"When I was about fourteen, we organized a youth team to play *fútbol* that we called *Ayacucho.* We had dark blue shorts and white sleeveless shirts. But although we played other youth teams, this club had only an ephemeral life."

Soccer, a Spanish import of British provenance, pre-dated baseball on the island. "I don't know if the Haitians played it during their occupation from 1822 to 1844, but it was played during my youth by people of Spanish descent. They had their clubs—*Ibéria, España,* the *Casa Velasquez,* and *Pindú*—but it declined." Although *fútbol* teams lasted into the 1930s and 1940s, soccer was soon eclipsed by baseball, just as Spain was overshadowed by the United States.

"The Spanish never really had much love for this country. They came here, made their money, and abandoned us. Nor did they leave us much. Perhaps that is the reason that Dominicans did not take to their sports—to *fútbol* or to *pelota basca, jai alai.* And then, it is maybe because of the frequent contact that we had with North Americans. Even though Cubans introduced the sport, it was during the epoch of the North American occupation that baseball was really ignited." Leaning forward in his seat and linking his long fingers together, Báez Vargas concludes, "But perhaps most of all, baseball was more appropriate for us. It's more exciting; it has more *acción*. Dominicans became more inclined to baseball the moment it appeared on the scene."

As young Dominicans mastered the game and clustered around the *Gimnasio Escolar* and the *Sociedad Recreativa Sport Club,* a number of self-organized clubs appeared. Playing for fun and eschewing any commercial connection, these youth began what is still called the romantic epoch of Dominican baseball. Clubs challenged each other for bragging rights to the city as the game's roots burrowed deeper without benefit of leagues or salaries.

Later that day, Pedro Julio Santana finishes the last of his newspapers and descends to the plaza below. He passes the remnants of the palace from which the Haitian occupiers ruled his country for twenty-two years early last century. A century and a half have done little to subdue the collective Dominican memory of Haitian atrocities. "A peaceful invasion of Haitians continues even as we speak," Santana reflects. Stopping only to buy a slice of melon from a pushcart vendor, Santana walks through the colonial zone until he reaches the home of *Don* Luis Alfau. Earlier, Santana instructed me, "To talk about something, you should not have just knowledge, you should have authority. *Don* Luis has that authority."

Now ninety-five, Alfau is one of the few left whose life spans the evolution of baseball on the island. A founder of *Los Muchachos* and later, *Escogido,* Alfau welcomes his friend with an embrace. Lighter-skinned and taller than the wiry, tawny-hued Santana, Alfau now lives with his daughter and son-in-law on the second floor of a house not far from where he was born in 1893. Stonemasons refurbishing the colonial zone hammer away on the streets below in anticipation of the upcoming quincentennial of Columbus's arrival. Closing the balcony's heavy wooden shutters, Alfau and Santana retire to mahogany and wicker rockers, a staple domestic item throughout the republic.

"There was not too much baseball when I was a boy," Alfau recounts. "It was played on Sundays, and when American ships came they usually had a team, so we would invite their team to play. My first team other than those we formed as boys was the *Nuevo Club*."

In the first decade of the century, teams formed out of the game's primal mix of Cubans, schools, and sport clubs. Two clubs, the *Nuevo Club* and *Ozama* (named for the river by which Santo Domingo was built), outplayed the rest. But a rival to their ascendancy soon appeared, one that would in time become the most celebrated sporting institution in Dominican history—*Licey.*

"The *Nuevo Club* was directed by Lulu Perez, who had assisted *Don* Federico Ramírez Guerra at the *Gimnasio Escolar,*" Santana explains. Lulu Perez had learned to play ball in the United States and transmitted his knowledge to Santo Domingo youth. His best student— Enrique Hernández—dominated the game. A dusky complexion that showed traces of the *Taino* indigenous to the island earned him the sobriquet of *Indio Bravo*—Brave Indian. Under Lulu's tutelage, *Indio Bravo* developed a curveball which the sporting elders claim was virtually unhittable.

Another gang of boys, many from distinguished families that had organized the *Sociedad Sport Club* and who had played together for several years without name or uniforms, decided to challenge *Indio Bravo* and his *Nuevo Club*. As one of them, Tulio H. Pina, later told Cuqui Cordova, "*Licey* had its genesis like nature, from the earth."

The youth gathered in a house on *El Conde,* then as now, the prime shopping street in the colonial zone, on a November evening in 1907. Before leaving that night, they decided to call themselves *El Club Licey.* It was the name of a river in the Cibao that the members found both *"suave y simpático."* While outfitting themselves at first in gray khakis, *Licey* would soon switch to blue and white striped flannels and henceforth be known as *los azules* (the blues). A *fiesta azul* is still celebrated each November, while their blue and white striped uniforms led to their nickname, *los Tigres.*

Licey's arrival in 1907 fanned Santo Domingo's sportive fires and thousands of *capitaleños* turned out for their encounters with *Nuevo Club, Ozama,* and the city's other self-organized teams during baseball's romantic epoch. The games were more than athletic contests; they became entertainment for both high society and the shirtless ones. "*Licey* and *Escogido,* which I helped found," Alfau offers, "were largely made up of boys from better-off families." Federico Fiallo, *Licey*'s captain and de facto manager, for example, would soon become General Fiallo, and infielder Frank Hatton would later direct the government's sporting bureau. "But as time went on and as economic factors come into play," Santana interjects, "things take a turn. There were boys who just spent a lot of time playing baseball. They didn't work or go to school and they were the prime matter from which baseball—and boxing—came from."

Baseball was still a diversion, played for "the love of sport," Santana insists, but with a passion that accelerated the game's development and subsequent commercialization. Many of *Licey*'s earliest members soon departed, unable to contend with *Indio Bravo,* whose hegemony was such that a frustrated *Licey fanático* stabbed him in his pitching arm. *Nuevo Club* won the first championship celebrated in Santo Domingo in 1912, but *Licey* rebounded and later that season won

"La Copa Francesa," a trophy offered by the French *chargé d'affaires* in Santo Domingo. More important, *Licey* began to expand its horizons, and by boat and mule train, the club went on the road.

San Pedro de Macoris was a relatively easy jaunt, by boat. Although only seventy kilometers to the east of the capital, San Pedro was more accessible by coastal vessels than by travel over the dirt road that connected the two cities. More cosmopolitan than Santo Domingo, San Pedro was then enjoying the rapid expansion of the Dominican sugar industry. Foreign investors controlled most of the mills, and their managers, a mix of foreign and native-born, mingled with a sizable Middle Eastern population. The San Pedro ball club reflected this heterogeneous cast, with a sprinkling of the sons of the Levant in its lineup. But not even these reinforcements could stop *Licey* in their initial 1911 encounter. They triumphed in a contest punctuated by twenty strikeouts and twenty-one stolen bases.

Santiago de los Cabelleros in the Cibao, the great valley north of Santo Domingo, posed greater logistical problems, and a match between *Licey* and Santiago's ball club was another decade in the making. But in August of 1921, the *Liceyistas* began their most challenging odyssey. Motorists can now reach Santiago from Santo Domingo in three and a half hours along the two—and sometimes four—lane blacktop. The *Aguilas* ball club bus driver makes it in about two and a half. But when *Licey* ventured across the mountains some seventy years ago, the trek took five days. By auto and then by mule, the ballplayers traveled northward, past tobacco leaves drying in sheds and the small garden plots of the peasants alongside their thatch-roofed huts. After two days of rest to recover, the boys in the tiger-striped flannels swept eight games against the best Santiago and La Vega could offer.

In the decade between *Licey*'s trips to San Pedro and Santiago, clubs emerged that would, in one form or another, give continuity to baseball in each of the republic's three major cities. Only *Escogido* had yet to appear to complete the quartet that has comprised the foundation of Dominican baseball for over sixty years. And *Escogido*'s birth was soon to come.

But before the creation of *Escogido, Licey* would gain, lose, and regain superiority on Santo Domingo's diamonds. Its route to the top internationalized the Dominican game as *Capitán* Fiallo went to nearby Puerto Rico to recruit reinforcements. A few Puerto Ricans, a Cuban pitcher known as *el Diamante Negro,* and even a *gringo* or two, appeared in their lineup. But the turning point occurred when *Indio Bravo,* after quarreling with his old club, jumped to *Licey.* He did so after no-hitting a team off the U.S. cruiser *Washington,* striking out twenty-one North Americans in the process. The loss of their ace was too much for *Nuevo Club* to bear and the team crumbled, only to see its nucleus soon regroup as *San Carlos*. When this rejuvenated nine surpassed *Licey*, the latter turned again to foreign reinforcements.

Their savior was a Puerto Rican, Pedro Miguel Caratini, who had first played in the Dominican Republic in 1916 as a member of the visiting *Ponce* club, the first foreign team to travel to the island (excluding those made up of ships' crews). This slick-fielding shortstop returned during the 1916–1924 United States Marine Corps invasion of the island. An employee of the occupation government, Caratini sized up the sporting balance and decided he could bring a new equilibrium to the game by joining *Licey*. Caratini would become *Licey*'s manager; and with *Indio Bravo* and a supporting cast that included Frank Hatton, Pedro Alejandro San, and *El Mono Ozuna*, the club regrouped.

Its unhappy competitors, however, did not stand pat. "In January 1921," *Don* Luis Alfau explains, "we formed a new team, *Escogido*, out of players from *San Carlos, Delco-Light,* and my club, *Los Muchachos*, which was not too old at the time. We formed out of rivalry with *Licey* and constituted their only true opposition." If *Licey* was the tigers, then *Escogido* would be the lions, and if *Licey* was blue, then *Escogido* would be red. "The name itself signifies the chosen or the selected," Santana explains. "The players were chosen from these three other clubs to challenge *Licey*."

"We tried to select a manager who would not be a partisan of the players from one of the three teams," Alfau remarks. "But Numa Parra, a Venezuelan whom we chose, returned to his country not long after, and I became *Escogido*'s manager." His lineup included Juan and Guaguá Vargas, cousins of Manuel Joaquín Báez Vargas and alumni of the *patio de los Báez*, José Sabino, who had learned the game abroad, and Fellito Guerra. A veteran of the *Gimnasio Escolar Beisbol Team* and *San Carlos*, Rafael "Fellito" Guerra was perhaps the only hurler of the day who could match up with *Indio Bravo*. Guerra shut out a Puerto Rican team for eighteen innings in an encounter between national squads and earned his credentials as a nationalist by refusing a contract to play ball in the United States because of the occupation.

Licey and *Escogido* played five games in 1921 and *capitaleños* were soon convinced that the rivalry between *los azules* and *los rojos* would forever shape Dominican baseball. *Indio Bravo* beat Fellito Guerra in their first encounter, and *Licey* made it two in a row when Pedro Miguel Caratini homered to tie the game 1–1 in the eighth and then repeated his feat in the tenth to win the second game. *Escogido* rallied to win the next two but *Licey* triumphed in the deciding game.

Scratch deep enough in the soul of a Dominican, one enraptured observer wrote, and you will find either *Licey* blue or *Escogido* red. "The essence of Dominican baseball is in these two colors," Santana agrees. "They are the two most authentic representations of baseball and rivalry in this sport."

The teams returned to the stadium *La Primavera* the following April, initiating a twenty-one-game championship called *el Campeonato de la Reina* (the championship of the Queen). Games were played each Saturday and Sunday afternoon as what was considered the best Dominican ball yet played captivated the island. The only import on the field was Caratini, whom most treated as if he were a native son. Although fiercely chauvinistic about Santo Domingo baseball, both clubs recruited players from the Cibao for the tournament.

That hardly lessened the sporting public's attachments. Rather, it extended this archetypal rivalry to the interior. More than twenty thousand paid to attend the games of this first championship at a time when Santo Domingo's total population was only a bit over thirty thousand. Given the size of the city and the number of men who passed through the clubs' directorates and lineups, most of Santo Domingo seemed to have had some connection with either *Licey* or *Escogido*—through family, friendship, work, or school. *Licey* and *Escogido* were not distant institutions, isolated by the megabucks of contemporary sport or distanced by television. They were close at hand, the teams' directors identifiable, and the players men with whom many rubbed shoulders in the course of a day in the tropics. More than mere ball clubs, these social institutions linked families, athletes, and fans in a lifelong sporting fraternity. And the rivalry, rather than crystallizing splits within the republic along the lines of class or color, actually allowed Dominicans to transcend these differences and join together in a larger sense of community. That has prevailed across the generations and even through the dark years of the dictatorship of Rafael Trujillo into the 1980s.

The Championship of the Queen in 1921 had its most memorable moments on April 30 as *Señorita* Esperanza Pereyra, the queen of the tournament, made her entrance into Santo Domingo. "It was a social event," Cuqui Cordova has written, as the young beauty of the Cibao (who happened to be Cuqui's aunt) made her way through the capital in an open car to the flower-strewn street where she would stay. Guitars and violins vied with the city's poets in paying homage to *la reina,* perhaps distracting *Licey,* who had asked Esperanza to grace the games. They would lose the championship thirteen games to eight. The hero of the series was Mateo de la Rosa, whose base-clearing blow during the April 30th game at which the *señorita* was toasted with champagne left him with the sobriquet, the batter who made the queen cry. At the house of the Vargas brothers in *Ciudad Nuevo* and throughout the capital, players and supporters sang of *Escogido*'s exploits through the night.

Yet even while the *fanáticos* caroused and devoured elaborate accounts of the series by sportswriters with handles like "Strong Silk," "Jimy Punch," and *"Bate"* (it was then customary for sportswriters to use a nickname for their byline), the romantic epoch of Dominican baseball was already beginning to fade.

"We played for the love of the game," Santana emphasizes. "It was a romantic baseball. It was *Licey* and *Escogido, Presidente* and *Nika*. Sport was not a profession. The yearning for lucrative gain had not awakened yet in the athlete. Instead they played for *la gloria deportiva* (for the glory of the sport). But in 1929, it changed."

Actually, Santana reflects, it had already begun to change earlier in the decade. Early on, as the teams began to collect money from spectators by passing the hat, the players would divide their take among themselves. The 1921 championship brought in over $7,000, netting each club almost $2,000. Commercial pressures led to a semi-professionalization of the sport, and bureaucracy and full-scale professionalization soon followed.

"Companies began to sponsor teams to promote themselves. They would put their names on the backs of the uniforms and the press would be sure to take care to mention them. A bakery might have a club and put some of its workers on the team and reinforce them with outsiders who don't work there to round out the team. *Presidente* was backed by *El Presidente* hardware store, *Nika* by a liquor company. *Delco Light* was a business that brought in batteries and electrical generators. Almost all the teams had some sort of support," Santana recalls.

"But sponsorship was limited. They would give the players uniforms and pay for bats and balls. The players were not put on salaries then. That came later. There was actually a lot more that they gave to the sport than what they got from it.

"Why did they do it you ask? To get to the souls of the people, the hearts of the customers. . . .

"But after 1929, we were lying to ourselves, fooling ourselves to call ourselves amateurs and these teams amateur—the boys are already getting an economic stimulus. They were hiring people and setting them up in hotels. Amateur was a euphemism by then."

As travel among the islands and countries of the Caribbean basin expanded during the 1920s, Dominicans went abroad to play and Cubans, Puerto Ricans, and North Americans returned the favor. *Li-*

cey, Escogido, and the clubs representing Santiago and San Pedro relied increasingly on *refuerzos*—reinforcements. These baseball paladins came to play—for pay.

While their directorate remained Dominican, *Licey*'s field manager was the Puerto Rican, Caratini. In 1922, Charles Dore, a black man from the United States who migrated to the island, became his assistant. When Caratini hung up his spikes and retired as manager, Dore succeeded him and guided the Tigers until 1936. *Licey* also engaged the services of Cocaína García in 1924. This legendary Cuban hurler was only one of a wave of island-hopping Cuban ballplayers who came east to play. In 1926, the tide went west, as Dominicans reinforced Cuban clubs in their league. The one player *Licey* could not hang on to was the boy who had been their mascot in 1921, Tetelo Vargas. Tetelo would join his brothers, Guaguá and Juan, on *Escogido* for the 1923 season. *Liceyistas* still rue the loss, likening it to the Red Sox selling Babe Ruth to the Yankees a few years before.

While fans of major league baseball will never cease arguing over which player was the greatest of all time, there is little controversy among Dominicans as to who can claim that title in the years before Jackie Robinson. Few would dispute that the honor belongs to Juan Esteban Vargas y Marcano. Tetelo Vargas left the backyard lots of *Ciudad Nueva* for a career that took him to Cuba, Puerto Rico, Venezuela, Panama, Colombia, Canada, and the United States. Blessed with speed, a strong arm, grace in the field, and prowess at the plate, Vargas played for thirty seasons. His resume contains virtually every possible honor in baseball, including several selections to the Negro Leagues' all-star contests and a Dominican batting championship in 1953, when Vargas was close to fifty years old. In exhibition games versus the New York Yankees, Vargas was seven for fourteen. He played too soon to cross the color line but left his mark in Caribbean and Negro League play.

Sometimes, a team representing the nation sallied forth, contesting Puerto Rican, Cuban, or Venezuelan squads for the glory of the nation. These games pitting the *Estrellas Dominicanas* (Dominican Stars) versus other national teams kindled fierce rivalries throughout the Caribbean basin.

And back in Santo Domingo, *Escogido, Licey* and other aspirants to the throne met in irregularly scheduled competitions. In July 1928, the reds and the blues played in a series dedicated to the soon-to-be-deposed President Horacio Vásquez. The trophy was a ball autographed by another lame duck president, Calvin Coolidge.

By the 1929 championship, playing for pay and importing reinforcements had become *de rigueur.* Dr. José E. Aybar, who would become a fixture in Dominican baseball and politics, assumed *Licey*'s presidency in 1929 and collected $12,000 from the club's wealthier backers. He used most of the money to import a half dozen Cuban stars. Three-time Cuban League batting champ Alejandro Oms, pitchers Cocaína García and Ramón Bragaña, second baseman Pelayo Chacon, and third baseman Pedro Arango donned *Licey*'s tiger-striped flannels. *Escogido* countered with their own assortment of Cubans, including the incomparable Martín Dihigo.

Arguably the greatest all-around ballplayer of any time, Martín Dihigo played every position but catcher. From his 1922 debut with the Havana Reds through 1947, Dihigo campaigned virtually every season, from Venezuela to the Negro Leagues. A "Have Glove—Will Travel" all-star, Dihigo is the only man in the baseball halls of fame of three countries: Cuba, Mexico, and the United States. A lifetime .304 hitter with a 256–133 won-lost record as a pitcher, Dihigo won batting, home run, total victory, total strikeout, and E.R.A. honors in the Negro National, Cuban, and Mexican leagues. For several seasons, he led his league in both pitching and batting. After the Cuban revolution, Dihigo returned to Matanzas to teach baseball and serve as his nation's minister of sport. His bust at *Estadio Latinoamericano* in Havana reads simply, *"El Inmortal."* A player for all seasons, Dihigo would be back in later years to figure in the greatest Dominican championship ever.

Escogido could also count on the services of Tetelo Vargas and home-grown pitchers Pedro Alejandro San and Fellito Guerra.

Two other clubs took part in the championship that year, the *Estrellas Orientales* (Eastern Stars) from San Pedro de Macoris and a ball club called *Sandino* from Santiago. The latter took its name from Nicaragua's Augusto César Sandino, who was then holed up on *El Chipote* mountain in his native land, with the United States Marines on his trail. The series that year enthralled the republic even while marking the end of the romantic epoch.

It is nearing the end of the day in Santo Domingo. The hammering outside ceases and *Don* Alfau opens the shuttered windows. The stonemasons are departing and the colonial zone is, by Dominican standards, at repose. Santana and Alfau clasp each other's arms and, after pleasantries with the younger generations in the household, Santana departs.

Santana walks across the centuries as he saunters down the hill to the *malecón*. The thick-walled, ochre-colored edifices of the colonial zone give way to air-conditioned, plate-glassed banks and frock-filled boutiques.

The patterns of the past hang heavily over the Dominican landscape. The Santo Domingo of Pedro Julio Santana's boyhood was a

relatively sleepy tropical town. The Santo Domingo of his elder states-
man days is a multimillion-member metropolis. It has grown from a
face-to-face, walking city of 30,000 in 1920 to one and a half million in
1988. Elements of both the nineteenth and the twentieth century co-
mingle. Horse-pulled carts vie with BMWs along the *Avenida* George
Washington—the four lane, cross-at-your-own-peril boulevard—along
the *malecón*, the walk by the sea.

Santana pauses until traffic slows, and walks across. On the *malecón,* he joins shoeshine boys and lovers, families and derelicts, and a
tiny boy selling peanuts that he roasts over charcoal in a jerry-built
contraption of two cans. Each comes to watch the dropping sun.

This republic's emergence as a "modern" nation tied into the
economic, political, and cultural currents of the developed world
awaited the arrival of the United States as their main connection to the
twentieth century. In between Cuba and Puerto Rico, the Dominican
Republic could hardly escape the onslaught of the Yankee Years early
this century. For the Dominican Republic, that would mean occupation
by the United States Marine Corps and Navy from 1916 to 1924. That
occupation, paradoxically, accelerated the cohesion of this nation and
prepared the way for the emergence of a sense of national consciousness. Somehow, baseball became a central part of that process
and provided this nation with a verve that frequently transcended the
difficulties of dependency and dictatorship.

The sun splashes into the Caribbean at the horizon and the sky
responds with delicious pastels. Many of the celebrants begin to leave.
Soon, the night shift—streetwalkers and hustlers as well as working
people seeking a breeze on a warm January night—comes on. Santana
sits on a concrete balustrade, taking it all in, as he has for the better part
of the century.

2
The Yankee Years

Juan Bosch knows about the marines. He knows about them all too well. Now 80, the silver-thatched, hawk-eyed intellectual *cum* politico won the first democratically contested presidential election held after the long darkness of the Trujillo years finally subsided. He donned the presidential sash on February 27, 1963, not quite two years after Rafael Trujillo was gunned down as he drove to San Cristobal to visit his mistress. But Bosch's ascension prompted unease in elite circles as well as in the U.S. State Department and he was ousted by a *coup* after only seven months. Bosch was on the verge of returning to power in 1965 after a rebellion of constitutionally-minded junior officers merged with Dominicans taking to the barricades; but the United States, still in those heady days before the Tet Offensive, sent in the marines to block his comeback.

Exiled to Puerto Rico, Bosch returned to contest the next presidential election, only to be defeated by Joaquín Balaguer, who had been titular president at the time of Trujillo's death. Bosch then left for Europe, his sojourn this time a voluntary one. His party, the *Partido Revolucionario Dominicano* (PRD), suffered from outright repression and internal bickering. Bosch finally split from its ranks in 1974 over whether or not to participate in the election that year, taking with him only a few score activists. Hardly anyone expected that Bosch's new party, the *Partido Liberacíon Dominicano* (PLD), would become a credible political force or that he would re-emerge as a viable presidential candidate in the 1980s. In May 1990, however, Bosch lost the presidential election to Joaquín Balaguer by the narrowest of margins in a race marred by charges of voter fraud.

But Bosch, perhaps his country's preeminent man of letters, dwells not so much on the landing of the marines in Santo Domingo in 1965 or even on his political future as on the making of his country's consciousness and social structure. Sitting in the offices of the PLD, a block from the fortress-like U.S. embassy in Santo Domingo, he points to a series of turning points and social forces that retarded his nation's emergence as an autonomous nation in control of its destiny and reconciled with its identity. Dissecting the fragmentation that has plagued the Dominican Republic, Bosch nevertheless points to its potential for coming back together in a more self-assured, independent fashion. A black-skinned bodyguard stands a few feet away, missing little that transpires around the man whose Phoenix-like rebirth from the ashes of the political wasteland has substantially affected the current political scene.

The Taino Indians who first peopled Bosch's homeland called their island Haiti, sometimes referring to it as *Quisqueya*. Dominicans today frequently call their land, as well as a beer and the ballpark in Santo Domingo, by that latter name. Columbus stumbled on the island during his first voyage and colonized it upon his return the next year. Acting as the Spanish realm's franchiser in the western hemisphere, he promptly renamed it *La Española,* which soon was anglicized to Hispaniola. But almost everybody in the western world knew it as Santo Domingo, the name of its capital city and the center for the Spanish conquest in the Americas.

The Spanish abused the island as a proving grounds for the mechanisms of conquest and colonization that they would carry to the rest of their new empire. The Tainos paid the heaviest price. By all accounts a peaceful lot, they subsisted on the fruits of the land and of the sea. Working their fields in common and worshipping the heavenly bodies as deities, the Tainos also played a ball game in a rectangularly shaped field rimmed by stone petroglyphs and engraved figures. Two teams kept a rubber ball made out of the fiber and sap of the *cupey* tree in the air without using their hands.

In his logbook, Columbus wrote that the Tainos were an "openhearted people, who give what they ask for with the best will in the world. . . . They bear no arms, and are all so unprotected and so very cowardly that a thousand would not face three; so they are fit to be ordered about and made to work. . . ." And order them about and work them the Spanish did—to the point of extinction.

Conservative estimates put the Taino population at over a million on the eve of Columbus's arrival. There would be hardly any left alive fifty years later. In their pursuit of gold, glory, and God, Spanish *conquistadores* easily subdued Taino resistance and proceeded to work to death those they did not kill outright or infect with epidemic disease, to which the Tainos had no resistance. Scholars doubt that any Taino blood remains in the national gene pool.

The Tainos' principal advocate arrived with the third Columbus voyage. After a decade as a recipient of Indian labor and tribute on Cuba and Hispaniola, Bartolome de las Casas renounced his life of ease and initiated a crusade on behalf of the indigenous Americans. The first priest ordained in the colonies, his carefully documented indictment of the Spanish stewardship of the Indians ignited a furor in Europe and the Americas over the conduct of the conquest. Las Casas argued that the Indians had rightful ownership of their lands and questioned the very legality of the conquest. Spain could convert them, but not enslave them. Ultimately, the crown agreed, but after it was too late to help most of the natives. Perhaps Las Casas should have turned his attention instead to those whose humanity would next be sacrificed to Western greed—the new African slave laborers, who began arriving in 1503 and soon composed the core of the workforce.

Gold and the easily-exploited Tainos attracted assorted rogues to Santo Domingo in its early years as it became the political nucleus of the Spanish Caribbean. But as the deposits of gold declined, as the Tainos curled up their toes and died, and as the discovery of the Aztec and the Incan empires with their fabled hoards of lucre shifted the center of the conquest to central Mexico and then the Andean highlands, Santo Domingo languished.

Dwindling prestige and a shrinking population could not be stanched; a quarter millennium of stagnation set in.

French and English corsairs, meanwhile, preyed on the colony and its shipping. France forced Spain to cede her the westernmost third of the island in 1697. They would call their part of the island Saint-Domingue (which reverted to Haiti) and, with the services of over half a million African slaves, make it into a profitable sugar plantation.

But Santo Domingo shriveled, reviving only when Spain liberalized its restrictions on colonial trade in one last attempt to break out of the stifling imperial system it had created. Population, down to about 6,000 in 1737, rebounded to 125,000 by the end of the century.

Saint-Domingue would soon play a pivotal role in Santo Domingo's future, and the haunting legacy of this interchange is only as far away as the Haitians who sell their wares on the streets outside Juan Bosch's offices and cut cane across the country. They are a daily reminder of the grim poverty that lies across the border of this also poor, but nowhere as desperate, republic.

The catalyst for Spain's departure from Santo Domingo was the French Revolution. Upon hearing rumors of this new French fad of "Liberty, Fraternity, and Equality," the slaves of Haiti stopped cutting cane and began chopping heads. The rebels allied themselves with Spanish forces stationed in Santo Domingo who were looking for payback against the French for seizing part of the island. But the French revolutionary tribunal's decree abolishing slavery throughout their empire brought the rebels, led by Toussaint L'Ouverture, back into the fold. They and the French army soon evicted the Spanish from Santo Domingo and L'Ouverture became governor of France's colony on the island.

As L'Ouverture waltzed into Santo Domingo and drafted a constitution that ended slavery, Spanish colonists set sail for more hospitable environs. Probably a third of the Spanish colony emigrated, including its most educated and propertied members. In just thirty years, population dipped to half of what it had been. Many of those who remained were neither Spanish nor colonist, but African, and newly emancipated at that.

Napoleon, envisioning a new empire in the Americas, brought L'Ouverture to heel, and like Columbus before him, the rebel leader was sent back to Europe in shackles. But the African and mulatto fighting men who followed him prevailed over Bonaparte's forces. On New Year's day, 1801, the victors proclaimed the independence of Haiti.

It took another eight years to drive the French troops off the island and return Santo Domingo to the Spanish empire. It didn't stay there for very long, however.

With their economy in disarray and the winds of national liberation pushing the Spanish out of their other colonies, Dominicans joined the rebellion against the mother country. In 1821, they sent the Spanish governor packing, declared their independence, and sought admission to Simon Bolivar's Republic of Gran Colombia. But before they heard back from Bolivar, Haiti re-occupied the fledgling republic and brought it under Haitian law.

Twenty-two years of terror and humiliation ensued. Whites fled and poverty became ever-present. Finally, a secret society organized and stormed the Ozama fortress in Santo Domingo on February 27, 1844. Haitian authority melted away and Dominicans regained their independence.

This time, they kept it for more than a few months. But autonomy was a fragile reed. Political intrigue, generals who saw themselves as the next *cacique,* and the ever-present shadow of Haiti cast a pale over the republic. If it wasn't an opportunistic military leader, it was Haitian forces crossing the porous border. The beleaguered Dominicans looked abroad for aid, offering to relinquish their sovereignty for protection. Neither England, France, nor the United States showed much interest, but in 1861, a revanchist Spain accepted the Dominican Republic back into the bosom of its empire. Spanish breasts, however, no longer bore milk, and as Spaniards usurped Dominican positions, profits shrunk and taxes climbed. Dominicans again rebelled. The third time was the final act for Spain; she left in 1865, never to return.

For the rest of the nineteenth century, the country shuddered through bouts of political anarchy, one long span of dictatorship, paranoia over Haiti, and fiscal dissipation. By the beginning of the twentieth century, politics were in disarray more often than not and the government was defaulting on European loans. With European powers threatening to send over their gunboats, there was an almost inevitable turn toward the new protagonist on the world stage, the United States.

In order to block European powers from penetrating this strategic island, the United States negotiated an agreement under which it took over Dominican customs operations—the government's chief source of revenue. The United States handed forty-five percent of the money back to the Dominican government and used the rest to pay off its creditors. That brought a temporary respite, which abruptly ended in 1911 after the assassination of the Dominican president who had cut the deal with the United States.

Political and economic chaos followed. Eight different governments formed and fell between 1911 and 1916. And the United States, fueled by a century of Manifest Destiny and frustrated by the Dominicans' inability to set their house in order, upped the ante. The State Department sought to place its own people in charge of finances and public works, subject to dismissal only by the U.S. Secretary of State. Meanwhile, North American warships steamed into Santo Domingo with increasing frequency, a reminder of what noncompliance might bring. But the Dominicans did not comply and the U.S. grew more bellicose. It demanded that the republic dissolve its military and replace it with a national constabulary controlled by a commander selected by the United States president. That, responded the Dominican government, would constitute nothing less than "an abdication of national sovereignty." Such a turn was not long coming.

In July 1915, the United States proclaimed it would intervene militarily if either the Jiménez administration or public order were in jeopardy. President Juan Isidro Jiménez had taken over in December 1914. His attempts to navigate between the Scylla of the North Americans and the Charybdis of Dominican nationalists would be too much for his shaky ship of state. It disintegrated in the spring of 1916.

With his minister of war in rebellion and the State Department pressuring him to request the Marines, Jiménez wavered. The rebels were in control of the capital, but Jiménez declined the offer of the Marine Corps and asked only for arms.

He got the Marines anyway. And once there, they stayed for the duration. With U.S. warships in his nation's principal ports and the Marines disembarking in Santo Domingo, Jiménez resigned. He pleaded that he could no longer occupy an office "regained with foreign bullets." The rebels also got the message and soon evacuated the capital.

The Marines did not advance without resistance, but they soon controlled the government and the major cities. Over the next eight years, U.S. forces would build roads, skirmish with guerrillas in the eastern provinces, and play baseball. But what lay behind this turn of events?

It probably goes back to the shining city on the hill the Puritans sought to create in New England. Their mission to recreate Eden on earth and offer asylum from the increasing degeneracy of Europe merged with expansionist sentiments to fuel the nation's bid for hegemony in the Caribbean basin.

That North Americans thought they could better handle the affairs of the people of the region than the people themselves was hardly in question. "History," Thomas Jefferson wrote after the Latin American wars of independence, ". . . furnishes no example of a priest-ridden people maintaining a free civil government." Neither Jefferson nor subsequent U.S. leaders expected much in the way of democracy or development in Latin America. What they did believe was, as Jefferson put it, that "America has a hemisphere to itself."

And as the United States flexed its supple economic and political muscle near the end of the nineteenth century, the Caribbean basin bore a disproportionate amount of the action. The Dominican Republic escaped any serious threat to their sovereignty from the U.S. until the 1860s when insecure Dominican leaders tried to sell Samana Bay to the States and sought annexation. A vote that would have made the Dominican Republic a protectorate of the United States failed on the floor of the U.S. Senate in 1870.

But as the United States toppled the remaining bastions of Spain's new world empire in 1898 in what we called the Spanish-American War, the Dominican Republic attracted greater attention. Situated between Cuba and Puerto Rico, the United States' spoils of war, the Dominican Republic possessed a strategic significance. Its Samana Bay was a choice harbor, from which a fleet could defend both the southeastern flank of North America or the Panama Canal. Moreover, North American investment on the island had been accelerating since the 1890s as the modern sugar industry took hold of the land around San Pedro de Macoris. Finally, with the outbreak of World War I, the United States feared German inroads on the island.

Given this confluence of forces, the Dominican Republic seemed likely to join the fraternity of basin nations invaded and occupied by the United States. The incursion went on with little fanfare in the United

States. But if the U.S. occupation made hardly a blip on its citizenry's consciousness, it caused a quantum disruption in the Dominican psyche.

The United States went into the Dominican Republic without a long-term plan. Its first goal was to restore order, although much of the disorder was a direct result of the invasion itself. The fiercest resistance was waged in the southeastern region, where rebel bands called *gavilleros* tied up the Marines for over five years. Elsewhere, the fighting was scattered, and in Santo Domingo, mostly verbal brickbats were thrown.

The second occupation goal, according to a U.S. Marine Corps brigade memo, was to "Contribute maximum to defeat of Teutons. . . . When so-called *Gabilleros* (sic) (i.e., bandits) were captured . . . they invariably . . . indicated that they had tasted of German propaganda." The United States saw German skullduggery behind every incident, in part because of their contempt for the capabilities of the Dominicans, and in part because Germany was the enemy in the war the U.S. had joined in 1917.

Occupation was not an unmitigated disaster. By building roads and establishing communications among previously isolated regions, the occupation brought the country closer together in a physical sense. By disarming much of the populace, subduing the local warlords, and creating a national guard in their place, it brought a greater degree of order. And by injecting some limited funds into education and public health, it helped improve the quality of life for a few.

But these reforms were not without costs and had the ultimate effect of Americanizing the Dominican economy, as well as aspects of Dominican culture. The occupation expedited the North American takeover of the economy as U.S. firms gained control of the sugar industry and opened up the Dominican market to U.S. goods. A taste for North American goods and styles grew, affecting language and music. Modernity, according to historian Frank Moya-Pons, became identified with the United States, while ties with Europe withered.

Although the guerrilla warfare did not compare with the more spirited resistance to the marines that Sandino's Nicaraguan irregulars put up, lives were lost and citizens brutalized. "The marines that came here were the pits of the U.S. military," Bernardo Vega said in the offices of the *Fundación Cultural Dominicana,* from which he has conducted exhaustive investigations of his country's history. "The elite troops were sent to Europe. Those that came here were badly trained and sent to Santo Domingo because there was no real fighting going on. And they felt bad about that."

Recently declassified State Department documents reveal how

some of those troops behaved during the occupation. Gently admonishing the occupation government, a State Department official reminds it "that the United States is not in the island as a mere military conqueror . . . the relationship between the United States and Santo Domingo is that of guardian and ward. . . ." He then rebukes the marines for their usurpation of justice, pointing to an incident where a hearing was held in the field ten minutes after the arrest of a suspected guerrilla, after which, the officer in charge pronounced, "Take the son of a bitch out and bump him off."

While the marines defended the sugar mills in the east and went into "Indian country" to search and destroy, resistance in Santo Domingo took on a more refined cast. Dominicans authored eloquent denunciations of the *Yanquis* in the press and on the stage, while peasants and artesans sang their protest in impassioned anti-Yankee verse. But while the guerrillas waged their hit-and-run campaigns in Seibo and San Pedro, Santo Domingo's youth played ball with them. Actually, they played more against them than with them.

U.S. Navy teams had played against Dominican teams while on layover for years before the occupation began. And as U.S. interests on the island grew, especially during the tense years before the takeover, these vessels appeared more frequently. With the occupation, the number of North American military men skyrocketed. So, too, did the number of confrontations on the diamond. These games became a point of positive contact for Yankees and Dominicans, as well as a chance for the latter to measure themselves against their occupiers. Baseball provided a rare glimpse of each other at play, transcending the often racist and violent images gained from other sorts of contact.

The marines probably played more ball than they fought. As *Scientific American* observed during World War I, "Uncle Sam has created not only an army of soldiers, but an army of athletes." Fighting was sporadic and the high command recognized that maintaining *esprit de corps* was central. U.S.M.C. Second Brigade Commanding General Harry Lee wrote his superior in 1922 that "The health and morale of the brigade is excellent. Lack of social life is the thing most keenly felt by the enlisted men, but this is combated, insofar as possible, by encouraging baseball and athletics of all kinds. . . ."

When the armored cruiser, the *Washington,* docked in the summer of 1914, players from the *Nuevo Club* and *Licey* buried their own rivalry long enough to defeat a team of marines. *Licey* and the ballplayers from another cruiser, the *Petrel,* played a nine-game series the same year. *Licey* won, six games to three. And to the delight of their fans, Dominican teams swept the other eleven games played against teams from North American ships of war that year.

After the occupation began, baseball suffered through the same disorientation that was striking all of society. But if at first hesitant to tangle with the marines on the field of play, Dominicans soon overcame their standoffish inclinations. A selection of Dominican players challenged a U.S.M.C. squad only three months after the occupation began. The marines could hit, but they couldn't field, and they lost a squeaker to the hometown lads.

Nineteen seventeen witnessed repeated encounters, with the marine teams suffering what baseball historian N. D. ("Strong Silk") Redondo called a series of calamities. Yet amity replaced enmity and Redondo, who affectionately refers to one team as "*Los* boys *del Capitán* Keenan," writes of these contests in virtually the same terms as games between two Dominican teams. *Licey* played a marine squad in a benefit for the Red Cross, while a Dominican selection did the same to raise funds for earthquake victims in Puerto Rico. As the occupation dragged on, Dominicans seemed to play North American teams far more frequently than they did each other.

"When the North Americans invaded in 1916," Manuel Joaquín Báez Vargas recalls, "they played the boys that came from the *patio de los Báez*. Vicente Pichardo got his nickname from this. We called him "Memphis," the name of a North American ironclad ship that invaded during the occupation. It ran aground in a storm on August 31, 1916, and we learned about it while playing on our lot. We started to call Vicente 'Memphis' because he was tall and strong, like the ship."

Thirty sailors drowned as the six-million-dollar cruiser broke apart on the volcanic reefs by the capital. More of the 700 men on board would have died if not for their rescue by Dominicans, who braved the hurricane to save them. It was a moment of cooperation soon lost, but Vicente Pichardo carried its symbolic import with him the rest of his career.

Báez Vargas moves from the personal to the political. "Even though the Cubans introduced the sport, it was during the epoch of the North American occupation that baseball was really ignited. These games with North American sailors and marines were very important. There was a certain kind of patriotic enthusiasm in beating them.

"In the east, the guerrillas were fighting the marines, but in the capital, we played ball with them. Yes, even here in Santo Domingo, there was some shooting, but there is something about sport that unites people. It makes people forget, or at least attentuates, the anger between them. There is nothing that unites people more than sport.

"Even though Dominican youth might have been angry and felt a certain resentment toward the North Americans, the spirit of sport allowed them to play. I can give you an example.

"In basketball, which is what I played the most in those years, we played at the *Gimnasio Escolar*. There were a number of young marines who were radio technicians at a station close by. They would come every afternoon and practice basketball. We boys would watch but were a little afraid of approaching them. After all, they were North Americans. Then one day, their basketball rolled toward us and my friend, Fernando, kicked it back to them. Soon we began playing with them and against them. Sport is like that. It caused some of that patriotic fire to just die down a bit and allowed for a certain camaraderie to develop. We were still patriotically enthused, but sport ameliorated it a bit."

When questioned as to the motives of the marines for playing so much baseball against Dominicans, Báez Vargas shrugs. "The North Americans were not trying to win our hearts and minds. They were men like any other men, and they just wanted to play baseball. When they came to play baseball, it is my sense that they did not do it to dominate or to impose their beliefs on us, but because they just wanted to play."

Dominicans, he adds, ". . . were there for the sport. We saw that there was a way to learn from them. In basketball, we learned quite a bit, and even in baseball. And of course, the enthusiasm for baseball was kindled a little stronger by the marines. We had to make a selection among ourselves, taking from two or three teams to get the best to play the marines.

"And the fans, whooooo! There were thousands of them, and of course, because of the whole occupation, there was immense patriotic enthusiasm. Sometimes we felt humiliated by the occupation, but in sport, we fraternized. The crowds were full of this fervor and wanted us to win because we were their team and because we represented the Dominican flag. But there were no demonstrations or rock-throwing or anything like that. Sport is aside, apart from everything else."

While Báez Vargas went to the hoop against the North Americans, Pedro Julio Santana wished to exchange fisticuffs with them. "The occupation troops had their boxing team and would box in front of *La Fortaleza*. But I was too young to box with them at that time," he sighs.

"The North Americans did not play in the interior—in the east. They did other things there—like fight. But here in the capital, their behavior was more civil. It was a good promotion for them. It would come out in the press that they were playing baseball and put forth an image of sportsmen that we were fighting, not of Yankee imperialists.

"Even *Don* Luis Alfau used to go aboard the ships to invite their ball club to come ashore and play in the *Gimnasio Escolar*. And they would agree happily and put together an all-star team to play the best of ours. With those great pitchers we had—Fellito Guerra, *Indio Bravo*— we were better. No doubt about it. Their teams were improvised, while ours were in training. Sometimes they won, but we were better. And we wanted to win more. If we rallied to win in the last inning of a game, there would be an explosion of joy and patriotism."

Juan Bosch remains less receptive to the benefits that accrued from competition with the enemy. A young boy during the occupation, the erstwhile organizer then played for a team he had assembled called *las Piratas,* along with his brother, Pepito. "The occupation did not do anything for our game because our teams were already formed and playing by then. These games were not a form of collaboration with the North Americans, nor would I consider them acts of friendship. These games manifested a form of the peoples' distaste of the occupation. They were a repudiation of it. And when a Dominican player would do something great, the people would shout their hurrays. The game was seen as to go beat the North Americans."

Pedro Julio Santana offers a more nuanced perspective. "Juan Bosch played in La Vega in his youth and demonstrated his love of baseball in later years by going to the games and sitting in the bleachers. I believe that Juan Bosch is a true sportsman, but as for the occupation, let me say this. We had gone through a sad experience. Eight years under the invaders' boots! This is a shameful thing for a country and there are scars that have been left on the body of our country. That is something for which the United States cannot be forgiven. One could, for instance, sympathize with the North Americans, but one cannot sympathize with their government.

"We have this thing inside us against the United States, a small rancor that always will continue to exist because you have to consider the dignity of a people. It should not surprise the United States. And remember that they came and stepped on us again in 1965 and kept Juan Bosch from the presidency. That also cannot be forgiven," Santana remonstrates before his frown transforms into a smile. "One can like a North American. One can love a North American. One can empathize with a North American. But with a government, one's warmth cools down, because it represents the state, and the state sometimes has a way of thinking that does not benefit the people."

Santana smiles again and points to the ambivalent love–hate relationship between his country and the United States. As an example, he remarks that Dominicans were fans of the unlikely combination of Augusto César Sandino and the New York Yankees.

"You remember that they used to call Sandino the eagle, *el aguila del Chipote*? They called him the Eagle of *El Chipote*. Those were the mountains where his guerrillas had their stronghold in Nicaragua. When we had a championship series in 1928 and again in 1929, the team from Santiago was called *Sandino.* Trujillo became president in 1930 so they did not use *Sandino* as their name after that. And in 1936, when there was another championship, the team from Santiago was simply called *Las Aguilas*—the Eagles.

"But we had an empathy, a symphathy for Sandino and the Nicaraguans. Here was this hero who was resisting the invasion of the United States, fighting patriotically for his country. He was a hero of enormous popularity in this country. Children were named César Augusto for him.

"There was a young Dominican, only seventeen, named Gregorio Urbano Gilbert, who rushed onto the docks in 1916 when the marines began disembarking in San Pedro de Macoris and fired his revolver at a group of officers. He killed one and wounded another. After he was released from prison several years later, he went to Nicaragua and became one of Sandino's aides. He fought with Sandino against the North Americans and all this drew admiration and solidarity. After all, we had been through eight years of occupation!

"You can say *Fuera los Yanquis!*—Yankees go home! Yet," he stresses, "when you are talking about the New York Yankees, it is a respected institution and symbol throughout the Dominican Republic which reaches the level of idol worship. The names of Babe Ruth, Tony Lazzeri, Lou Gehrig, and their teammates are venerated here. Their names are at the same level as any notable figure of Dominican sport. I, myself, of course, was a Detroit Tigers fan. Mickey Cochrane, Charlie Gehringer, Hank Greenberg! That was my team. . . .

"You must understand that baseball is not thought of as the sport of the Yankee imperialists. That is a stupid way of thinking. Baseball is the national sport of the United States and it is the greatest thing that the United States has given us and the other countries of the Caribbean. They have not given us anything else that, in my opinion, is of any value but baseball! And here, baseball is the king."

If Báez Vargas, Bosch, and Santana each put a slightly different spin on the impact of the occupation on Dominican baseball, they all agree on what was perhaps the invasion's most significant legacy— Rafael Trujillo. "Trujillo," Bosch argues, "was the product of all the historical forces that have opposed the development of the Dominican people since Columbus discovered the island."

He was all that, and more.

"En esta letrina, Trujillo es el jefe," ("In this latrine, Trujillo is the chief") is scrawled on the door of the bathroom by the visitors' dugout at *Estadio Quisqueya* in Santo Domingo. How far the mighty one has fallen. At one time, virtually every house in the republic bore a sign that read "In this house, Trujillo is the chief." Santo Domingo was renamed

Ciudad Trujillo, and his name adorned the highest mountain peak as well as provinces, towns, and streets throughout the land. Rafael Trujillo ran this country as if it were his own private fiefdom for thirty-one years. But in the years since Trujillo's death on May 30, 1961, his personality cult has crumbled to the point where a North American ballplayer gestures to the bathroom graffiti and asks a Dominican teammate, "Who's this Trujillo guy? Can he play?"

"This Trujillo guy" was the man the marines left behind when they returned to the States in 1924. As the occupation forces quelled dissent, they disarmed the gun-toting populace and disbanded the Dominican army. In its stead, the marines organized a National Guard composed of Dominicans but commanded by North Americans.

The marines tried to recruit Dominicans to serve as officers in this national constabulary, but found few takers among the elite, the traditional source of military leadership. Better-off Dominicans shunned the Guard, creating rare openings for men from the middle echelons of society who could exploit military service as a means of mobility. Among the latter was a young *mulatto* with an uncertain past who would become the Guard's commander and use that as a fulcrum to leverage his way into power in 1930.

Rafael Leonidas Trujillo Molina could trace his lineage on one side to Haiti and on the other to a former Havana chief of police who had spent a few months in the Dominican Republic during which he tried to spy on Cuban exiles, and incidentally fathered a son, who in turn fathered Rafael. Despite the considerable Haitian blood on his maternal side, Rafael would go to great lengths to declare his "whiteness." Once in power, he would attempt to promote immigration by Caucasians to diminish the African portion of the population.

He was born in 1891 to a middling successful businessman in San Cristobal, a small town about twenty miles west of the capital. Trujillo's youth and career before joining the National Guard have been clouded by his supporters' revision of history. In 1907, he found work as a telegraph operator and held that position for three years before embarking on pursuits that likely had some criminal content. In 1916, he was an associate of a gang that robbed stores in the cane fields and engaged in acts of mild extortion. In 1917, Trujillo went to work for the sugar industry, by then the dynamo of the Dominican economy.

He worked at both the San Isidro and Boca Chica sugar mill estates as a weigher in the fields, toting up the amount of cane transferred by a cane cutter from an ox-drawn cart to a railroad car. He then became a *guarda campestre,* a sugar estate policeman. Part security guard, part sheriff, the *guarda campestre* could exploit his small realm of authority to bully the mill workers and demand a cut from the cockfighting concessions. It was a smooth transition for Trujillo to move from the mill to the National Guard.

After requesting a position in the Guard, the twenty-seven-year-old, five foot seven inch, one hundred and twenty-six pound Trujillo was commissioned as a second lieutenant in January 1919. Army life, with its martial trappings and opportunities to display power, appealed to him. Frank Moya Pons, the director of the Foundation for the Advancement of the Social Sciences in Santo Domingo, has written of the psychological effects of the occupation's policy of disarming the people. The revolver, he notes, was not only an instrument of force and social respect, but a symbol of virility and the male rite of passage. This mass disarming thus constituted a collective castration. While most Dominican males were to find some sort of substitute in bat and ball, Trujillo would stick to his guns.

Stationed in Seibo in the southeastern sugar region, Trujillo saw limited action against the guerrillas. His exploits, however, went through an after-the-fact enhancement by those seeking favor with him. After a brief stint in a military academy, Trujillo was promoted to captain in 1922, bypassing the first lieutenant rank. By the time the marines left, he was third in command of the Guard, and by 1928, he had become Brigadier General and the Chief of Staff of the National Army, the heir to the Guard.

Along the way, Trujillo divorced his first wife, married a second, and impregnated a third woman, his mistress, Maria Martínez. She gave him a son, Rafael Leonidas Trujillo Martínez, whom later generations knew as Ramfis. He was his father's pride, joy, and sorrow.

During his apprenticeship with the marines as an officer in the Guard, Trujillo was schooled in counterinsurgency. He learned how to gather intelligence with an emphasis on preventing potential disturbances. The internal apparatus he built controlled population movement and discouraged the slightest display of dissent. Dominicans soon internalized a fear of being singled out that would have bordered on paranoia if it was not so well-founded.

As commander of the army, Trujillo built a network of alliances that focused power in his personage. By 1930, he was ready to make his move. He instigated a revolt and then switched his allegiance to the provisional revolutionary government that resulted. Trujillo declared his candidacy for president in the ensuing elections and eliminated any opponents by one means or another. On May 16, 1930, he won election without opposition.

Within weeks after Trujillo took office, Santo Domingo was leveled by a hurricane. Hurricane *San Zenon* destroyed all but four hundred of the ten thousand buildings that comprised the capital. It killed over two thousand, injured six thousand, and left thirty thousand without shelter. But the hurricane was probably Trujillo's finest hour, as he channeled his enormous energies into relief and reconstruction.

"The first years of the Trujillo era were constructive," Manuel Joaquín Báez Vargas acknowledges. "I was not politically oriented. I worked with education all my life, but I am an observer of politics. In my work with the secretary of education, I could see that Trujillo appointed the best men—the most prepared, the most intelligent, the most morally sound. And in those first years, he disciplined us. He committed crimes and he was ruthless, but he accustomed us to respect our national anthem and our flag, which until then had not been respected by us. He instituted a great discipline, which he himself learned from his association with the North Americans."

His visage darkening, Báez Vargas continues. "But around the middle of his era, around 1945, his physical and mental faculties began to wane. As you know, we say that power corrupts. The period of power begins to corrupt the mind, to make it rot, and as the mind rots, it has to inflict more power and force to maintain itself. And with that force, you see atrocities.

"In the last phases of his life, it was awful. The atrocities were committed not only by him, but by those who accompanied him. There came a point when he had surrounded himself by people with inferior qualities in terms of their ethics, and the last half of his government was disastrous. He did not govern; he lost control. He was sick."

Raising a long finger and jabbing the air with it, Báez Vargas cautions, "Trujillo cannot be judged fairly yet. He cannot be dealt with coolly. Even twenty-seven years after his death, the passions are still high and a lot of those same people who were around are still around. Those who were his enemies are still around, too. Perhaps history might be able to judge him, but only years from now, when the passions of his friends and enemies have diminished."

As Trujillo consolidated power in the 1930s, he humbled opponents and kept even his supporters on a perpetually shaky footing. All authority became centralized in his august body. Death squads eliminated potential rivals and the survivors soon learned that there was only one way to conduct oneself—Trujillo's way. With the creation of the *Partido Dominicano* in 1932, there was only one political party in the country and its sole purpose was to advance Trujillo. He would be elected to cries of "God and Trujillo" in 1934, with a vote count thought to be ten times the actual number of ballots cast.

With his monopoly over political power came near-monopoly over the Dominican economy. He, his family, and their retainers would ultimately own half the sugar industry, about a third of all cultivable land, and the core of the country's commercial and manufacturing sectors. If *el Jefe* wanted it, *el Jefe* got it. Many either concealed their true wealth or purposely prevented it from accruing so that Trujillo would not confiscate it. By the time of his death, with a portfolio reputedly worth as much as a half billion dollars, Trujillo was one of the richest men on the globe.

Nouveau riche that he was, Trujillo demanded adulation and constant massage. His associates and underlings went to great lengths to enhance this cult of personality. That need to honor and acknowledge his omnipotence penetrated every aspect of Dominican life, even baseball.

By the time of Trujillo's inauguration in 1930, baseball had evolved from a network of self-organized clubs into a semiprofessionalized arena for both sport and entertainment. Trujillo's ascendency assured that baseball would gain a political connection, too.

"But he did not like baseball, he liked the horses," Cuqui Cordova protests. "And women, too," he adds with a Latin lilt. "He really liked women. But he helped baseball. He knew that it was good for him to have the people seeing baseball because then they don't pay attention to politics. Always, the dictatorships do that." Indeed, one often hears Dominicans say that there will never be any political trouble during the baseball season, only afterwards.

But if Rafael Trujillo was not an aficionado of the Dominican pastime, his family was. "Now Ramfis, Trujillo's son, was a great backer of *Escogido,* and his brother, Petan, and most of his sisters were *Liceyistas.* But Trujillo himself, no. He was not such a fan." Those who backed Trujillo, Cordova notes, were also quite often ardent fans. Dr. José E. Aybar, a dentist whose political savvy opened the door to the inner sanctum of power, had been a *Licey* mainstay since the late 1920s. General Federico Fiallo, Trujillo's principal military chief, had pitched for *Licey* its first season and remained ever loyal to his team. Francisco Martínez Alba, Trujillo's wife's brother, would become *Escogido*'s chief executive in the 1950s. And Ramfis, as commander of the Air Force *(Aviación),* would make this branch of the armed services virtually an *Escogido* farm club. These men were not above manipulating their positions to advance their teams or exploiting the game to add to Trujillo's prestige. Given how closely Trujillo supervised business and political dealings, baseball might have been one of the few safe outlets for rivalries among the elites. And even there, overstepping the bounds could lead to jail.

After the hurricane *San Zenon,* baseball collapsed in the capital. The ballparks had been atomized by the storm and recovery took precedence over recreation. But barnstorming teams called the *Es-*

trellas Dominicanas and *Generalísimo Trujillo* carried the Dominican sporting banner to Cuba and Central America. "They were not really professionals," Pedro Julio Santana explains. "The spirit of these teams was amateur and their purpose to project the image of Trujillo and our country."

The sport soon rebounded, as *Licey* and *Escogido* reassembled and the island became more integrated into the fervor of Caribbean basin baseball. By the 1930s, Latin ball was a melange of native players, black Americans from the Negro Leagues, and white major leaguers playing winter ball as the game's national borders were pierced by the players' itinerant style. Given that racial boundaries still kept the major leagues off-limits to any but those who were white or who could pass for it, these Caribbean alternatives probably surpassed, at least on the field, the more capitalized and publicized major leagues of this era. Dominicans like Horacio Martínez, Tetelo Vargas, and the three Grillo brothers played for *Almendares* and *Havana* in Cuba, while Cubans, Puerto Ricans, Venezuelans, and Negro Leaguers would up in the Dominican Republic.

In 1933, both the *Cuban Stars* of the Negro Leagues and *Richmond* of the International League played series on the island. Venezuela's *Concordia* came next, bringing with them Negro League *nonpareil* Josh Gibson and other black American reinforcements. *Escogido* and *Licey* responded with their own recruits, including Cuban hurler Luis "Lefty" Tiant and Puerto Rican Perucho Cepeda, father of Orlando and perhaps the greatest player from that island until Roberto Clemente. Finally, in 1935, the Cincinnati Reds became the first major league squad to visit, beating both *Licey* and *Escogido* in the process.

These encounters whetted Dominican appetites and set the stage for professional championships during the 1936 and 1937 seasons. By the end of the summer of 1937, Dominicans had begun to realize that they had just witnessed possibly the best ball played anywhere in the world that year. Paradoxically, that season's end also began a fourteen-year hiatus for pro ball.

3
Have Baseball—Will Travel

J ames "Cool Papa" Bell sits quietly in the Pirates' dugout at Three
Rivers Stadium on a warm September night in 1988. A banner
commemorating the Homestead Grays' 1948 Negro League World Series championship, the last ever played, flutters over the left field stands.
Bell, a handful of survivors from the Grays' 1948 team, and several
other men who helped make Pittsburgh the center of black baseball in
the Americas during the 1930s and 1940s, await a moment of recognition on the field before the evening game. As the field crew disassem-
bles the batting cage and rakes the base paths, Bell, now 85, reminisces
about his season in the Dominican sun more than fifty years ago.

"Trujillo!" he exclaims. "That man took Gus Greenlee's ball club
and put it in Santo Domingo. He just took them right off Gus. But he got
himself a ball club. Nobody could touch us."

Bell should know. The Starkville, Mississippi, native thought to be
the fastest man ever to play baseball was a member of Gus Greenlee's
Pittsburgh Crawfords as spring training began in 1937. The 1935
Crawfords had won the Negro National League championship with five
future Hall-of-Famers in the lineup: Oscar Charleston, Judy Johnson,
Josh Gibson, Satchel Paige, and Bell. But three of these men, Gibson,
Paige, and Bell, as well as a half dozen other Crawfords, and some of
the finest Negro League and Cuban players that money could buy
wound up in the Dominican Republic for the summer of 1937.

"He got Satchel first," Bell relates, "but Satch figured he needed
some help so he called me. I'll tell you, we played some baseball that
summer."

Like Bell, most of the other Negro Leaguers honored that night
had played in Latin baseball, which, until the 1950s, often played both
summer and winter seasons. For them, Mexico, Cuba, Puerto Rico,
Venezuela, and the Dominican Republic offered either an alternative to

34

the Negro Leagues or a chance to continue playing during the winter months. Few could afford to pass the North American off-season idly.

There were other reasons, too, as Willie Wells pointed out when he wrote to the *Pittsburgh Courier* to explain why he had left the Newark Eagles for a club in Vera Cruz, Mexico. "Not only do I get more money playing here, but I live like a king. . . . I am not faced with the racial problem. . . . I didn't quit Newark and join some other team in the United States. I quit and left the country. . . . I've found freedom and democracy here, something I never found in the United States. . . . Here, in Mexico, I am a man."

A few Negro Leaguers likely would have played in the 1937 championship in any event, but it took defeat by both *Licey* and *Escogido* in the 1936 season to bring them there *en masse*.

The capital's teams had lost to the *Estrellas Orientales* from San Pedro de Macoris in the 1936 *Campeonato Mayor Trujillo*. Rafael Antun remembers it well. Sitting in his kitchen on a residential street in the almost never tranquil San Pedro, the seventy-seven-year-old Antun cuts tickets out of cardboard for an upcoming cockfight. His hands and white, V-necked tee-shirt are blotched with purple magic marker, which has also managed to mar his orange bermuda shorts.

"At one time, during Trujillo, I was very important. If I didn't take care of baseball, there would have been no baseball in Macoris. When the San Pedro team began in 1912, it was mostly Dominicans then, from the upper classes—a pharmacist, two doctors, engineers—and perhaps one or two Cubans and an American who played. In 1936, when we re-formed the ball club and called it the *Estrellas Orientales*, there was an association of prominent men, including myself and Federico Nina, who backed the club. It made no money then," Antun laughs. "It cost! It cost *mucho*! And the players were mostly *Cubanos*."

So were many of those who played for *Licey*, *Escogido*, and Santiago's *Aguilas Cibaeñas*, the three other teams in the league. A few Dominicans such as Tetelo Vargas, Horacio Martínez, and Pedro Alejandro San held spots in the lineup, but foreign reinforcements dominated the game. When San Pedro's Cubans beat the other clubs' recruits, that did not go down easily in *Ciudad Trujillo*, as Santo Domingo had been renamed.

"Trujillo's friends put politics into baseball," Antun argues. "Those who were close to him took advantage of politics, but in baseball there should not be politics. I had a friendship with Trujillo. He was the godfather of my son, but I was not interested in what I could get from him. He wanted to make me an official but I turned him down." Digressing for several minutes to sketch several complex business transactions with Trujillo that netted the Antun brothers enough profit to make Antun chortle decades later, Antun suddenly exclaims, "I don't want to talk about politics. Don't complicate my life!"

But as an unreconstructed *Trujillista,* Antun cannot stay off the subject. "Trujillo was what this country needed. You think at that time that there were any communists here? The communists were seven feet in the ground. You think there was any theft?" Antun's face reddens and he spits out "The person who would steal a chicken . . ." before emotion overwhelms him and he does not finish the sentence. "You could sleep with your door open. Now you have to sleep with irons on the door. If you didn't mess with Trujillo, you were in peace. But if you tried to harm him, whoooo!"

Returning to the events of the 1937 season, Antun grins. "We had a Cuban team here and they were the only ones that could beat *Ciudad Trujillo* [*Licey* and *Escogido* were combined to form the *Ciudad Trujillo* club that season], so the army came and arrested all our Cubans before the game one day. We could play only with *Criollos*—Dominicans. This happened two or three times and then they would free them after the games. Why did they do this? Because they said that *Ciudad Trujillo,* a team with Trujillo's name, could not lose."

Federico Nina agrees. Like his father, Federico Nina Santana, and his son, Federico Nina *hijo,* Federico Luis Nina is an attorney. He practices law in San Pedro, on a street close to the central square. Rain beats against the wooden shutters in his second floor office as Nina traces his father's career. "He was born in Santo Domingo in 1900 but came to San Pedro in 1924, after law school, when he was named a judge here. . . .

"When I was very young, he played baseball. Before he came to San Pedro, he had been one of the directors of *Los Muchachos* and a founder of *Escogido.* Here, he built his house next to the ball field. There were always teams from the *ingenios* (sugar mills) playing there.

"Finally, in 1936, he and a group of friends organized the *Estrellas Orientales.* All during that time, the team was losing money. It was something that was supported by romance. I remember that every Monday from this very office, we would look for some money to pay the ballplayers that were sitting out there in the hallway, waiting for their pay. They played every Saturday and Sunday then, and it cost a lot of money. We never made that much money and my father used to go on Monday mornings with a few leaders of that group to the offices of the people involved in the organization of the team and say 'Give me five thousand *pesos*' or 'Give me three thousand *pesos*' till they could scrounge up enough."

In 1936, San Pedro's club won the championship. "*Señor* Trujillo—that was, of course, his era—did not like to lose. And since he didn't like to lose, he made a team out of *Licey* and *Escogido,* called *Ciudad Trujillo,* and brought to the country the best ballplayers of the North American black leagues. For Trujillo, baseball was secondary. He did not like the city of *Ciudad Trujillo* to lose so he created this invincible machine so that it would never happen again."

Like Antun, Nina discounts direct political rivalries between the directorates of the San Pedro, Santiago, and *Ciudad Trujillo* ball clubs. "I suppose that you understand that Trujillo did not allow enemies. They did not exist. You have to understand that anyone that declared himself an enemy of Trujillo could not operate openly. Anyone that would have been a declared enemy of Trujillo could not have operated a team."

But even competing with the team bearing Trujillo's name could be risky. Dr. José Aybar, who ran *Ciudad Trujillo,* was not satisfied with his Cuban and Puerto Rican imports, even though they included some of the basin's finest talents. He went to New Orleans where the Pittsburgh Crawfords were training. His objective was the lanky Leroy "Satchel" Paige. With his "bee ball," hesitation pitch, and pinpoint control, Paige was not only the Negro Leagues' greatest attraction, but one of its finest pitchers. He was also keenly aware of his worth, both on and off the field, and willing to jump teams if it was in his best interests. And he knew of the bankrolls that Latin clubs were flashing to prospective recruits. The *Crawfords'* owner, Gus Greenlee, was not a man without resources, controlling the numbers rackets in Pittsburgh's Hill District from a seat at the bar of his *Crawford Grill* nightclub. But Gus, the "Caliph of Little Harlem," was no match for Trujillo.

As Paige reconstructed events of the 1937 championship a quarter century later to his biographer, David Lipman, a man introduced himself as Dr. José Enrique Aybar and said, "I direct the baseball team in *Ciudad Trujillo.* . . . We are interested in your pitching. President Trujillo has instructed me to obtain the best pitcher possible for his team and our scouts recommend you." A suitcase full of money helped Paige overcome his qualms about jumping the Crawfords and he was soon en route to *Ciudad Trujillo.*

He arrived to a "hero's welcome" and a press conference. "Seems like some of these hungry peasants," he later wrote, "was crying because all that money was being spent on ballplayers and Dr. Aybar wanted to straighten things out." Aybar told the press that the money to hire Paige had been "subscribed voluntarily by enthusiastic baseball fans. . . . Neither the president of the republic, Dr. Trujillo, nor the government had to intervene. . . . Baseball in Trujillo City is not commercial. . . . Money makes no difference. Baseball is spiritual in every aspect, as indulged in by Latin races."

Spirituality aside, Paige appraised the competition and saw that the Santiago ball club had Martín Dihigo, Luis Tiant, and Horacio Martínez, each a *bona fide* Negro League star. And San Pedro could counter with an imposing mix of Cuban and Dominican talent. He then called his Crawford roommate, Cool Bell, to tell him of the pecuniary joys of island ball. Bell liked what he heard. Along with Josh Gibson, Sammy Bankhead, Cy Perkins, and a few other Crawford teammates, he soon boarded a Pan American biplane for a new venue.

The *Dragónes* of *Ciudad Trujillo* had more Negro Leaguers on its roster than it did Dominicans and Cubans combined. Its team photo features eight Negro Leaguers, six Cubans, one Puerto Rican, one Dominican, and Dr. Aybar. The other clubs took notice and went shopping themselves.

"I was only eleven or twelve then," Federico Nina recalls, "but I lived that season from the dugout. I remember it with an amazing amount of love and fondness. I would like to live that season again. But there were some difficult moments. My father went to Pittsburgh with *Don* Luis Mendez, an employee of the Dominican consulate. They were at the ballpark [Pittsburgh's Forbes Field] checking out some players that they wanted to bring here, and after the game, they were jailed and accused of robbing players from Pittsburgh. Of course, this was true."

The arrest set off a minor diplomatic tiff. Telegrams shot back and forth among the Dominican legation, the State Department, and Pittsburgh, where Nina and Mendez spent a weekend in jail before being freed on $500 bond. The Commonwealth of Pennsylvania charged the two with conspiring to defraud the Pittsburgh Crawfords and Homestead Grays of the services of six players that the teams had under contract. The Dominican *chargé d'affaires* wired Secretary of State Cordell Hull in response that the arrests were both improper and irregular.

Power cuts out and Nina unshutters his window before the airconditionless room steams up. The rains have ceased but the street below approximates a lake. "I do not know if it was the intervention of the Dominican government or a lack of evidence, but charges were dropped after about two weeks." Meanwhile, word of Dominican salaries, which were substantially higher than what the Negro League clubs could pay, spread.

As a result, most of the players that Nina had been accused of soliciting ended up on the island. But when he returned with several of them, he found *Licey* stalwart General Federico Fiallo there to meet him.

"San Pedro was the port for Pan American Airlines then. They flew hydroplanes here that landed on the *Rio Higuamo* right there in front of the main church. Everybody that came from the outside ended up in San Pedro.

"But when the best ones that my father picked up over there arrived—I think that there were four of them—officers of the army were waiting for them. They took them all to the capital and made them play for the *Ciudad Trujillo* team. So, my father had to go back to the United States for more players, and this time when he returned to San Pedro, they arrested him!" Nina would spend another week in jail before returning to his city and his ball club.

This would not be Nina's last run-in with the forces of Trujillo. A dispute over the drafting of a thousand young Dominicans, including his son and Cuqui Cordova, to fight alongside the North Americans in Korea, eventually caused him to drop off the San Pedro team directorate. "They accused him of subversive propaganda and rumors against the state," his son explains. "Upon him going to jail, the other directors of the *Estrellas Orientales* decided to substitute for him, because at this point, he could not continue to be in the forefront of the team—not as a recognized enemy of Trujillo. From then on, he couldn't be involved in anything of importance. And once that was all over, he never again wanted to become a member of the directorate." Nina was rehabilitated to some extent for his lifelong efforts in sport, however, by his election to the Dominican Hall of Fame in 1982, a few years before his death at 85.

The play on the field that summer somehow transcended the machinations off of it. And while the season was a fiscal folly that sidetracked pro ball on the island until 1951, it left indelible memories on a generation of Dominicans, who still recall the thunderous blasts from Gibson's bat, Paige's eccentricities on the mound, and the lithe Bell roaming center field like no one before him.

"My older brother used to carry me to the ball fields," Roberto Caines recalls in an English heavily accented by the lilt of his parents' Virgin Islands origins. "I remember everything I see then. I saw Gibson, Cocaína García, Arango, Bell and I'll tell you this. Martín Dihigo, that was the greatest ballplayer God ever gave the world." Caines lives in the Consuelo sugar estate, about ten kilometers from San Pedro. "Paige, Bell, and those boys used to come here to play golf on the estate's golf course. Only black men to do that!"

Like Caines, Coleridge Mayers is a descendent of migrants from the British West Indies and a lifelong sugar mill employee at one of San Pedro's *ingenios*. "I knew Satchel Paige, and Joshua Gibson, William Perkins, Bell, Bragaña, García, Perucho Cepeda. I knew them personally. Those who played here in San Pedro would dance on Monday nights and we would get to know them.

"That Gibson, he could hit the ball from here to the sky. One Sunday, he was playing and Bragaña strike him out twice and he says to Paige. 'Goddamn! that ball is dropping hard. I can't hit him.' Paige says you'll get him the third time. When Joshua comes to bat that third time, he has two strikes and a ball, I remember like it was just now. Paige says 'Stoop a little more. Stoop a little more.' Whooooooo! It was the biggest home run I ever saw in all these Lord's days."

With games on weekends only, each contest took on greater significance. Paige and the other Negro Leaguers speak of armed guards and not-so-veiled threats that *Ciudad Trujillo* should win or else. *Kansas City Monarch* ace Chet Brewer, pitching for *Aguilas* that summer, recounts searching for Paige one day so that they could have a beer. He couldn't find him, and a small boy came up to him and said Paige was *"En la cárcel."* ("In the jail.") Trujillo, Brewer explains, "had put them in before they were going to play us so they wouldn't rouse around." Federico Nina, whose father's team would come in last that summer, adds his grievances. "The interests of Trujillo began to play too important a role and to affect the game. For instance, Dominican umpires did not dare call out decisions against *Ciudad Trujillo* and sometimes there arose disturbances on the field and when the military forces came to break it up, they would always clobber the ones on the other side of *Ciudad Trujillo*. I saw this with my own eyes. I was a batboy and more than one time I saw it."

But Pedro Julio Santana discounts Trujillo's involvement. "That's something that has been made up. Baseball is born of the breast of those who come dragging with them their devotion to the sport. With Gibson and Bell, you don't have to think of Trujillo to find the reason they won. Trujillo had nothing to do with their winning. He did not have anything to do with any of that. . . . Those things were manipulations of the directors and that has always been done here."

Cuqui Cordova also protests that these accounts of interference and Trujillo's role in them have been overdrawn, but both he and Santana join those who attest to the championship's calibre of play. He considers the *Ciudad Trujillo* team the "most potent baseball machine" ever assembled on the island and the championship the best celebrated there. Gibson batted .437 to lead the league, hit for the cycle in one game, and added Dominicans to the legions with a story to tell that usually begins, "It was the longest home run I ever saw. . ." Paige, 8 and 2 for the season, sometimes pitched and won back-to-back games on weekends. And Bell, stealing bases and winning ovations for his play in the field, had the fifth highest batting average for the season.

The finale of *"El Campeonato Nacional de Base Ball 1937: Pro Reelección Presidente Trujillo"* came in early July. A week after Chet

Brewer one-hit *Ciudad Trujillo,* his *Aguilas* and the *Dragónes* met for the last time. Brewer started again and was coasting on a 2–0 lead when *Ciudad Trujillo* chased him not only off the mound, but off the island, erupting for eight runs in the fifth inning. The key blow was a grand slam by shortstop Sammy Bankhead off Martín Dihigo, who left center field to relieve Brewer. *Aguilas* rallied in the ninth, scoring four runs to make it 8–6 before Paige came in to shut them down.

As Aybar, joined by the directorates of the other clubs, offered the championship trophy to the Honorable Dr. Trujillo, the jubilant crowds spilled out of the stadium. The celebration along *El Conde* in *Ciudad Nueva* went on through the night, but when the visiting Negro Leaguers and Cubans departed a few days later, the pro game went with them.

"We spent much money to bring these players here and because they were the best in the world, it cost too much," Cordoba explains. "That killed baseball here." Pedro Julio Santana agrees. "The costs were ruinous. It could put you in the poorhouse to have a championship. There was no money after 1937." And there was no pro ball either, until 1951.

But baseball, by then on the island for almost half a century, could not be denied. Although the best Dominicans would play in other countries during the 1940s, the game's roots had burrowed deep in Dominican soil. The land was fertile and the game would soon blossom again.

Fernando Arturo "Bolo" Vicioso is asleep at his desk on the fourth floor of the *Centro Olímpico* in the heart of Santo Domingo. It is a sensible mid-morning strategy for this 83-year-old veteran of the sporting wars on a warm, muggy June day. Power cuts off and with it the fan that had been gently lifting the soft white hairs on Vicioso's head. Vicioso snaps awake soon after I arrive and adopts a conspiratorial edge while tracing his not insignificant role in the making of a Dominican sporting establishment.

"I was born in 1905 on *Calle Sanchez* in *Ciudad Nueva.* When I was a child, I went to the *Gimnasio Escolar.* Professor Ramirez Guerra called me over once one day and started out, 'When you grow up, you are going to be a man of about five foot five inches. You're not going to grow any further than that. I am going to assign you to different teachers because when you grow up, you're going to be a leader in sport—not an athlete. You are not going to practice sport anymore. You are going to learn to teach it.'"

While still in his teens, Bolo left the republic for the United States and then Central America, where he represented an Italian publishing house. He lived in Nicaragua between 1924 and 1942 and began working with that country's sporting program.

A secretary enters to attend to her boss and wipes a pool of my sweat off the desk. Bolo, in a white guayabera shirt embroidered with powder blue flowers, does not seem to notice the heat or the lack of electricity.

"While in Managua, I proposed to a group of Nicaraguan sportswriters that they write their government, soliciting it to create some sort of institution regulating sports. I drafted the letter for them. This request was successful and the National Commission for Sports was created. I became an advisor for it and managed the Nicaraguan baseball teams for the Central American and Caribbean Games.

"During that time, I also helped the team, *General Trujillo,* which had run aground in Panama and needed assistance. I contracted for them to play a series in Nicaragua and went with them to Guatemala and Mexico. But I had much more influence on Nicaraguan sport at that time than in my homeland."

Anastasio Somoza García ran Nicaragua then. Like Trujillo, he won his spurs in the national constabulary created by the marines during their early twentieth century occupation, and later gained hegemonic control over his country's economy. Unlike Trujillo, Somoza was a genuine baseball fan. When he visited *Ciudad Trujillo* in the summer of 1952, he stood on the mound amidst frenetic well-wishers and tossed out the first ball at a game. Fernando Nina, whose *Estrellas* were playing *Licey* that day, asked that the game be dedicated to his "*Excelentísimo Señor Presidente de Nicaragua, Gen.* Anastasio Somoza." After the opening ceremony, Somoza and Trujillo, who was decked out in a crescent-shaped hat with long ostrich plumes, left the field for the dignitaries' box. But Somoza did not like being seated so far from the play and after a few innings, he left Trujillo for a seat behind the dugout.

"Somoza loved baseball *muchísimo,*" Vicioso recalls. "Much more than Trujillo. He played baseball at one time and was always a great fan." Only three days before his assassination of Augusto César Sandino in 1934, Somoza took in a ball game with United States Minister Arthur Bliss Lane, whom he later claimed had authorized the murder.

"I met Somoza when he was still a civilian and we became friends. When he was in the National Guard, we used to hang out together. We used to go to baseball games together. When he achieved power, he called on me to organize sports."

Despite this entree to Nicaraguan sport, Vicioso kept in touch with the Dominican sporting scene. "When I was in Mexico in 1938 as the Nicaraguan delegate to the inauguration of the Sports Federation of

Mexico, I asked the Dominican ambassador to Mexico why in the Dominican Republic, the government did not take sport in hand and organize it. When I went back to Nicaragua, I wrote down my proposal and sent it to the republic. They wrote back and said it was a good idea but that it would be better if I returned to the country myself to implement the project. At that time, I was at the height of my activities in Nicaragua and had a great deal of prestige. But a few years later, I did return."

Back in his homeland in 1942, Vicioso advanced new versions of the project, modeled for the most part after Cuba's *Dirección General Nacional de Deportes*. "One day, just before they approved the project, they took me to *el Jefe*, General Federico Fiallo, and he questioned me. 'You have been in Nicaragua. What were you, a liberal or a conservative [the two opposing sides in a decades-long struggle there]?' I said I was *nada*—nothing—that I had been a sportsman and that I've never been in politics and never intended to become involved in politics."

Given a clean bill of political health, no doubt helped by his brother, a member of the armed forces' inner circle, Vicioso organized the *Dirección General de Deportes* (DGD) in late December, 1943. Frank Hatton, former *Licey* second baseman and operator of *Radio Voz,* was appointed its director, with Vicioso second in command. Frank Hatton had been a pioneer in both Dominican sport and broadcasting. The son of a North American father and Dominican mother, Hatton first broadcast the World Series on the island by translating a radio account and simulating ballpark sounds from his Santo Domingo studio.

Another, perhaps equally important, impetus for the *DGD* came from Dominican emulation of Cuba. "The idea for the *DGD* came in part from Juan Marine y Montes, the director of the *Dirección General Nacional de Deportes* in Cuba," according to Pedro Julio Santana. "Marine came here and was honored for his role in sport. He spoke to Trujillo and there were exchanges between sporting elements and we began to copy these Cuban ideas. We had, you remember, good relations with Cuba then."

Bolo Vicioso, meanwhile, defined the DGD's agenda and directed its revamping of amateur sport. And like so much else in this tropical land, baseball reflected Trujillo's drive to centralize power and make the Dominican Republic a world player.

Soon local tournaments channeled sporting energies into an annual series of regional competitions. "Each region would organize its teams and then have eliminations," Pedro Julio Santana explains. "There were four regions, one here in the capital and one each to the east, west, and north. The team that won the region would absorb the best players of the losing teams and then come to the capital for the championships." An extraordinary organizer, Bolo developed a set of armed forces teams based in the Air Force, Army, National Police, and Marines. He later helped the sugar industry create a similar sporting infrastructure on an *ingenio*-by-*ingenio* basis. Vicioso then brought these clubs, as well as community and privately-backed teams, into the tournaments. "The fruits of these competitions were the Alou brothers from Haina, Manuel Mota from Santo Domingo, and Juan Marichal from Manzanillo," Pedro Julio Santana offers.

About the same time that the *DGD* was centralizing Dominican ball on an amateur and semipro level, the nation elected to participate in the *Mundiales*. "This world amateur championship," Santana recounts, "began, ironically enough, in England in 1938." Only the United States showed up and it came in second best. "But the series took on a more serious character after that and they were renewed in Havana." Held in the basin throughout the 1940s, with Cuba hosting five consecutive tournaments, the *Mundiales* had a decidedly Latin flavor and became the most important sporting competition in which these nations competed on something approximating equal footing, both with each other and with the United States. Basin nations won every championship from 1940 through 1972, with Cuba winning eleven out of eighteen times.

National aspirations and international rivalries sometimes spilled onto the ball field. An irate Anastasio Somoza fired the Nicaraguan manager in the midst of one *Mundiales* and took to the dugout to direct the team himself. National honor was restored only years later by a victory over Cuba in the final game of the 1972 series, an event still celebrated as one of the Central American nation's greatest sporting exploits.

Trujillo, meanwhile, had come to fancy himself as a world leader. He tried to mediate the Chaco dispute between Paraguay and Bolivia and offered to admit 100,000 Jews fleeing Nazi-controlled Europe in 1938. But the South Americans scoffed at his efforts to intercede and only a few thousand Jews ever made it to Sosua, the site of Trujillo's proposed Jewish refuge. Just a handful remain there now, and Sosua has subsequently evolved into a chic beachfront catering to a mostly European and Canadian clientele, albeit with the country's best deli. Where Trujillo did get results from his international intrigues was closer to home, in the Caribbean.

And baseball, naturally, was perceived by sportsmen and politicians alike as a way to advance both the national image and their leader's prestige across the basin. "The government," explains Santana, who was then vice-chairman of the National Baseball Commission, "became concerned with encouraging baseball—as a sport but also because they were aware that by helping sport, they would help the stability of the government. Sending Dominican teams to other places demonstrated the progress of baseball in this country. It showed them that we were not stagnating." Except for Haiti, the countries with which the Dominican Republic interacted the most played baseball. Besting Cuba, Puerto Rico, or Venezuela at the ballpark alternated with less pacific means of conflict and mattered just as much to most Dominicans, from Trujillo's upper echelons down to the boys washing cars along the *malecón*.

The Dominican Republic first entered the *Mundiales* in 1941 and returned to Havana and other Caribbean tournament sites throughout the decade. In 1942, the Dominicans went into the ninth game of the twelve game round-robin series tied with the Cubans. They faced a United States team made up primarily of university students. Cuban fans, known for their zealotry throughout the region, shouted the *Yanquis* on to a lead in the game. The scene that day at *Estadio La Tropical* was more of a madhouse than a ballpark, argues Cuqui Cordova. The bedlam in the stands soon aggravated play, and a hit batsman led to a brawl in the *Yanqui* dugout. Cuban fans began throwing bottles and assorted ballpark comestibles at the Dominican players, and Dominican manager Burrolote Rodriguez flung a bat into the stands in retaliation. "He hit two fans," Cordova explains, "and the Cuban police took him to jail." The skipperless Dominicans regained their poise but not the lead. An indignant Trujillo ordered the immediate return of the team but then countermanded his orders. Cuba ultimately triumphed with the Dominican Republic coming in second in the games.

Cuba and Venezuela dominated the championships, but at the tenth competition, held in Managua, Nicaragua in December 1948, the Dominican Republic broke through. It came just months after a plane carrying the national champion team, *Los Caballeros* from Santiago, crashed by the *Río Verde,* with all aboard killed.

The country cut loose as radio transmissions from Managua announced the Dominican victory. Strangers embraced on the streets, rum flowed like water, and as one journalist wrote from the midst of carousing Santo Domingo, "The people jumped, screamed, and shouted 'Long live the victors and the Government!'" Winning the *Mundiales* was more than a sporting triumph. It marked the end of a national mourning period after the crash at the *Río Verde* and provided one of the rare moments when this nation could unabashedly celebrate something other than the grandeur of Trujillo. Defeating Cuba, Venezuela, and the United States in the one cultural arena they held in common was heady stuff. No series was held in 1949, but when the

Dominicans returned to Managua in 1950 and successfully defended their title, professional ball was not long in the offing.

"And where does the stream of amateur baseball finally flow?" Santana asks and then answers. "To that great river of professional baseball."

4
Peloteros *in the Banana Fields*

Tony Peña pops out of his low-slung crouch behind home plate and dives for the ball squibbing down the third base line. Grabbing it bare-handed, he rolls to his feet and fires to first before his momentum carries him back to the turf, where he lies facedown on the grass as an explosion of noise from the stands tells him the runner is out.

While skyrockets flash above the palm trees behind left field and the band begins to *merengue,* Peña snaps to his feet and dances back to the plate. Three months before, Peña caught for the St. Louis Cardinals in the World Series, but on this twilight evening in January, Tony Peña is playing baseball in the *Estadio Cibao* in Santiago, and he couldn't be happier. The Cardinals, like the Pirates before them, had hoped that Peña would take off the winter season. But by mid-January, after being named the Most Valuable Player on a major league barnstorming tour of Japan, Peña is back in the lineup, catching full-time in anticipation of the winter league playoffs.

"How could I sit out?" Peña demands. "It would be like slapping the people here in the face. Besides," he grins, "you've got to be crazy to play this game and I love to play this game. I just love to."

He always has.

Earlier that day, Peña has had, at most, four hours' sleep as he eases his BMW 735i up to a roadside fruit stand outside Santiago de los Caballeros, his winter home. "Best breakfast in *el mundo,*" he smiles before biting into a slab of pineapple and pulling back onto the highway. The day before, Peña had ridden the team bus from Santiago to San Pedro de Macoris for a night game and then back afterwards. This morning, he is on his way to Palo Verde, about 125 kilometers away, to pick up his father before returning for a game against league-leading *Escogido.*

"I come back to Palo Verde as often as I can," Peña explains. "I love the land, and the people there are my real friends. I care more

47

about what people there think of me than anywhere else. I don't want them to see me any different than I was. I would not be Tony Peña if I didn't come back."

The two-lane blacktop that winds its way northwest from Santiago slices through the *Cibao,* the island's most fertile valley. Urban sprawl runs flush against fields of shimmering green tobacco plants. Sheaves of tobacco leaves hang drying in open-sided, thatched roof sheds while old women with bandannas covering their heads rake coffee beans on the roadside. Entire pigs slowly turn on barbecue spits nearby. The sugar cane harvest has begun and cane cutters hack their way through a field of fifteen-foot-high plants. Most are Haitian, but Peña points to a group of Dominicans. "You see how they use their *machetes?*" he asks. "That's what gives us our arm strength."

About halfway to Palo Verde, the tobacco fields give way to rows of banana trees. Peña drives as he plays, with seeming abandon. He weaves through a cluster of motorcycles, the drivers of which are clutching propane gas cannisters, and waves jauntily at a traffic policeman who tries to pull him over.

Peña soon passes the sandlot in Villa Vasquez where Julio Martínez, an *Aguilas* coach, took him in the summer of 1975 to work out for Howie Haak, then the Pirates' Caribbean scout and still the maven of Latin talent. "Howie wanted to sign him, but Tony's parents wanted him to go to college instead," Martínez remembers. Haak won.

Outside Villa Vasquez, Peña decelerates, takes the cap off his head, and crosses himself. "Did you know Ramón Lora?" he questions. "He was a hell of a good ballplayer—a catcher—from Palo Verde." The cross by the roadside marks where Lora died in a car wreck, just a few days before the start of the 1986 winter season.

In nearby Monte Cristi, Peña points out *Liceo* José Marti, the high school named after the Cuban independence leader who visited the city during one of his exiles. Peña graduated from Marti shortly before the Pirates signed him. "My father didn't like baseball too much, then," Peña recounts. "It was my mother, Rosalia, who was the *pelotero* (ballplayer) in our family." Palo Verde's top female softball player, Rosalia Peña also taught school in a room of the family home. "She's the one who showed me and my three brothers how to play. She'd pitch and we'd play two against two."

Peña identifies the sporting progeny of each passing town. "Ozzie Virgil, the first Dominican to play in the majors, was from Monte Cristi. But he moved away when he was a child and grew up in Puerto Rico." Virgil's family left the island after his father fell into disfavor with Trujillo. "Over there, from Güayubín, came Diómedes and Chi Chí Olivo." The Olivos still rank among the all-time pitching leaders in

Dominican baseball. Diómedes debuted with the Pirates as a 41-year-old rookie in 1960. "Rafael Belliard and Felix Fermin are both from Valverde de Mao. So was Pedro Borbón." Both shortstops, Belliard plays the field for the Pirates, while Fermin, once with Pittsburgh, has since been shipped to Cleveland, where he solidifies the Indians' defense. Borbón, selected the best right-handed pitcher in *Licey*'s history, starred in the Cincinnati Reds' bull pen during their reign as the Big Red Machine in the 1970s. "On the way back, we'll go by Laguna Verde, the birthplace of Juan Marichal."

Pulling off the highway onto a rutted dirt road, Peña negotiates the car through a herd of goats attended by two little girls on burros, to Palo Verde, a town of about 6000, ten kilometers down the road. It sits on a line of five similar banana *bateys* (villages) that date to the coming of the United Fruit Company to the region in the early 1940s. By a bridge over the *Rio Yaque del Norte,* Peña stops to exchange greetings with old friends. Eusebio Valenzuela, Peña's first manager, clasps Tony to his chest, then takes him aside for a moment. "He needs uniforms for a youth team," Peña later explains. "Maybe I can help."

"I wanted to be a ballplayer for as long as I can remember," he says. "I would fall asleep at night listening to *Aguilas* play. When we made up sides, no one else wanted to catch but me. I wanted to be like Enrique Lantigua [considered one of the best Dominican catchers ever]. I made a mitt from cardboard, and my brother Ramón and I made a ball by cutting the tube of a tire into strips and wrapping it together. The bats we made from pieces of the *guasima* tree."

A cloudburst leaves behind a rainbow that seems to touch down in the nearby banana fields. For decades, bananas—both the large *plantains* for frying and the tiny sweet *guineos*—provided the livelihood for Palo Verde and the other *bateyes*. During those years, the Grenada Company, a subsidiary of United Fruit, pumped capital into a region underdeveloped even by Dominican standards.

Based in nearby Manzanillo, the Grenada Company sponsored ball clubs for its workers. "The banana company built the fields and gave us a half day off work to play," explains Octavio Acosta, an *Aguilas* coach who played for the Grenada Company team. "All the good *peloteros*, like Juan Marichal and the Olivos, got their start on the Grenada Company teams. Either our fathers worked for the banana company, or they recruited us to play for them."

But too many years of cultivation robbed the soil of its fertility. The Grenada Company, unable to get enough water to irrigate its fields and facing a restive labor force after the death of Trujillo, pulled up stakes in 1967. "The land is tired," Peña acknowledges. "Things are worse now than when I was young."

Peña pauses briefly to inspect work on the ballpark he is building for the town. On the stadium wall is written "*En Memoria de* Ramón Lora," Peña's boyhood friend. Tony is godfather to his children. A few goats gambol in left field, a young boy watching them from the shade of the outfield wall.

Peña takes a few cuts at an imaginary ball and heads next to the aquamarine-painted house of his youth. Eighteen years ago, this son of a banana company worker painted a circular strike zone on an adobe wall across from his home and defied his younger brother, Ramón, to hurl a homemade ball by him. That circle is still there, and so, as often as he can be, is the boy who drew it.

"It hasn't changed much," he notes, glancing at the goats and chickens in the yard and the banana fields across the way. Peña hugs the elderly woman now living there, slipping a fistful of *pesos* into her bathrobe when he thinks no one is looking.

Outside, two little boys play ball. The younger one, naked, with a stick in his hands, stands in front of the circle Tony drew when he was a boy. As a band of children gather round, Peña reaches into the car's glove compartment for a pistol and fires it into the air. The children cheer and four older men look up from their dominos game and call over. "Tony is the same *muchacho del campo* (country boy) that he was then," swears one of the players. "And he still plays baseball all the time. He has not changed."

Seventy-three-year-old Octaviano Peña came to Palo Verde over forty years ago and worked as a foreman in the banana fields. After Rosalia hit the lottery, a Dominican passion ranking behind only baseball and strong coffee, the Peñas bought a small rice farm. They lost it during a drought when Tony was fifteen. "We had a couple of bad years," he remembers, "but my parents made me stay in school."

Peña caught for Palo Verde's community team, which traveled on the back of a banana truck to play other town teams. "The Sunday games were the biggest show in town," he recalls, "but they didn't prepare me for professional ball. When I got to the minors in 1976, I wasn't strong enough to play behind the plate every day. I was shy and couldn't speak much English and thought about going home."

The Pirates almost agreed. "At first, Tony didn't show us anything," remembers Branch B. Rickey, then the club's minor league director. "He didn't have an above-average arm in the Instructional League, and he was too young, too physically immature, to put up with the daily routine. Frankly, I was worried about whether he could take the pounding."

But Pittsburgh, a pioneer in scouting the Caribbean, did not give up on Peña. After moving him around in the field, the club tried him again as a catcher. "As he gained in strength," Rickey explains, "his exceptional defensive abilities started to show." In 1978, despite his hitting only .230 at Shreveport in the Class AA minors, the Pirates placed Peña on their 40-man roster, which protected him in the minor league draft.

"When God gave me that good luck, I decided I was going to work till I break in two pieces. My dad always said that no matter how hard a man worked in the fields, he never saw one break in two. I went back to Palo Verde and people thought I was crazy. I ran and threw every day. We took the seed from the *guasima* tree, and Ramón pitched that to me instead of a ball, so I could learn to hit fastballs better. For curves, he threw me bottle caps."

Rosalia and Amaris, his Palo Verde sweetheart whom he wed in 1975, shagged balls for him. Peña also worked with Pablo Cruz, the Pirates' head Dominican scout and godfather to young Latin players in the Pirate organization. "Cruz told me, 'Tony, you are a line drive hitter—not a home run hitter. Try to hit from shortstop to right field. Hold the bat like it's a little bug and don't squeeze it too tight.'"

The next season, Peña hit .313, with 34 home runs and 97 RBIs in the hitter-friendly confines of the Buffalo park in AAA ball. After a comparable season in 1980, the Pirates brought him up in September, and a year later, made him their regular catcher.

Peña also began playing winter ball for *Aguilas* in 1977, and by the 1979 season, he was starting, pushing aside Manny Lantigua, son of his old idol, Enrique, in the process. Winston Llenas became *Aguilas'* manager in 1980, and immediately made Tony the team's captain. "He played so hard and wanted to win so badly," Llenas recalls, "and his body had finally caught up with his spirit.

"And he still plays that way," Llenas had testified on the bus back from San Pedro the night before. "Every Dominican understands that every time Tony puts on his uniform he's risking his career. They know he's not playing winter ball for the money, and they know he's not cheating them, his teammates, or himself. He's not only the best Dominican catcher ever, he's the most respected ballplayer in this country today."

But Peña rides the bus like everyone else. And the rides through the night, the cold-water showers, and the urine-stenched locker rooms don't seem to bother him much, if at all.

In fact, he was all smiles as he slapped his way down the aisle of the bus and slid into a game of spades the day before on the way to San Pedro. The bill of his cap turned up, Peña flicks each card onto the jerry-built table. Miguel Diloné, his lean, muscled torso stripped to the waist, scratches his Charlie Chaplin mustache and harasses Ramón Peña, who is losing hand after hand. The stakes are dinners and Diloné enumerates the feasts he envisions at the younger Peña's expense.

Rock and *merengue* escape from the headsets of the other players, a mix of Americans and Dominicans in various stages of sleep. The Dominicans seem to be having an easier time dozing off.

After a food stop, the bus departs, but brakes sharply when someone notices Peña furiously chasing it down the highway. Half the players shout, "*Vamos!* Leave him here," while the rest heckle as Peña, two sheets of lottery tickets in hand, sheepishly climbs on board.

"He's still the same boy now with all that money as he was before," coach Octavio Acosta observes from his spot on the bench later that night in San Pedro. When Peña chases a curve in the dirt to strike out for the second time in the game, Acosta snorts in disgust and calls to Tony as he walks by, "Still haven't learned?" Peña scowls as he hands his batting helmet to the team's 50-year-old batboy, but does not stay upset long. "Tony's anger is like a big wave," Winston Llenas contends. "Once it breaks, it's all gone."

Peña grew up in an environment in which major league ball was already a magnet for the best Latin players. Along with players like Alfredo Griffin, Joaquín Andújar, George Bell, Tony Fernández, Pedro Guerrero, and Julio César Franco, he came to the major leagues in the second Dominican wave, during the 1970s and 1980s. The first came in the late 1950s and 1960s, when Ozzie Virgil, Juan Marichal, the Alou brothers, Manny Mota, and Rico Carty splashed up on North American shores.

By the time Peña was born in 1957, professional baseball had resumed on the island and was about to become a conduit to the majors. Resurrected as a summer circuit in 1951, the Dominican league switched to winter play in 1956 after formalizing its relationship with major league baseball in the States.

The four-team pro league, with *Licey* and *Escogido* in Santo Domingo, the *Estrellas Orientales* in San Pedro, and the *Aguilas* in Santiago, was buttressed by the extensive amateur network set up by the *Dirección General Deportes* in the late 1940s. This government-sanctioned network held a series of local and then regional tournaments to select squads representing the four regions of the country that would play for a national championship. It also served as a hothouse to stimulate the growth of the best talent on the island. In the Cibao, that first meant the *Caballeros* from Santiago, the team that perished in the 1948 plane crash at the *Rio Verde*. After their demise, it meant the Grenada Company's Manzanillo ball club.

Manzanillo is only a few kilometers away from Palo Verde, on the northwestern tip of the Republic, near *La Linea* or the Line, as the border with Haiti is called. The aptly-named *Rio Massacre* empties into Manzanillo Bay by the town. Haitian peasants had spilled over the Line for years, squatting on Dominican soil. Efforts to negotiate their re moval during the 1930s, soon after Trujillo seized power, met with little success. As part of his objective of "whitening" the country, Trujillo ordered the execution of all Haitians in the Republic on October 2, 1937.

No one counted as perhaps 25,000 Haitians were rounded up and slaughtered. A young lawyer, Freddie Presto Castillo, surveyed the carnage of bodies tossed into the *Rio Massacre,* and later wrote a book about it called *The Massacre Can Be Crossed by Foot.* In Santiago, the morbid phobia of Haitians led to decapitations in the courtyards of government buildings, while in Monte Cristi, the victims were bound and thrown alive into the sea.

The massacre escaped more than passing notice in the world press, which was then focused on the twin spectres of world depression and the rise of fascism. Fifty years later, the sounds of Haiti can be heard on Tony Peña's car radio as he steers towards Manzanillo. And more than a few Haitian visages can be seen along the roadside.

The green hues of the banana fields halt abruptly where the irrigation canals end, and cacti sprout from the arid hillsides. Peña pauses to give a ride to Celestino Cruz, a former banana company worker dressed in faded jeans and a Houston Astros cap, hitching into town. Cruz, who once played for the Manzanillo ball club, sells lottery tickets there now. "Business is bad," he laments. "Not too many people have jobs here now. Many are on pensions." Peña buys ten tickets after dropping Cruz off in the center of town.

Manzanillo has a wild west, almost ghost town ambience these days. Cattle graze on what once was the finest golf course, albeit the only one, in that part of the country while the ballpark sits in disrepair by the bay. The wind whips pieces of paper and plant life into spirals along the dusty streets. A handful of old men, pensioners from the banana company, sit at an open-air restaurant and dispute each other's recollections of this once bustling port.

"There was nothing in Manzanillo then," Jamie Marchena would tell me several days later on the veranda of his home in the comfortable Arroyo Hondo section of Santo Domingo. *Bougainvillea* and *flamboyant* trees offer a canopy of red, purple, and orange blossoms. "I remember it very well. When I first went to Manzanillo in 1942, there was only a small military installation there. But the bay was a natural port. The water was 36 feet deep by the wharf, just what was needed to bring in banana boats."

Marchena, like Pedro Julio Santana, was born in *Ciudad Nueva,* the original center of Santo Domingo, in 1913. "Pedro Julio is like my brother," the silver-haired Marchena attests. "We would go watch Dominican teams play the marines when we were boys, and we were both sportswriters. I wrote for *Listín Diario* and *La Opinion,* while Pedro Julio wrote for *La Nación* and *El Caribe*. My nickname was Jimy Punch. He called himself Peter.

"I began working for the Grenada Company in December 1939, soon after they had gotten a government concession to build an enclave in Manzanillo. Nobody before had any success planting there, but the United Fruit Company said that they could grow bananas at a profit. It was good land for bananas and close to the United States market. A boat could get to Miami in two days, to New York City in only three, and to Europe in a week and a half."

As Europe plunged into war in the late 1930s and Asia followed suit, United Fruit raced to put additional Caribbean basin land under cultivation. Intent on keeping as near a monopoly as possible over fruit production, United Fruit maintained extensive holdings throughout the basin. Known in Guatemala as the Octopus, because it had its tentacles into almost everything, United Fruit created the Grenada Company for its Dominican operations.

"The name was a big mistake, made by a typist at the headquarters in Boston," Marchena explains. "When they make the contract, instead of putting Granada, the name of the city in Spain, they wrote Grenada, like the British island. When they go to sign, somebody say this is not the Spanish city, but the name of a West Indian island, but the lawyers protested that we could not do anything at that point."

Manzanillo was a company town, and the five 1000-acre-sized *bateyes,* where the bananas were grown, were its appendages. Stretching along a single dirt and rock road, Batey Madre, La Cruz, Isabel, Maguaca, and Palo Verde cultivated the tall Johnson banana trees with their small sweet fruit and sent them to Manzanillo for export to breakfast tables in Europe and North America. The company, one of the largest in the country, employed a couple of thousand workers, but most of the other men and women working in the region indirectly depended on it for their livelihood.

"You maybe can't believe it," Marchena argues, "but for me, the Grenada Company was a real example in the Dominican Republic of good will with employees. The single men lived in barracks with kitchens, while the families got homes. Electricity, water, and rent were all free. And to almost ninety percent of the people we gave free the furniture.

"The first thing the company built after the houses was a hospital, and then an American school for the Dominican employees' sons who wanted to learn in English. There were two Dominican schools, too, and education was free for everybody. They charged only fifty percent for the cost of the books. I mean, you know what happen when you give something for free.

"There was a big *bodega,* a store, which sold rice, beans, and everything the laborers needed at a reduction in price. I can assure you that at that time, the Grenada Company was the best place on the island for a worker, yes sir! We had no labor problems, not until the final years when political people with wrong ideas came from the outside after Trujillo died. They came and tell the workers that they will be the owners of the houses and everything, and they cause a strike. But they gained a foothold only because of politics, not because of trouble the company has with the workers."

The top echelon of management, mostly men from the United States, lived on a hill overlooking Manzanillo. Marchena, the highest Dominican in the company hierarchy, represented United Fruit in Santo Domingo, and made the seven-hour drive to Manzanillo twice a week. "It's a pleasure to go there now, because you can fly. But I don't want to go back any more. It looks like a city after it has been destroyed. There is no work, and the *bodega* has burnt down. In the old days, it had a golf course with nine holes, and a church, and clubs for the workers. The Grenada Company built all of this. It was a model for this country."

But the Grenada Company has long since packed up and left the island. If it was a model for the Dominican Republic, its lasting legacy was not on the economy but on the diamond.

"The company," Marchena explains, "understood that sponsoring sports helped in worker relations. It makes people feel happy. They have something to do besides work. It gives them a diversion, some entertainment, and what else was there to do in Manzanillo?"

The club began in 1950, after Rafael de la Maza, the superintendent of the stevedores, approached Dave Cloward, the enclave's manager, and Warren Brick, Cloward's assistant. Moca-born Maza had left the island as a 14-year-old in 1938 when his widowed mother took her family to the States. Maza, who became a U.S. citizen, joined the United States Navy after high school. After World War II, he began working for United Fruit in Honduras and transferred to the Republic in 1950.

"They already had a club in *Batey Madre,*" Maza remembers in his home in Charleston, South Carolina. The company let Fernando Badia, Batey Madre's manager, use its tractors to maintain the field, but took little interest in the game.

"At that time, there was no entertainment whatsoever for the people, but Cloward and Brick liked baseball very much and they decided to sponsor two teams, one in Batey Madre, the other in Manzanillo. Brick was the Godfather down there. He was a very popular guy who could talk to the workers. The guys up on the Hill, the American managers, didn't mix with the people down below. Only Brick could do that."

The Batey Madre team was primarily for the workers and their sons in the countryside, while the Manzanillo team was composed of workers in town. The two teams fielded a common squad for the playoffs and ultimately merged. "None of the Americans played on the team, just Dominicans," Marchena recalls. "Some of the Americans played on the softball team, but mostly they liked golf. Every single player on these clubs had a connection to the company. We didn't have to recruit," Marchena snorts. "The *Aviación,* Ramfis Trujillo's team, would come and recruit from us.

"The company paid for everything, including a bus for transporting the team. The ballplayers had the liberty of practicing every afternoon after one o'clock and played every Saturday and Sunday; sometimes, on Wednesdays, too. And when they played—whooooo! This portion of the island at that time didn't have many forms of entertainment and everyone from the countryside came to the games. We have two or three thousand people at the stadium, for sure."

Rafael de la Maza, who had 400 men working under him on the docks, could always find a job for a good player. Another of his cousins, Fernando Lara, managed the team for a season and put many of the players on his building and grounds staff. "They would water the flowers and prune the bushes on the Hill, by the Americans' homes," Maza laughs. "We made sure they had a soft job, so they wouldn't be too tired to play. We had a kitchen right there on the docks, because when you were loading you worked round the clock. Marichal and the other ballplayers would always be there eating."

In addition to Lara, who led the team to its 1956 national championship, former New York Cuban and Dominican national team star Grillo B (Andres Julio Báez) managed the team. Julito Martínez, the *Aguilas* coach, helped train it while Maza acted as its cheerleader. "I went to the games with a battery-powered siren and bought all our fans rum. Then I would get them hollering in unison. We gave *Aviación* such hell when they were here that I thought they were going to put me in jail."

The Manzanillo and Batey Madre clubs were soon the *Cibao*'s best, and represented the region in the national tournament. "We were good from the beginning," Marchena recalls. "I think we win the national championship three times in the 1950s. And look who played on those teams—Danilo Rivas, Chi Chí Olivo, Octavio Acosta, Juan Sanchez, and, of course, Marichal. He used to cut the grass on the golf course before Trujillo's boy took him away from us."

Despite its success on the base paths and its connection to United Fruit, the Caribbean's fruit corporation supreme, the Grenada Company did not turn a profit. "We always lose money, except for one year," insists Marchena, "because we cannot improve the plantations due to a lack of water. We pump from the *Yaque* River, and when we started, we had enough. But as Santiago grew and the farms on its outskirts began taking water from the *Yaque* for their irrigation, there was not enough for us. We are near the last part of the river where it opens into the bay. It was a big mistake by the engineering company, not thinking about that happening."

Maza disagrees. "Certainly, we could have used more water, but after the revolution, there was trouble with unions. There was always some Commie hollering 'Yankee Go Home!' and leading a strike while we were trying to load the boats. That's why United Fruit decided to shut down the Grenada Company and get its bananas from its other operations."

United Fruit bailed out, virtually giving its land and capital to another company, Marchena says, "Just so that they don't close down operations and so that the people have somewhere to live. But it don't progress. They try sorghum and tomatoes, but now the government is the owner and you can't compare Manzanillo now with what it was then."

The ball club had already declined before the Grenada Company folded. "Things started falling apart all over the country in 1959, the year of the invasion and the terror," Maza argues. On June 14, 1959, a C-46 airplane loaded with would-be freedom fighters who had trained in Cuba landed at Constanza, in the central mountains. Six days later, two yachts filled with their compatriots approached the coast between Puerto Plata and Monte Cristi. Most met their end shortly after the invasion, for Dominican intelligence had thoroughly penetrated the rebel operation.

Many young Dominicans, including sons of elite families that had been pillars of the Trujillo regime, were apprehended in the wake of the invasion, and charged with complicity. Several were close friends of Trujillo's children, Ramfis, Rhadames, and Angelita. Some were tortured, others executed. With the economy already in decline, this wave of repression further alienated Trujillo's base of support.

Trujillo's status outside the island was also slipping, as his meddling in the affairs of other nations undermined the relationship he had gained with the United States due to his anti-communist stance during the Cold War. In 1960, the CIA station chief in Santo Domingo began making overtures of assistance to conspirators plotting Trujillo's assassination. In May 1960, President Eisenhower approved a contingency plan for a *coup*. The next month, Trujillo tried to kill Venezuelan president Romulo Betancourt with a bomb concealed in a car along the leader's route to work. Although Betancourt's Cadillac was set on fire by the bomb, the president survived. After the botched effort was traced to Trujillo, the Organization of American States severed diplomatic relations with the Republic. The Central Intelligence Agency, fearing that the Dominican Republic might go the way of Cuba, stepped up its machinations to bring about Trujillo's downfall.

These plans, however, came too late to save an exiled graduate student at Columbia University. His death would lead to Trujillo's and also, hasten the end of the Manzanillo ball club.

Late on the night of March 12, 1956, Jésus de Galíndez was seized by Trujillo's agents as he walked home from the subway. A loyalist during the Spanish Civil War, Galíndez had gone into exile in the Dominican Republic at the conflict's end. He lived there until 1946, when his work in the Labor Department during a strike wave in the sugar fields attracted Trujillo's ire. He wound up in New York City, where he began work on a doctoral thesis about the Trujillo era at Columbia University.

Few grad students have had their work-in-progress taken so seriously. After Galíndez refused an offer of $25,000 for his manuscript, Trujillo ordered the Spaniard's seizure.

Two weeks after defending his dissertation on February 27 (Dominican Independence Day), the 42-year-old scholar was seized after leaving the subway near his home, sedated, and flown back to the island, where he was killed.

The search for Galíndez soon reached an impasse, but the North American pilot of the flight, Gerald Murphy, was unable to maintain the discretion that such intrigue demanded. He disappeared several months later, his car found on a cliff overlooking the sea near a slaughterhouse. The spot, which attracted an unusually heavy concentration of sharks due to the remains from the slaughterhouse, was known as the 'swimming pool' because many of Trujillo's enemies took their final dip there. Like Galíndez, Murphy's body was never found.

"After they killed Murphy," Rafael de la Maza explains, "there was an investigation by the U.S. State Department. Trujillo needed a fall guy and they went to my cousin, Octavio de la Maza, and arrested him."

The government's scenario called for de la Maza, a pilot and close friend of Ramfis, to confess to the murder of Murphy, saying that Murphy had made homosexual advances and that while defending himself, he had pushed Murphy to his death.

Octavio de la Maza refused to go along with the plan, so the government revised their original plan. De la Maza's jailors hung him with a noose made from mosquito netting and left a suicide confession note at his side.

Trujillo's efforts to cover up his government's involvement failed and further investigation linked Murphy's death to the Galíndez case. Trujillo would never recover his standing in the U.S. Congress, and American foreign policy became increasingly hostile.

The death of de la Maza accelerated the plotting against Trujillo. "At Octavio's funeral," his cousin Rafael de la Maza explains, "his brother Antonio said 'This cannot end like this!' and swore he would kill that son-of-a-bitch."

An Action Group of eight men, including Antonio de la Maza, began plotting Trujillo's death. "I found out about the plot in October 1960," Rafael de la Maza recalls. The de la Maza clan, centered in Moca, had a well-deserved reputation for its close-knit, *macho* style. Octavio's brothers, in particular, were under scrutiny to see if they would seek revenge. Even their cousin, Rafael, felt the heat. "Trujillo's police were suspicious of me and I started making plans to leave the country. Before I got out of the country, I left my shotgun with Antonio, who ran a sawmill not far away. Antonio, by the way, donated the lumber that we used to build the ballpark fence in Manzanillo. He used my shotgun the night they got Trujillo.

"I lost my job with United Fruit when I left the country and went to work with the Merchant Marine. I was working on deck as we were making our way to Puerto Rico a couple of months later, when someone yelled down that they'd killed the son-of-a-bitch. I knew who they meant immediately."

The ball club not only lost de la Maza, but Warren Brick, who had transferred back to the United States. When de la Maza came back after Trujillo's death and resumed working for the Grenada Company, there was still a ball club, but it received less company support.

Professional baseball, both on the island and in the United States, was by then beckoning to the better ballplayers. Amateur ball suffered, as it could no longer hold on to its prospects when faced with competition from Dominican and North American teams. Manzanillo kept its club but the team slid into mediocrity during the 1960s.

Dominican baseball, however, was on the ascent. If one man symbolizes the amazing trajectory of the island's sport since then, it is the man who once rode a tractor as he cut the fairways of the *Club de Golf de Manzanillo,* Juan Marichal.

"He was the best," Tony Peña pronounces without hesitation later that afternoon at the *Restaurante Cocomar* on the coast, a short but dusty ride from Palo Verde. "He showed that a Dominican could play in the majors and be the best." Spooning heaps of *cangrejos y salsa roja* (crabs in tomato sauce) onto pieces of fried *plátano,* Peña looks at his father, Octaviano, and confesses. "When we were kids, Ramón and I used to listen on the radio after we were supposed to be asleep when Marichal was pitching in winter ball. Ramón [who broke into the majors with the Detroit Tigers in 1989] would pretend he was Marichal. I would fall asleep and dream that I was catching him."

Now young boys fall asleep dreaming of becoming another Peña.

A decade of catching in the majors, supplemented by extensive winter play during his so-called off-season, has taken its toll on the 32-year-old backstop. After hitting near .300 over his first five seasons and winning three consecutive Golden Glove awards, Peña's average tailed in the late 1980s, and other, younger players usurped his fielding honors.

On April Fool's Day, 1987, the Pirates traded Peña to St. Louis for Andy Van Slyke, Mike Lavalliere, and Mike Dunne. A tearful Peña appeared on the news, protesting his unhappiness at leaving Pittsburgh.

But a few days later, Peña was grinning again, albeit in the uniform of the Cardinals, and by the end of the season, he was playing in the World Series, for the first time in his career.

He would be named to the National League All-Star team twice more before the end of the decade, but by then, Benito Santiago, the San Diego Padres' young Puerto Rican backstop, had taken Peña's place as the best Latin catcher in baseball, and prospect Todd Zeile was threatening his future as the Cardinals' starting catcher.

As he approaches the conclusion of his tenth year in the major leagues, Peña's future as a ballplayer is in some doubt, but there is no question that the boy from Palo Verde will play as hard as he can and as often as he can until they won't let him come on the field. (After the 1989 season, the Cardinals do not offer Peña a contract. A few months later, he signs a three-year, $6.4 million contract with the Red Sox.)

Draining a demitasse of coffee, he urges, "*Vamonos.* I will show you where Juan Marichal grew up."

5
The Dominican Dandy

Laguna Verde, birthplace of the Republic's most famous sporting emissary, looks like any of the other small farming towns dotting the Dominican countryside. The streets are dirt and half-clad children fill them. Clumps of soil and vegetation cling to the power lines overhead. Tony Peña points out the house of *Doña* Natividad, Juan Marichal's 86-year-old mother. Her son no longer lives there. These days, Juan Antonio Marichal Sánchez splits his time between a house in San Francisco and his home in the posh El Millón section of the capital.

On this January day, Marichal is in the States, where he directs Latin American scouting for the Oakland Athletics. Six months later, I track him down at *Estadio La Normal,* an aging ballpark in downtown Santo Domingo. It's late June and I've been trying to make contact with him for several days.

The day before, I had set out in the morning for a small complex that Epy Guerrero runs for the Toronto Blue Jays in Villa Mella, on the outskirts of Santo Domingo. I was to talk with Marichal there as he evaluated talent in the Dominican summer league that had just begun play.

One wrong turn and I find myself lost in the city dump instead. Smoke from mountains of burning garbage envelops an army of scavengers picking through the refuse. Most have rags covering their mouths and noses. Many are children, others gnarled and gray. They separate reusable sheets of plastic, rags, and pieces of cardboard from the decay. A few carry their prizes back to the collection of stick and cardboard hovels on the edge of the site where they live. With a quarter of the Republic's citizens unemployed or underemployed, these dump denizens are far from the worst off of Santo Domingo's poor.

Epy Guerrero's complex might as well be in a different time zone than the dump. Well off even the un-beaten path, (all the better to hide his prospects, Guerrero's competitors say) the Villa Mella complex was the most advanced effort of its kind when Guerrero began building it a decade ago. With a dormitory for players, a weight area, and two well-manicured ballparks, Guerrero offers Dominican teenagers a chance to

61

strengthen their bodies and prepare their minds before venturing off the island. Those who make it will never again smell the stench of the dump that lies hidden behind the hills only a few kilometers away, beyond the thick scrub vegetation shielding the complex.

"Latin players need more time to develop," offers Guerrero, a 46-year-old former Dominican pro who has become the island's foremost scout, as he explains the purpose of his operations. "They are not as physically mature as young North Americans. They are not as big, they haven't had the nutrition. And going to the States to play is tough when they don't speak the language and are away from home for the first time. We give them a chance to get a summer of play in here first, and see if they can make it. We teach them a little English and feed them good. Some go home after a few weeks, but others you will see in the United States in a few years. You can count on it."

Guerrero's employers, the Toronto Blue Jays, have savored the offerings that he has heaped upon their plates in recent years. The Blue Jays of the 1980s frequently fielded four, even five Dominicans at a time, with all-stars like Alfredo Griffin, Dámaso Garcia, George Bell, and Tony Fernández pushing them to the brink of championship play. Griffin and Garcia have since been traded, replaced by representatives of the seemingly endless flow of middle infielders from San Pedro de Macoris. Overall, a third of the 200 ballplayers in the Toronto organization comes from the Dominican Republic or elsewhere in the Caribbean basin.

"But Marichal?" Guerrero says. "He is not here today. They changed the schedule. Maybe tomorrow, he will be here."

He's not. I find him instead at *Estadio La Normal,* not far from where the Ozama River drains into the Caribbean, watching the Oakland A's summer league team play a club composed of Yankee minor leaguers. Tiers of houses that look no more substantial than those built of playing cards line the ravine down to the river. When it floods, many wash out to sea. Outside the park, boys sell hubcaps by the curbs of the pitted streets and women crouch on the sidewalk to fill plastic jugs with water from an underground spigot.

Now 51, Marichal is more the "Dominican Daddy" than the "Dominican Dandy" as five-year-old Juan Antonio Marichal Jr. climbs all over him. Dressed in charcoal slacks, an Oakland A's cap, and a gray and black checked shirt with purple and pink threads running through it, Marichal's sanctified status is reflected only by the gold *Sálon de Fama* medallion around his neck and the attention he draws from the other men, who gesture his way as they talk to their own sons.

"I played here once," Marichal says. "In fact, when I first came to Santo Domingo to play for *Aviación* in 1956, I lived for awhile in the

locker room inside this stadium with some other ballplayers. We were
training for a youth tournament in Mexico that year."

Juan Jr. throws his arms around his father, imploring "Papi?"
Marichal fishes some *pesos* out of a brown leather bag and calls to the
small boy circulating through the stands with roasted peanuts for sale.
The child shows his *estufa* (a stovelike contraption of two cans, the
upper one with peanuts, the bottom with charcoal), to Juan Jr., who sits
and shares his purchase with his new acquaintance.

"We had a farm," the tall, still sturdily-built Marichal resumes.
"We called it a *parcela,* a parcel of land, a few kilometers outside
Laguna Verde, when I was growing up. It was small, something like 60
acres, and we grew mostly rice, *platanos,* and beans. Now it's bigger,
because when I started making a little money, we started buying more
land and I bought a tractor for it. It's over a thousand acres now."

Juan's father died when he was three, but *Doña* Natividad held the
family together with the help of relatives. "I don't think my father
played baseball, but I know that he used to live for the *gallos,* for
cockfighting. I think that's why I've got that in my blood. I love
roosters. I'm a member of a club that has an arena for *peleas de gallos,*
cockfighting. In the Dominican Republic, *gallos* come right after baseball."

Laguna Verde numbered about four hundred residents then and is
only up to two or three thousand 50 years later. While the *casa de
Marichal* was comfortable by peasant standards, with indoor plumbing
and a tank of water that could be filled by hand for bathing, like the
other homes in Laguna Verde, it lacked electricity. "We had propane
gas for cooking, just like most people still do. And we had a battery-
powered radio on which I listened to the ball games. There was a player
then from Laguna Verde, *"Gallo" Martinez,* and when he did something in a game, his father would shout *'Ese es mi gallo!'* (That's my
rooster!) I would tell my mother that some day she would listen to the
radio and shout *'Ese es mi Juan!'* "

During the morning, Juan worked the *parcela,* before walking eight
kilometers to school in *El Duro* each afternoon. "We didn't have any
money but we had a lot of food. Almost everything that we needed to
eat we had right there. My mother had a herd of goats and one of my
brothers and I used to take care of them. I grew up on goat milk."
(Could that be the source of Marichal's incredibly high leg kick?)
"Later on, I used to send my mother five hundred dollars every 15 days
and when I got back here I see she has been buying cattle and more
goats with it."

As Marichal recounts the saga of his youth, he misses little on the
field. When a player slides at home and misses the plate, Marichal is on

his feet, shouting "He missed the plate!" to the catcher. The umpire, who had not yet made his call, waits until the catcher follows the runner into the dugout and tags him to signal out.

"In 1947, when I was nine years old, I almost died," Marichal continues. "We had been working on the farm, doing what we called *en junta*. That is when you invite all the families around you to help when you are doing something that needs lots of hands. You would feed them for their efforts and go to their farm when they needed help. We were harvesting and cleaning rice. After the work was done, my mother fed all the children first so that they would go away and not bother the adults while they ate.

"We started swimming in the canal right away after eating and I got cramps. The next thing I knew it was a week later. When the doctor looked at me after they fished me out of the canal, I'm told he said 'I don't see too much chance. But be sure to give him lots of baths with very hot water.' They sent me to the house of one of my uncles where they gave me lots of baths but nothing happened. On the seventh day of my coma, the doctor looked at me and told my mother that if I did not come out of it by midnight, I was not coming back. At fifteen minutes to midnight, I awoke. . . .

"It seems like all I did as a boy was work on the farm, go to school a little, and play ball. We swam in the canals, and hunted and fished some, but mostly it was baseball.

"All the boys in my town played baseball. I used to love baseball and dream of playing it. And I will tell you, I feel very proud that, coming from that little community, I went all the way to Cooperstown."

A persistent five-year-old interrupts the reveries of the only Dominican in the Hall of Fame. Extracting a few more pesos, Marichal calls "Tito, *por favor*," to a handsome young man concentrating fiercely on the field of play. Tito Fuentes Jr., son of the former Cuban major leaguer who played with Marichal on the Giants, swoops down on Juan Jr. and carries the boy off to find him a mango. After completing high school in San Francisco, Tito has come to Santo Domingo to play ball and see if he can interest a major league organization in his services.

Fuentes, like Stanley Javier, Ivan Calderon, Danny Tartabull, Roberto and Sandy Alomar, and Moises Alou, is the son of a Latin major leaguer. But while their fathers grew up in dirt-floored, thatched-roof homes in the countryside, these sons have known little but the affluence of suburban life in the States and an elevated status in their homelands. "They are not as hungry as their papas, they don't have the same drive, but some of them can play. . . .

"Tito still has to learn just about everything," Marichal muses. "He is almost a man, but he hasn't played that much. He's just starting, compared to a kid here at that age."

By the time Marichal was Tito's age, he had been playing ball for a living for several years. "Baseball was strong around *La Línea*. And we seemed to produce more pitchers than anything else, then. There was a ballplayer in the 1920s and '30s from there, Pedro Alejandro San, who pitched for the Cuban Stars in the Negro Leagues. And there was Bombo Ramos, who I will tell you a story about, and the Olivos, and Juan Sánchez. These days, this part of the country is producing some hitters, too, like Tony Peña, and this boy, Junior Felix, who plays with Toronto.

"All we wanted to do then was play ball. We made our own bats from branches that we cut from the *guasima* tree and dried in the sun. For gloves, we would take a piece of canvas, the kind of stuff they used to cover trucks, and fold it around a piece of cardboard and then sew up the sides. And for balls, we would get some golf balls from the golf course at Manzanillo and wrap nylon stocking or tape around them, and then take them to the shoemaker who would sew a leather cover around them. And then we would play! Later on, my brother, Gonzalo, would give me spikes or a glove."

Laguna Verde was too small to have a team in the DGD-organized amateur network, but it did have a town team for the men and a youth club for the boys.

"We played all day, every day, whenever we were not in school or working. We played on a field that we made ourselves, but now we're planning on building one there. Laguna Verde had a team for the boys that would play youth teams from other *bateyes*. We traveled to those towns on horseback or on the back of a dump truck or they would come to Laguna Verde, every Sunday. If they came to Laguna Verde, we would have a meal for them after the game, with goat meat, *enchiladas*, rice, and beans. Sometimes we would go from house to house, asking for contributions so that we could feed the other team. Often, Ramón Villalona, who was a bit better off and helped coach us, would give us money so that we could have a little *fiesta* after the game."

While Juan played for the town's youth team, his older brother Gonzalo campaigned for a team in Monte Cristi. "Gonzalo was the best ballplayer in our family," Marichal swears, slipping back into the hero worship of his youth. "I became a baseball player because of all the help he gave me." Seven years older than Juan, Gonzalo frequently returned to Laguna Verde to play for its adult team. Juan would ride to Monte Cristi on a horse to watch Gonzalo play Saturdays for his team there and the two rode back together on Sunday mornings for the game in Laguna Verde, Juan interrogating his brother on baseball the entire way. "He played all the positions then, while I was a shortstop—until I saw Bombo Ramos play. That's when I became a pitcher.

"I think I was 11 or 12 years old. *Los Caballeros* from Santiago were playing against Monte Cristi. The game had been announced in the area for a long time. There were posters for it up everywhere. My brother-in-law got me permission to go. Even today, I remember watching Bombo Ramos pitching. I get goose bumps thinking about that day. He pitched for Monte Cristi, and you see that man over there, the groundskeeper—he was the catcher that day. Bombo would turn all the way around, like Luis Tiant, but he never used to raise his head up like Tiant. He would throw sidearm, too. He was something to watch! He shut out *Los Caballeros* that day. That was what converted me to pitching. When I went back home I told my friends that I was not playing shortstop anymore—that I had to become a pitcher like Bombo Ramos. He inspired me and I tried to pitch just like him."

The horseback seminars with Gonzalo turned to the art of pitching. On the mound, Juan imitated his new hero and delivered the ball sidearm, turning his back to the plate during his windup. Under Gonzalo's guidance, and with an arm strengthened by years of farm work, Marichal developed a good curve and was soon trying a screwball. "I had control, too," Marichal remembers with the trace of a smile.

Only fifteen, he was ready to play for the adult town team, but *Doña* Natividad was none too pleased with that. "I was always getting in trouble with her when she found out I was playing ball instead of being in school. And she thought I was too young to be playing with the men." But Juan did play with the town team, and almost always pitched them to victory.

Marichal completed the primary school in *El Duro* when he was fifteen but could not afford to continue his studies in Monte Cristi. Instead, Juan went to the capital for a visit with Gonzalo, who had moved there to operate a small fleet of dump trucks for their uncle. The visit turned into a stay of a year, and Marichal did not return to school. "I never finished school, and that was something that my mother reminded me of even when I was in the major leagues. I regret not finishing," he admits.

In Santo Domingo, Gonzalo taught Juan how to drive a truck and arranged for him to play on the Esso Company team. When he returned to Laguna Verde in 1955, Marichal joined a team called *Las Flores,* that the Bermúdez Rum Company sponsored, in time for a tournament in Monte Cristi. *Las Flores* won and the best players in the city, including Marichal, were selected to represent Monte Cristi in the regional tournament. That was Marichal's first encounter with the Grenada Company's Manzanillo team.

Sweeping through the sub-regional tournament, Marichal led Monte Cristi to victory in Santiago, and then to the national amateur championship tournament in Santo Domingo. "We played the best amateur teams from all over the country—from San Pedro de Macoris, Santo Domingo, and of course, from the armed forces. I cannot remember, though, how we did. I'll ask Gonzalo. He'll remember."

The Bermúdez Rum Company covered the team's expenses, but provided no stipend for the players. "It was typical that a tractor driver tilled the soil Saturday night so that work could be done early Sunday morning. On Saturdays, I would go around to the bigger farms until I found a tractor driver that wanted to carouse instead of work that night. I would drive his tractor from six in the evening until six the next morning, and then clean it, lubricate it, and fill it with gas. All that for five *pesos!* Then I would wash up in an irrigation ditch, go home and get my uniform, and wait on the road for a ride into Monte Cristi."

Marichal did not stick with the Bermúdez Rum team for long. His pitching attracted the attention of the manager of the Manzanillo club, which offered work, meals, a little bungalow to live in, and 25 *pesos* a week.

"It was an easy job," Marichal recalls. "All the players used to do was to go down to the docks when they loaded a ship with bananas and check to see if there was a mashed one. I didn't really consider it a job. They just had us do it so that they could say we were working. They treated the players first class, like the way a nice lady was to be treated.

"When there weren't ships to be loaded, I drove a tractor to water the trees and flowers in town, because Manzanillo doesn't usually get much rain. Sometimes, when it did rain a lot, I drove my tractor all over the golf course, cutting the grass."

Manzanillo had a core of veteran company players and traveled across the Republic in a bus. "It sure was more comfortable than the dump truck in Laguna Verde," Marichal says. Winning the regional tournament in 1956, the club picked up a few of the best players from other teams, including Danilo Rivas from Puerto Plata, and then swept through the national tournament.

"Soon after that, *Aviación* came to Manzanillo to play. I threw a four-hitter and we beat them 2–1. That night we celebrated. The next day, I was drafted."

A sudden downpour sends the fans scurrying for cover. Marichal clasps his son's hand in his own and asks, "Why don't you come to Las Palmas when the Oakland team plays there next week? We can talk more. It's near San Isidro, where I served with *Aviación*."

Las Palmas is a swatch of Dodger blue in the multihued green Dominican countryside. A first class, first world operation, the Los Angeles Dodgers' state-of-the-art baseball academy opened in the spring of 1987. About an hour's drive from the capital, Las Palmas abuts Batey

Mojara, a group of dilapidated huts where Haitian cane cutters from the nearby *Ingenio Rio Ozama* spend the hours they are not sweating in the fields.

It's July 4th and the United States flag flutters in the languid breeze over center field, alongside the banners of the Dominican Republic and the Los Angeles Dodgers. *El Campo* Las Palmas might be dedicated to the youth of the Dominican Republic and their love for baseball, but it pays homage to a pantheon of Dodger heros. The thirty or so young Dominicans living there emerge from the Roy Campanella locker room to play ball on Manuel Mota field. Evenings, they study English in the Al Campanis classroom. While Campanis has fallen into disregard since his confused comments on "Nightline" regarding the capacities of blacks to manage and hold front office positions, the former Dodger general manager is still respected in the Dominican Republic. There, his image is that of a man free of racial prejudices and more than willing to accommodate Latin ballplayers. And the players eat in—where else but the Tommy Lasorda dining room?

Like the Epy Guerrero complex in Villa Mella, the Dodger academy offers youngsters the chance to make the transition to organized baseball without adding culture shock to the complexities of hitting curveballs. Over a dozen pro organizations run some sort of complex in the Dominican Republic, at which they can host a prospect for several weeks before they must either sign him to a contract or tell him to hit the *calle*. But none of the other organizations offers facilities that can compete with *Las Palmas,* complete with dish antenna and VCR.

"Look at this," Juan Marichal commands with a wave. "There is nothing like it in all of the Caribbean." The Dodgers, who have occupied baseball's *avant garde* since Branch Rickey came aboard in 1942, broke baseball's color line in 1947, but were slow to jump into the Latin market. The club utilized former Negro League talent better than any other in the 1950s, as Jackie Robinson, Roy Campanella, and Don Newcombe led them into the World Series in six of the first ten seasons after integration. But only a few Latins stuck with the club until the 1980s when their major league roster began to carry at least three or four Latins annually, including Mexican Fernando Valenzuela and Dominicans Pedro Guerrero (since traded to the Cardinals), Alfredo Griffin, Alejandro Peña, Mariano Duncan, and Ramón Martínez. Overall, one-fifth of its players at all levels were Latin in 1989, including several of the top prospects in the minor leagues. "It's awfully tough to compete with this," Marichal says, as much to himself as anyone else.

A few Haitian children from the *batey* watch impassively from the shade of the palm trees that ring the field. Several snazzily dressed motorcycle cowboys with punkish sunglasses perch on their scooters nearby. Marichal takes to the mound and throws a few pitches before making the ceremonial toss that opens official summer play at *Las Palmas*. Afterwards, he stands in the shadow of the dugout talking shop with prospective pitchers from both rookie teams. He emphasizes control and timing, rather than sheer velocity or an array of pitches.

When play begins, Marichal joins the Dodger brain trust in the shade behind the backstop. One Dodger coach takes copious notes, while another evaluates the pitchers' velocity with a JUGS speed gun. Rafael Avila, who administers Las Palmas, talks with Marichal about Pedro Guerrero's brother, Ramón Guerrero, and half-brother, Domingo Michel, two prospects in the Dodger organization.

Like Avila, the other Dodger coaches are transplanted Cubans, men who made the jump from their island to the major leagues and stayed with the latter when their homeland embarked on its revolutionary adventure in 1959. Havana-born Chico Fernández, who played briefly for the Orioles, shakes his head dolefully as he contemplates Cuba since Fidel. "They've fucked everything up there. It once was a beautiful place. You could get anything you wanted—women—gambling—anything. And the *beisbol* was almost as good as in the United States. But now, it's shit." Like Fernández, Avila has since settled in the Dominican Republic. There, he runs Las Palmas, coaches *Licey,* and has won acclaim as one of the most capable and astute baseball men in the basin.

Marichal settles into a lawn chair and accepts a soft drink from one of the Dodger groundskeepers who hover nearby. Clad in blue jumpsuits with Dodger patches, the attendants are the most enthusiastic fans at the game. For Marichal and the coterie of expatriate Cubans, the game is an opportunity to evaluate talent, to see if any of these youngsters has a legitimate chance. "Once the Dodgers sign a boy," Avila says, "we try to keep him at least two years. We want to be fair to them. If they are released before then, it is usually because of something they did off the field, not because of their performance on it."

Most of the players on these rookie teams received between $3,000 and $25,000 to sign with a major league club. During the season, they make about $700 a month, a little less than what the Dominican minimum wage would pay a worker for an entire year. And if they make it to the majors . . .

The road from Santo Domingo to Las Palmas skirts the San Isidro air force base, the primary air force installation in the country and long a pillar of Trujillo's power. In the 1950s, Trujillo's favorite son, Ramfis, commanded the *Aviación* and took special interest in its ball club, which competed in the amateur network organized in the 1940s.

And beating *Aviación,* as Marichal discovered after pitching Manzanillo to victory in a 1956 encounter with Ramfis' team, had its consequences. "We beat *Aviación* on a Sunday in Manzanillo. I remember that we had quite a *fiesta* after that, but early the next morning, there was a lieutenant from the Manzanillo installation at the door of my bungalow. He had a telegram for me from Ramfis saying '*Favor de Reportarse de inmediato al Equipo de la Fuerza Aerea.*'

"I told him that I had to talk with my mother." The officer and his conscript got in a jeep and drove to Laguna Verde. *Doña* Natividad might not have been an aficionado of the game, but she was politically savvy enough to know that her youngest son's success on the ball field would attract Trujillo's attention. Almost anything out of the ordinary did.

"She didn't have much to say at first. I didn't want to pressure her and kept quiet myself. At four that afternoon, another military man showed up with a second telegram asking whether I had left yet for Santo Domingo. My mother looked at it and finally said, '*Bueno,* my son. You know that to these people you cannot say no.' "

Even at 17, Juan knew that one did not turn down a summons from God. After a cry with *Doña* Natividad, the new recruit returned to Manzanillo to pack up his belongings and was soon riding the highway that bisects the island from North to South. Before dawn the next day, he was at the San Isidro base.

"The next morning, they took me to meet General Fernando Sánchez, Ramfis' assistant. He gave me a hundred *pesos,* and remember that a hundred *pesos* was worth a hundred dollars then, and told me to go to *Estadio La Normal* in Santo Domingo, where they were having tryouts for a youth team for a tournament in Mexico. I lived under the stands there for a few weeks while they picked the team and then I was off to Mexico."

Joining Marichal in Mexico were Danilo Rivas, Manuel Mota, Manuel Emilio Jiménez, and Mateo Alou. It was the Laguna Verde youth's first airplane trip and first time out of the country.

"It was something, I'll tell you. Sometimes you tell this story and people don't believe it. I started against Puerto Rico and beat them, and was used to close another game that we won. Finally, we were playing Mexico for the championship. The stands there were low, like in Dodger Stadium, so the fans were right on top of you. And these Mexican fans had guns and knives and were threatening us with them. Our manager sent us to the bull pen to warm up, but it was impossible! We didn't want to come out of the dugout. Those people were crazy the way they rooted for the home team. It is not fair dealing with kids that way."

Mexican police guarded the dugout, and stood alongside the relievers as they warmed up in the bull pen, but Mexico won the game.

Returning to the island, Marichal reported to the air force base at San Isidro. Like other draftees, he had his head shaved and was handed an ill-fitting khaki uniform. But unlike the other new recruits, whose salary was 27.50 pesos a month, Marichal was making 52.50 pesos. "We were specialists," he grins.

Nor did Juan don his military threads very often. "That was for when we were off the base. At San Isidro, I mostly wore a baseball uniform."

And he mostly played baseball. "That was my job in the air force, playing ball. We played intersquad games every day of the week on the base. If we played in the morning, we practiced in the afternoon. If we practiced in the morning, we played in the afternoon." And on Sundays, this more than amateur but not quite professional team traveled into the interior or hosted other clubs at the San Isidro base.

Although Néstor González Pómares managed the team, Marichal's mentor was Francisco "Viruta" Pichardo. Viruta, as he was known throughout Dominican baseball, was the team's trainer and probably the best instructor in the country during the 1950s. He had answered Ramfis' call to make *Aviación* the best "amateur" squad in the nation.

He did it, with equal parts of tough discipline and astute instruction.

"Viruta trained us to be winners," Marichal explains, "and we beat everybody in the country. We even flew in an Air Force plane to Puerto Rico and Curacao to play. In the fourteen months I was on the *Aviación* team, we hardly ever lost."

The *Aviación* club was made up of two groups, a contingent of young prospects like Marichal, whose potential had yet to be reached, and a number of veterans in their late 20s, who would never play at a higher level. Viruta put up with these 'lifers' while focusing his unrelenting efforts on the younger players.

Among that group were Marichal, Manuel Mota, Pedro González, Danilo Rivas, and the Jiménez brothers. Each starred in Dominican winter ball and all but Rivas, who played in the Giants organization, played major league ball, too.

González, Jompy Jiménez, and Manny Jiménez were from sugar mill *ingenios* in San Pedro de Macoris, an advance guard of the army that surged out of the cane fields in the 1970s and '80s. Manny hit .301 as a rookie for the Kansas City Athletics in 1962, sixth best in the American League. Manuel "Geronimo" Mota, a native of Santo Domingo, played 20 seasons in the majors, mostly with Pittsburgh and the

Dodgers. He hit .304 over his major league career and totaled 150 pinch hits, the most ever, before retiring in 1982 to become a coach with the Dodgers. In winter ball, the three-time batting champ holds the best career batting average (.333), hit .300 a record 11 times, and retired from active play in 1981 with 800 hits, then the third highest lifetime total in Dominican ball. After that, Mota managed *Licey,* the Dodgers' Dominican affiliate, to consecutive championships in the 1983–84 and 1984–85 seasons.

In the air force, Marichal ate better than the other servicemen, and was given vitamin supplements, too. Most nights he spent at Gonzalo's home in Santo Domingo, which was still named *Ciudad Trujillo* at the time. At five each morning, he would grab a ride in a truck to the base.

Despite the relatively soft treatment off the field, Marichal and his *compadres* never worked so hard on it. "Viruta had us running wind sprints from foul line to foul line, and doing calisthenics to build up our endurance. And he insisted that we practice something until we did it the way he wanted us to do it."

When players tried out for the team, Viruta hit them grounders and flies until they dropped. "If an infielder missed a ball and said, 'Viruta, it took a bad hop,' Viruta would say 'Then why didn't you take a bad hop with it?' I saw a guy miss two ground balls in a row during a tryout and say to Viruta, 'I don't know the field too well.' Viruta walked over, grabbed him, and pulled him down so that his face was touching the dirt and said, 'Ground, this is so and so. I want you to get to know each other.' "

If a player feigned illness, Viruta marched him over to the clinic and stood there while the doctor diagnosed and treated him, and then usually brought the player back to practice.

He brooked little interference with the sport. Not long after Marichal arrived, a few of the veterans persuaded him to go drinking with them one payday. "They taunted me, saying I was a *niño de faldas,* a mama's boy. I was only 17, and had never really been drunk before, but I was unable to tell them no. We drank rum, straight. You had to down the glass and then turn it over with a slap to show that there was nothing left in it.

"The next day, Viruta ran us from foul line to foul line in the sun, until most of these guys were puking their guts out. I didn't do that, but I assure you, I felt sick. But Viruta didn't say anything about the drinking the night before."

He didn't say anything to Marichal the entire next week. Finally, as Juan was putting on his uniform to play a game at San Isidro, Viruta confronted him.

"He said, '*Mira,* look, Juan, you see these star players on the team, these veterans? The North American scouts don't want to sign them. They have no future in baseball, and it was with them that you drank last week!'

"He told me that he thought that I had a real future in baseball and that if I wanted to, I would pitch in the major leagues. I don't know if I was ready to hear that then, but I listened to Viruta. I listened to everything he said and tried to pitch like he told me to—with attention, above all else, to control. He said that control was more important than velocity."

After Marichal had been with *Aviación* for a year, he returned to Manzanillo to play against his old teammates. Marichal started the first game of the doubleheader and lost 1–0. Danilo Rivas, who had pitched for Manzanillo against *Aviación* the previous year, pitched the second game for *Aviación* against Manzanillo. The banana company boys won that game, too.

Ramfis was beside himself. "I don't think he ever played baseball, but he loved to watch us," Marichal recalls. Twenty-eight at the time, Rafael Leonidas Trujillo Martinez, whom everyone knew as Ramfis, was the son of *Doña* Maria, Trujillo's mistress and lifelong companion. They wed in 1935. Ramfis was made a colonel in the Army at his fourth birthday, a festivity that the entire Cabinet attended, and advanced to the rank of Brigadier General by the age of nine. Taller and more handsome than the father who adored him to the brink of idolatry, Ramfis fancied himself a sportsman. Like papa, he had boundless sexual appetites. But unlike the elder Trujillo, Ramfis had little interest in politics. Captain of the *Ciudad Trujillo* polo team, which he led on forays abroad, Ramfis took a special interest in the *Aviación* ball club.

After the astounding double defeat to the Grenada Company team, Ramfis ordered a special commission to go to Manzanillo and find out why his squad had lost both games. While the commission interrogated the players and investigated the events preceding the games, the *Aviación* players were confined to base.

"The commission declared that the players had been drinking before the game and that was why we had played so poorly," Marichal recalls. "But you must remember that Manzanillo was a good club, and the truth is not that we were drinking, but that the water had made many of the players sick. I had a very high fever that day."

Despite their protestations, the players were fined and jailed for five days. The manager and team captain were confined for a month.

"But we never lost a doubleheader again while I was there," Marichal concludes.

In 1956, while Juan was playing for *Aviación*, Monte Cristi native Ozzie Virgil became the first Dominican to play major league ball. Like a host of dark-skinned Cubans, Puerto Ricans, and Venezuelans, Virgil's debut had been made possible by Jackie Robinson, whose 1947 voyage across major league baseball's color line irrevocably altered the sport.

Major league scouts descended upon the Caribbean, eager to sign ballplayers they had coveted during countless winter seasons past. Cuba, long the center of basin baseball, sent the first and most players northward, but during the 1950s, the Dominican Republic began to follow suit.

"By the time I was with *Aviación*," Marichal says, "Virgil was playing for the Giants and winter ball was strong again on the island. I knew I wanted to become a professional, but I was only 17."

The first scout he met was Carlos "Patato" Pascual, brother of Washington Senator pitching star Camilo Pascual. Carlos had only had a sip of coffee in the majors, and was scouting the Caribbean for the Senators. He saw Marichal strike out sixteen when *Aviación* played in Aruba and spoke to him afterwards about signing with the Senators, but didn't follow up.

Back in the Dominican Republic, *Licey* president Ignacio Guerra approached Ramfis about signing Marichal and second baseman Pedro González. He wanted González to play winter ball for *Licey* that season and for both players to then sign with the New York Yankees. Ramfis, a *fanático* of *Escogido,* granted Guerra permission to sign González but refused to let him have Marichal.

By then, Mota, Mateo Alou, and Danilo Rivas had turned professional, signing with the New York Giants. Marichal was not long in joining them.

For some time, Horacio Martínez had been talking to Gonzalo Marichal about signing his younger brother to a contract with *Escogido* for winter play and the New York Giants for major league ball. Martínez, the Santiago-born shortstop who Dominicans still revere, was bird-dogging for Alejandro Pompez, the New York Giants scout.

The Cuban-born Pompez had barnstormed a team called the New York Cubans through the Negro Leagues during the 1930s and '40s. With one foot in the numbers rackets (which likely had its origins in the Caribbean game of chance called *la bolita* and gave sustenance to independent black baseball in those decades before Robinson) and the other in Caribbean ball, Pompez jumped into organized baseball after integration. As a scout for the Giants, he helped recruit Monte Irvin, the Giant's first black player and future Hall-of-Famer, and signed Manuel Mota, Danilo Rivas, and Felipe and Mateo Alou.

Martínez, along with Tetelo Vargas, had played for Pompez's New York Cubans, and while coaching for *Escogido* in the 1950s, he scouted the island for Pompez. He talked to Gonzalo, Gonzalo talked to Juan, and they both sought Ramfis' approval. With that final hurdle cleared, the brothers Marichal got in a Lincoln Continental on the afternoon of September 16, 1957 and went to the home of Francisco Martínez "Paquito" Alba, *Escogido*'s president and Rafael Trujillo's brother-in-law. There Juan signed to play for the *Leónes* of *Escogido*. The next day, he signed to play for the New York Giants. His bonus was $500.

That night, a team of touring major leaguers led by Willie Mays played in *Ciudad Trujillo*. Marichal watched in awe from the *Escogido* dugout but caught up with Mays a few seasons later, in San Francisco.

In March, 1958, Marichal flew to the Giants' spring training camp in Sanford, Florida, along with countrymen Mota, Mateo Alou, Danilo Rivas, Julio César Imbert, and René Marte. Alejandro Pompez was there to greet them and ease the transition to both the majors and a new culture.

"Like the other Latin players, I had problems with the food and got homesick. There was a group of us from here that would play *merengue* after practice. But that made me so sad that I finally took my records and broke them one by one and stopped listening to any Dominican music at all."

When camp broke, Marichal was assigned to Michigan City, Indiana in Class D ball. After two days in a bus riding north, Marichal met racism, North American style, for the first time. Along with René Marte, José Tartabull and Julio Santana from Cuba, and a few black American players, Marichal encountered hostility on the street and an unwillingness to serve him at restaurants in the town and on the road.

"I didn't speak any English at all then," Marichal says with a frown. "I used to eat a lot of fried chicken because a restaurant there gave a meal of fried chicken to the pitchers for every game they won. They only gave us $2.50 for meal money and I won lots of games that year. Sometimes, I would see what someone else was eating and point to his plate."

On the field, Marichal blocked out the racial and cultural indignities of his new venue and led Michigan City to the championship. Pitching to his compatriot, René Marte, Marichal won 21 games and lost only eight, with a 1.87 ERA and 246 strikeouts. He won two more games in the championship series.

That won him a promotion to Class A ball the following year, where he pitched for Springfield, Massachusetts. His salary jumped from $250 to $450 a month. He was also reunited with Mota and Alou, and shared an apartment with them. "That's where I learned how to cook," he recalls proudly.

Although his record slipped to 18 and 13, Marichal helped pitch

Springfield to their league championship with two postseason victories and continued to please the Giant organization. When Giant Hall-of-Famer Carl Hubbell had observed Marichal during his first spring camp, the former screwballer noted that Marichal possessed a poise rarely seen in players that young. Unbeknownst to Marichal, Hubbell directed Giant pitching coaches in the minors to keep their hands off the young Dominican and let him develop on his own. He did, picking up an extraordinarily high leg kick and a screwball along the way. The leg kick became Marichal's trademark in the majors.

In addition to the two hundred plus innings he worked each of his first two years in the minors, Marichal was throwing another hundred innings during the winter season. He began his third season in the minors in Tacoma, Washington in AAA ball and showed he could win there, too. Mid-season, the 5'11", 160 pound 21-year-old received a telegram from the parent club requesting he report to San Francisco. "That was better than the telegram from Ramfis!"

Marichal's totals for two and a half seasons in the minors were 54 wins, 26 defeats, an ERA of 2.35, and 575 strikeouts in 655 innings. And true to Viruta, he allowed only an average of 1.8 walks per game.

A week after being called up, Marichal debuted on July 19, 1960 in Philadelphia. He no-hit the Phillies into the eighth inning, when Clay Dalrymple singled with two outs. It was the only Philadelphia hit. Four days later, Marichal tossed a four-hitter to beat the Pirates, who would win the World Series that fall, and in his next start, he beat Warren Spahn and the Milwaukee Braves. The league quickly began to take notice of this latest Latin import. Marichal finished the season with a 6–2 record, his play marred only by a shoulder injury that would plague him throughout his career.

The Giants, who had followed the Dodgers into the black American and Latin talent markets, already had Felipe Alou and Puerto Ricans Orlando Cepeda and José Pagan on their roster. Mateo Alou and Manuel Mota would soon join them, followed by the youngest Alou brother, Jesus, in 1963. Felipe, the senior Dominican on the team, arranged for Marichal to room with Blanche Johnson, a black woman who lived near Candlestick Park. Mateo Alou did the same when he was called up.

Marichal won 31 games and lost 21 over the next two seasons. In 1962, the Giants came from behind to beat the Dodgers in a West Coast reprise of the 1951 pennant playoffs and went to the World Series. Marichal pitched shut-out ball through the first four innings of the fourth game, but when he tried to bunt a runner up in the top of the fifth, the pitch smashed into his fingers and he was forced to leave the game.

He did not return to play in the series and the Giants succumbed, losing the seventh game 1–0 when Bobby Richardson snagged Willie Mc-Covey's line drive with two out and two on in the bottom of the ninth.

For the rest of the 1960s, Marichal compiled a simply astounding record, winning more than twenty games six of the next seven seasons, leading the National League twice in victories, shut-outs, and complete games, and once in ERA and winning percentage. Overall, he had an ERA below 3.00 nine times, struck out more than 200 batters six seasons, and won at least 25 games three times. In 16 seasons, Marichal won 243 games, lost 142, and had a career ERA of 2.89. He completed over half of the games he started and struck out 2,303 batters. An eight time All-Star, he won two of these contests and no-hit the Houston Colt 45s on June 15, 1963.

Marichal was the best Latin pitcher of his times, and perhaps any time, his celebrity dimmed only by the brilliance of a trio of stellar National League pitchers with whom he shared the stage during the 1960s—Koufax, Drysdale, and Gibson.

Dodger lefty Sandy Koufax was considered even better than Marichal during these seasons. Few could argue against the two-time Cy Young award winner who pitched four no-hitters and won 111 games against only 34 defeats between 1962 and 1966 as he led the Dodgers to three pennants and two World Series triumphs. But Koufax's career totals were only 165 wins and 87 losses, as arthritis shortened his brilliant career. Joining Koufax on the Dodgers was the intimidating right-hander, Don Drysdale, whose 58 consecutive innings of shut-out ball set a record that lasted over twenty years. Right-hander Bob Gibson, who hurled St. Louis to three World Series appearances and also won the Cy Young award twice, posted career marks that approximated Marichal's stats. During this trio's tenure, the Dodgers and the Cardinals appeared in seven World Series. Marichal's Giants, meanwhile, came up empty in 1962 and the club did not return to the fall classic until 1989. Each of these men wound up in the Hall of Fame, although Marichal's route to Cooperstown was the most tortuous.

In 1959, during the winter season, Marichal met Alma Rosa Carvajal, a pretty 15-year-old neighbor of the Alous in Santo Domingo. Her father, a pensioned army officer, was good friends with General José García Trujillo, who was the Secretary of the Armed Forces, a cousin of Rafael Trujillo, and an aficionado of the game.

"The General used to send for me every morning during the winter season just to talk about baseball. He followed Cuban baseball as well as major league ball. I was nervous, a young kid talking to a general, while he would sit back and drink vodka while we talked.

"Alma's family lived near the palace of Trujillo, and her father's relatives had a lot of money and land. That made them very, very close to Trujillo.

"I didn't know anything about politics as a kid. The only thing I knew was that Trujillo was the biggest man in the country. It wasn't until I went to the United States and lived there for six months that I started learning what had been happening in my country. I didn't know the things Trujillo used to do to people—the political repression and murder—because Trujillo controlled the media here.

"When I started playing with lots of Puerto Ricans, they used to know more about what was happening in Santo Domingo than I did. They called the Dominicans *chapitas*. A *chapita* is a bottle cap. They said that Trujillo's medals were only bottle caps that he wore to make him look like a big man. They called Trujillo a *chapita*, too." Indeed, by then, Rafael Trujillo had accumulated a chestful of decorations and several pages worth of titles, collecting such honorifics the way a laterday autocrat, Imelda Marcos, collected shoes.

As Marichal's career was ascending, Trujillo's reign was coming to an end. An increasingly isolated figure in the Caribbean, the man they called the goat went down to a hail of assassins' bullets on May 30, 1961.

"I was afraid at what was going to happen to my country. After 31 years with the same man, I didn't know what to think. I was engaged to Alma by then and extremists were threatening to bomb her family's house. After I went to spring training with the Giants in 1962, I got worried about her. I asked Alvin Dark, who was my manager, if I could go back to get married and he said yes."

They wed on March 28, 1962 and made their first home together in San Francisco, where they shared a house with Felipe Alou and his wife, Maria. The next year, Mateo and his wife, Teresa, moved in, too. "We got along very, very well together," Marichal remembers. Mateo, who had caddied at the Santo Domingo Country Club as a boy, taught golf to Felipe and Juan, while the three women helped each other adjust to the trials they encountered on foreign shores. "Felipe is godfather of my oldest daughter, Rosie, and I am the godfather of a daughter of his. And Mateo is the godfather of my second girl, Elsie, while I'm the godfather of his daughter. That is a serious obligation for a Dominican, to be a godfather."

Marichal and his housemates returned each fall to the island, where winter play began on October 24th, Trujillo's birthday, and lasted until the play-offs in January. The winning club then played in the Caribbean Championships the first week of February.

During the 1960s and '70s, Dominican winter play flourished, in part due to the collapse of Cuban league play following the revolution. As North American and Cuban major leaguers joined the growing numbers of Dominican major leaguers on Dominican winter team rosters, the calibre of baseball soared. Imports such as Frank Howard, Gaylord Perry, Steve Garvey, Dave Parker, Phil Niekro, and Willie Stargell made Dominican ball frequently as competitive as summer play.

Marichal played eight seasons of winter ball, all for *Escogido,* the club most associated with the Trujillo family. Joining him were Giant teammates Willie McCovey, Andre Rogers, Manny Mota, Tito Fuentes, and all three Alou brothers. *Escogido,* which had established a relationship with the Giants, got first pick of the club's players for winter ball, while *Licey* threw their lot in with the Dodgers, *Aguilas* with the Pirates, and *Las Estrellas* of San Pedro with the Braves.

After signing with *Escogido* in 1957, Marichal struck out the side in his first appearance, a relief stint in late December. He threw over a hundred innings each of the next three seasons.

"It wasn't easy doing that," Marichal protests. "After pitching for two or three hundred innings in the States, it was hard to come down here and be expected to play winters. There was a lot of pressure on you to play. But there was also pressure from the Giants not to play, because they wanted me to rest my arm.

"But if you don't play, the whole country gets on you."

Marichal compiled a 36–22 won-lost record in winter ball, a career winning percentage second only to that other Manzanillo hurler, Güayubín Olivo. His cumulative ERA of 1.87 is still the best among all pitchers with over 300 innings of work, and his 32 complete games behind only Güayubín and his brother, Chi Chí.

But because Marichal did not play every season, he became the focus of criticism in the press and by fans. Nor did his injuries or heavy workloads for the Giants fend off the constant nagging as to why Marichal was not playing winter ball. While his spectacular success in the United States was appreciated, Dominicans wanted to see Marichal play on the island. And there, the game's *fanáticos* were even more demanding than their counterparts in the States.

Injuries, the need for rest, and the four daughters born during his playing days, however, were enough to keep Marichal away. "I finally built a house in San Francisco and stayed there one winter so that I would not have to go home and listen to them asking on the radio as to when I was going to pitch. They were having a rough time with baseball then, anyway. After Trujillo's death, and then the military's overthrow of Juan Bosch, they didn't play winter ball for awhile."

While Marichal skips over the shoulder and back injuries that

plagued him, these ailments made playing a painful process and sometimes hospitalized him. Often, the only comfortable place he could
sleep was the floor.

Marichal even tried bathing in the *Río Sanate,* near the shrine of
the Virgin of Altagracia, a pilgrim's destination in Higüey that looks like
a huge McDonald's Golden Arches. "Mateo Alou had a dislocated
shoulder and would go to the *Sanate* to bathe. If you did that on the way
to Higüey, it was supposed to heal you. It seemed to work for him and
with all the problems I had, I went to that river every year."

In the 1980s, as salaries escalated in the major leagues to the point
where most established Dominican ballplayers did not need the relatively small pay that winter ball provided, fewer and fewer Dominican
major leaguers continued to play. "I cannot criticize them," Marichal
says. "Look at Tony Peña, playing almost every inning in the majors
and then most of the season here. I don't agree with what he is doing. I
don't care how much he loves the game. When a team starts paying you
over a million dollars in salary, they want you to produce for them. I
don't think a guy who plays that much can be ready for the whole
season."

A pitch sends an Oakland rookie sprawling and when he takes a
few steps towards the mound and shouts at the pitcher, Rafael Avila
quips, "Juan, show him how it's done."

The oblique reference to the darkest moment in Marichal's career
brings a grin to Chico Fernández's face and the hint of a smile to
Marichal's.

That the Dodgers and Giants were waging war between the lines in
the summer of 1965 was little surprise. This Brooklyn versus the Bronx
rivalry in the senior circuit had reached new heights with the Giants'
come-from-behind victory in the 1951 pennant play-off and then traveled west as both clubs deserted New York City in 1958. The Giants
bested the Dodgers again, in the 1962 play-offs, with Los Angeles
rebounding to win the World Series in 1963.

By late August 1965, the two teams were virtually tied for first
place when the Dodgers visited San Francisco for a four game series.
Both clubs were known for their aggressive approach to the game, with
pitchers laying claim to the inside portion of the plate, *caveat* batter. A
batter who crowded the plate would invariably be knocked down. In the
1950s, Giant pitcher Sal Maglie, a.k.a. the Barber, for the close shaves
he gave batters at the plate, set the tone. In 1956, Maglie was traded to
Brooklyn, where he tutored the Dodgers staff in the art of intimidation.
Among his eager disciples was Don Drysdale, who went on to set a
major league record by hitting 154 batters in the course of his 14-season
career.

Earlier in the summer, Drysdale had decked Mays twice, prompting Marichal to respond that, "If he keeps that up, somebody's going to find out we can protect our hitters." Such payback was *de rigueur* and batters expected that their pitcher would retaliate when they were thrown at. Willie Mays had made a point of telling Marichal that early in his career. After Marichal's intemperate remarks to the press, National League President Warren Giles tried to halt the escalation by threatening to impose a thousand dollar fine if Marichal or anyone else did so.

In the final game of the August series, Marichal came to bat with the Dodgers leading 2–1 in the third inning. Marichal had decked Maury Wills and Ron Fairly in the second inning, and Sandy Koufax, on the mound for the Dodgers, had sent Willie Mays sprawling in the bottom of the inning.

John Roseboro, who stepped into the void created by the car crash that ended Roy Campanella's marvelous career, was catching. Neither he nor Marichal could have been immune to events off the field that spring and summer. In late April, constitutionally-minded junior officers in the Dominican military had backed the protests of the supporters of deposed president Juan Bosch, who had been ousted in a 1963 coup. A bloody civil war broke out with aerial bombing and house-to-house fighting in Santo Domingo. President Lyndon Baines Johnson, seeing Red, sent in 23,000 U. S. troops with the backing of the Organization of American States to support the anti-Bosch forces, and thousands more died as the summer played itself out. Roseboro, meanwhile, was a black man living in Los Angeles in the midst of that summer's Watts uprising, the worst outbreak of racial rioting since World War II. Thirty-four died and Watts, a neighborhood where sixty percent of the people were on relief, went up in flames.

Koufax's second pitch to Marichal was low and inside and Roseboro dropped the ball. According to Marichal, when Roseboro fired the ball back to Koufax, it clipped his ear. Marichal whirled and shouted "Why did you do that?" Later, Marichal said, Roseboro replied "(expletive deleted) you!"

As Roseboro moved toward Marichal, the Dominican pitcher clubbed him three times with his bat, gashing the Dodger catcher's scalp.

A small brawl erupted. After the umpires restored order and ejected Marichal, Koufax retired the first two batters before walking the next two. Figuring that under these circumstances, Koufax was not going to jam him, Willie Mays stepped into the batter's box expecting a pitch over the middle or outside of the plate. He got one and hit a three-run homer that won the game for the Giants.

Marichal subsequently argued that Roseboro had deliberately tried to hit him with the ball, but did not try to defend attacking him with a bat. League president Giles fined Marichal $1,750 and, more important, suspended him for eight playing days. The Giants staggered through the suspension, and reclaimed the league lead in mid-September, before folding in the stretch.

Marichal's record was 3–4 the remainder of the season, and the incident haunted him the following year. "I didn't throw inside to anybody the remainder of that season, and into '66. I didn't even realize that was happening until Tom Sheehan, the pitching coach, pointed it out to me. That's bad enough for any pitcher, but especially for a control pitcher, and that was what I was."

Far worse than the immediate effect on Marichal's pitching was the impact on his image, and, by extension, that of all Latin players. That it was a Latin player on the Giants, who had more Latins on their roster than any other team, probably made the attack seem even worse.

Marichal's teammate, Puerto Rican-born Orlando Cepeda, had battled Giant managers repeatedly, holding out each spring and drawing the charge that he was a lazy, undisciplined player. In 1958, the Pirates' Bob Friend and the Giants' Rubén Gomez, also from Puerto Rico, threw repeatedly at each other's batters in a game at Forbes Field. Bench jockeys, including Pirate manager Danny Murtaugh, and his Giant counterpart, Bill Rigney, tossed further invective at each other from the dugout. Gomez decked Friend and later in the game, Friend returned the honor in kind. Feeling the need to come to Gomez's defense, Cepeda grabbed a bat and went on to the field after Danny Murtaugh. Only a shoestring tackle by Willie Mays saved the Pirate skipper. But the image of Latin players as hotheads had been firmly imprinted on the sporting public.

"They call us hot-tempered and say that we don't play under control—that we are too emotional," Marichal protests. "But there are a lot of American players that do the same. It's part of the game. It's excitement that makes you act like that."

Marichal had waged a few holdouts with the Giants over his contract, too, but what irked him most about his relationship with the club was manager Alvin Dark's questioning of his courage.

"Alvin Dark to me was one day the best man in the world and the next day, he was the worst. I love the guy, I love him, but I think you have to love people with all the defects that they have. He did things for me that I still appreciate, like when he let me come back to get married during spring training. But I saw Alvin Dark do things that hurt me deeply."

The problem, Marichal explains, was that Dark did not believe him when he said his back hurt too much to pitch. Dark charged Marichal with not wanting to pitch and not having the guts to play with a little pain.

Dark, a Barry Goldwater supporter and fervent Christian, had difficulty keeping his political and religious views out of the clubhouse. During the 1964 season, communication with his players deteriorated. In late July, Dark was quoted by *Newsday*'s Stan Issacs as having said that the problem with the Giants was the presence of so many black and Latin players who ". . . just are not able to perform up to the white ballplayer when it comes to mental alertness. You can't make most Negro and Spanish players have the pride in their team that you can get in the white player. And they just aren't as sharp mentally. They aren't able to adjust to situations because they don't have that mental alertness."

Dark's comments came at a time when the Giants not only had Marichal as their ace, but fielded a team that started three American-born blacks and three Latins. Dark did not return to manage the Giants in 1965. He was replaced by Herman Franks, a Spanish-speaking, former Puerto Rican winter ball manager whom the players found a great deal more *simpático*.

The image of Latin and black players as malingerers was not an uncommon one. What Marichal encountered in San Francisco, Roberto Clemente confronted in Pittsburgh. The graceful Pirate right-fielder from Puerto Rico had a medical history that rivaled Marichal's and both were devotees of chiropractic medicine. And both were viewed as hotheaded showboats on the field.

"Roberto Clemente was beautiful to watch," Marichal attests. "He was something getting to that ball, even if it meant hitting the wall. Roberto used to go to the field to beat you. But look at how he was treated!"

The stereotyping of the Latin ballplayer lingers in the late 1980s, with Dominicans Joaquín Andújar, George Bell, Julio Franco, and Dámaso Garcia a few of the latest to be castigated in the press for their alleged shortcomings.

After splitting his time between two societies for thirty years, Marichal offers one last thought on cultural conflict. "I have always thought that food is a great thing in life. With the Giants, Alvin Dark would sometimes come into the clubhouse after a loss and kick the spread of food set out for the players onto the floor. It was as if he couldn't stand the sight of us eating after we had been defeated. I remember Felipe Alou bending over after Dark did this one night, picking up some of the food off the floor, and eating it while looking Dark right in the eye. I think that is why Dark approved of trading Felipe. He couldn't understand that for us, even if you lose, you don't kick food on the floor. You just don't do that."

Marichal recovered from the Roseboro incident on the field and was the National League's winningest pitcher between 1963 and 1969. He could not quite, however, recoup the loss that his persona had suffered. The Giants remained a first division team until 1972, when the club fell to fifth place in the National League West. Management decided to revamp the club. They traded Mays, the club's icon, to the Mets, largely so that the Say Hey Kid could salvage a bit of financial security from the game, and Marichal and future Hall-of-Famer Willie McCovey were next to go.

Marichal had dropped to 6–16 in 1972, his first losing record. After he went 11–15 in 1973, the Giants shipped him to Boston in the junior circuit. Marichal was 5–1 for the Red Sox, but pitched in only 11 games.

The Dominican Dandy finished his career the next year in, of all places, Los Angeles. "Not many people know this, but I was a Dodgers fan for awhile when I was a kid," Marichal reveals. "They came to Santo Domingo in 1948 during spring training, with Jackie Robinson, Pee Wee Reese, Gil Hodges, and Duke Snider. I was nine then and it made an impression."

Dodger fans seemed to have forgiven Marichal his transgressions now that he was wearing Dodger blue. But sixteen seasons in the majors and eight in winter ball had taken something off Marichal's fastball. He pitched only twice for the Dodgers in April, 1975 before deciding to call an end to his career.

The rookie game is over and Marichal talks to some of the players before walking to his car. "I stayed in San Francisco for about two years, then came here in November 1977. I played golf, made a few investments, and traveled some. Then, almost four years ago, I got a call from Oakland to see if I was interested in working in their organization. Bill Rigney, who had managed the Giants when I came up, recommended me to them. And since then, I've worked for the A's. I spend more time here, but I also have to travel a lot, to Oakland and throughout their minor league system. And I'll tell you, I don't like to fly anymore.

"Baseball has come on real strong here the last ten or fifteen years. I don't think it has peaked yet, either. It's better organized every year and the players are better prepared. There's better instruction all the way up the line. I'm afraid that some day they will stop so many Dominican players from coming to the United States. There is already a visa system. Oakland has only twenty visas for Latin players for the entire organization."

Major league baseball, the United States Department of Labor, and the Immigration and Naturalization Service have developed a quota system over the last fifteen to twenty years that limits the number of foreigners eligible to work as professional ballplayers. Most teams get between twenty and twenty-four work visas each year, using them for foreign-born players who will hold positions that they argue cannot be filled by U.S. citizens. The total of these visas represents the ceiling on the number of foreigners (mostly *Latinos*) who can play either minor or major league ball. Some years, there are not enough visas to go around.

Marichal leaves Las Palmas behind and returns to Santo Domingo. The visiting players board the bus, while the Dodger rookies head for the showers.

In 1981, five years after Marichal retired, he became eligible for election to the Hall of Fame. His affirmative vote total fell short of the 75 percent of the ballots cast by members of the Baseball Writers of America needed for election. Also on the ballot for the first time that year was Bob Gibson, who was voted in, with 100 more votes than Marichal. Gibson told the press he didn't think that he was a hundred votes better than Marichal, whom he called the best pitcher during the years that they, Koufax, and Drysdale were playing.

The Roseboro incident had clearly hurt Marichal. Protests were raised across the Caribbean and by some writers in the States as well. The following year, 68 additional yes votes were cast, but the Dominican Dandy still came up seven votes short.

More and more voices in the baseball world decried the refusal of the electors to decide for Marichal. In a moment fraught with symbolism, Roseboro and his wife, Barbara, came to the Dominican Republic in late October, 1982. Marichal had invited his old nemesis for a golf tournament he hosted in Puerto Plata. Roseboro told the press that the events of 1965 should be forgotten and urged Marichal's election to the Hall of Fame in the January 1983 vote.

As the island held its collective breath, the Baseball Writers of America announced on January 12th that Marichal had finally won election, with 83.6 percent of the votes cast.

Marichal said he didn't believe that there existed a man happier than he was anywhere else on earth and dedicated his honor not only to all Dominicans, but all *Latinos*. They share in my triumph, he said, because it is their triumph, too.

Congratulations came from Venezuela, Mexico, and Puerto Rico as well as throughout the United States. But nowhere was the jubilation greater than on Hispaniola. Marichal had become the foremost Dominican ever, beating the *Yanquis* at their own game.

"For three years, they didn't want to give, how you call it, the *mérito,* to be in the Hall of Fame," Marichal had said earlier in the day. "After I made it, I told them that if they had come to my country and seen where I grew up and how I grew up, and then thought about how far I went in baseball, I would have made it a long time ago."

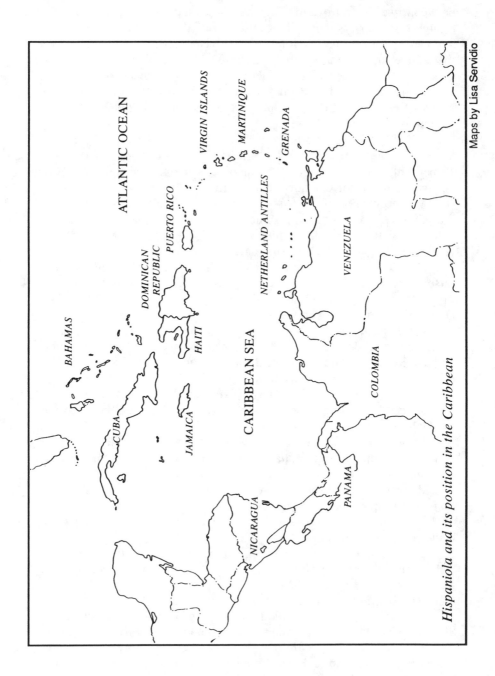

Hispaniola and its position in the Caribbean

Maps by Lisa Servidio

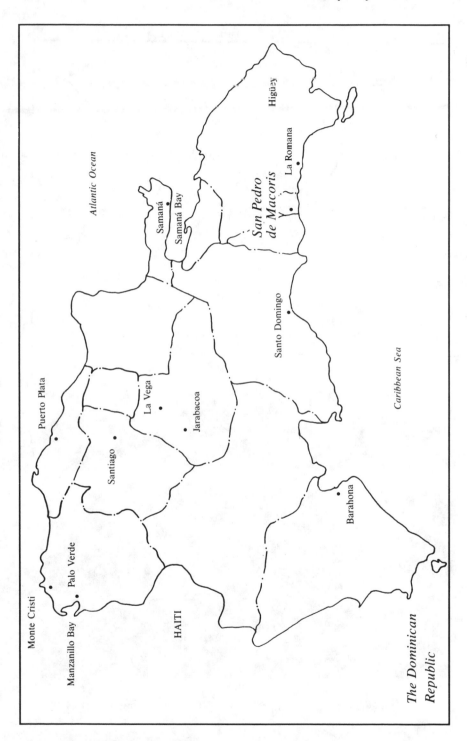

Atlantic Ocean

Higüey

San Pedro
de Macorís

La Romana

Samaná
Samaná Bay

Santo Domingo

Caribbean Sea

Puerto Plata

La Vega

Jarabacoa

Santiago

Barahona

Monte Cristi

Palo Verde

Manzanillo Bay

HAITI

The Dominican
Republic

San Pedro de Macoris

Boys play ball in the canefields at *Batey* 59 against a backdrop of the central mountain range.

They named the ballpark in San Pedro de Macoris for the *Estrellas'* legendary Tetelo Vargas, whose fields of play ranged from the Caribbean to North America's Negro Leagues. Photo courtesy of Cuqui Cordova.

Negro Leaguers, including Cool Papa Bell, Satchel Paige, and Rodolfo Fernández, on an excursion during the 1937 series. Photo courtesy of Craig Davidson/Refocus Films.

Flame swallowers and conjurers perform atop the dugout roof at the stadium in Santiago.

Winners of what was probably Caribbean baseball's greatest championship, the 1937 *Dragones* of Ciudad Trujillo. L to R: Standing: Josh Gibson (C), Harry Williams (2B), Tony Castaño (OF), Rodolfo Fernández (P), Robert Griffin (P), Perucho Cepeda (IF), and Cy Perkins (C & OF); Kneeling: Lázaro Salazar (1B, P, & Manager), Dr. José E. Aybar (Club president), and Satchel Paige (P); Sitting: Enrique Lantigua (C), Leroy Matlock (P), Huesito Vargas (OF), Cool Papa Bell (OF), Sammy Bankhead (SS), Silvio García (3B & P), and Cuco Correa (IF). Photo courtesy of National Baseball Library, Cooperstown, NY.

Hall-of-Famers James 'Cool Papa' Bell and Josh Gibson jumped the Pittsburgh Crawfords and the Homestead Grays of the Negro National League to play ball for the team bearing Rafael Trujillo's name in the summer of 1937. Photo courtesy of Craig Davidson/Refocus Films.

Highkicking righthander Juan Marichal played his way from Laguna Verde to Cooperstown. Here he pitches for *Escogido* in winter ball. Photo courtesy of Cuqui Cordova.

Boys with nets afixed to the ends of long poles sit on the outfield wall of
Tetelo Vargas Stadium in San Pedro de Macoris and try to snare a ball
during batting practice.

Former big leaguer Winston Llenas managed the *Aguilas* (Eagles) of
Santiago for most of the 1980s, before becoming its general manager.

Tony Peña plays as hard in winter ball as he does in the major leagues or did in the banana fields of Palo Verde, near the border with Haiti, where he grew up.

In the locker room before a winter game, a masseur works on Tony Peña while the *Aguilas* catcher plays cards with his brother, Ramón, and Miguel Diloné (L). Catcher Rubén Rodríguez lifts weights in the background.

Tony Peña and *Aguilas* coach Luis Silverio in the dugout during a winter game.

Amateur ballplayers in one of *Central Romana's* leagues take batting practice before a game in La Romana.

Johnnie Cuevas, an Atlanta Braves minor leaguer, during a workout at the stadium in San Pedro de Macoris, baseball's Dominican Mecca.

The sugar mill at Santa Fe, one of the six *ingenios* in or around San Pedro Macoris. "It's sugar," says Dodger coach Rafael Avila, "that makes San Pedro baseball so sweet."

Hall-of-Famers Henry Aaron and Juan Marichal with Cuqui Cordova, the foremost chronicler of Dominican baseball (L to R). Photo courtesy of Cuqui Cordova.

All-Star Julio Franco in the bleachers at Consuelo, after working out with boys from this sugar milltown outside of San Pedro de Macoris.

Men like Roberto Caines fought to make the milltown of Consuelo a decent place to live and to play. Of *Cocolo* origins, Caines helped steer the milltown's sporting energies from cricket to baseball.

A boy with a machete walks through the ballfield that Tony Peña is building in his native town of Palo Verde.

6
The Winter Game

Jackie Robinson's leap across the color line in 1947 sent shock waves throughout Caribbean baseball. It meant that black and *mulatto* ballplayers from the Dominican Republic, Cuba, Puerto Rico, Venezuela, Mexico, and the lesser baseball-playing locales could now think of careers in major league ball. With that stimulus, Caribbean ball entered its golden age and the pro game soon returned to the Dominican Republic.

For decades, the Dominican Republic had fit into a Caribbean baseball network that had its epicenter in Cuba and extended northward into the Negro Leagues. In that network, color did not matter. Any ballplayer—white, black, *mestiza,* or *mulatto*—could play in the winter and summer campaigns held in Cuba, Puerto Rico, and Venezuela.

Only the United States, of all the baseball-playing nations in the Americas, segregated its professional leagues. Major league baseball maintained a fairly rigid color line from the late 1890s, when the last black Americans were driven out of baseball, until Robinson's signing in October 1945 and subsequent debut with the Brooklyn Dodgers in 1947.

At least one Latin, Cuban Esteban Bellan, played pro ball in the United States before the raising of the color barrier. But Bellan's major league career was short-lived and after the color line was drawn, only Caucasian and lighter-skinned Latins came north to play major league ball.

Colombia's Luis "Jud" Castro broke ground in baseball's modern era, after the creation of the National and American Leagues, but Cubans, for the most part, led the way. While Castro played part of the 1902 season for the Philadelphia A's, Rafael Almeida and Armando Marsans spearheaded a Cuban invasion that left its imprimatur on the game and numbered over thirty players before integration. Another ninety or so Cubans followed afterwards.

The crucial factor controlling the entry of Cubans and other Latins to the major leagues was skin color. The *Cincinnati Enquirer* greeted the signings of Almeida and Marsans in 1911 with relief, introducing them as "two of the purest bars of Castilian soap to ever wash up on our shores," but many Cubans simply could not pass. They and other darker-skinned Latins had two North American options. They could barnstorm the United States or play in its Negro Leagues.

The Cuban Stars and the New York Cubans were popular draws as they roamed their way across the United States, injecting talent and a tropical allure to the North American game. On these pan-Caribbean aggregations, Cubans Martín Dihigo, Alejandro Oms, Luis Tiant Sr., Orestes "Minnie" Miñoso, and Silvio García were joined by Dominicans Horacio Martínez, Pedro Alejandro San, and Tetelo Vargas, Puerto Rican Peruchin Cepeda, Panamanian Pat Scantlebury, and sometimes several black North Americans passing for Cubans. Most Latins played for the Cuban Stars, a team that had no home field but which became a mainstay of the Negro Leagues that began play in 1920 and lasted until soon after baseball's reintegration. A few, though, could be found on the rosters of the Pittsburgh Crawfords, the Homestead Grays, and the Kansas City Monarchs, the three best franchises in Negro League history. The Negro League play of Hall-of-Famer Dihigo, powerful outfielder Cristobal Torrienti, and José de la Caridad Méndez, *"el Diamante Negro,"* enhanced Cuba's baseball mystique.

On the other side of the racial divide, in the major leagues, lighterskinned Cubans made their presence felt, too. Perhaps the greatest Cuban major leaguer in the epoch before Jackie Robinson was Adolfo Luque, a pitcher whose twenty big league seasons were capped by a brilliant 27–8 record in 1923 and a winning relief stint of shut-out ball in the seventh game of the 1933 World Series. Following that game, Clark Griffith, whose Washington Senators lost the Series, decided to back a scouting exhibition to Cuba. He sent Joe Cambria.

"I loved Papa Joe," Rafael Avila remarked when tracing his own journey from a sugar estate in Camaguey to pro ball in the United States. "Papa Joe Cambria signed all the good Cuban players who played with Washington—Camilo Pasqual, Pedro Ramos, Roberto Estalella, everybody. When he signed us, we got $75 a month, no bonus, and a plane ticket from Havana to Key West. The rest of the way from Key West was by bus, and there was no air-conditioning then."

Papa Joe stocked the Senators with Cubans. Among his first signees was Roberto Estalella, from the sugar cane mill town that Hershey Chocolate operated in Cardenas, Cuba. The arrival of the dusky-skinned Estalella indirectly breached the color line. While no one challenged his signing, Red Smith wrote afterwards that he suspected "there was a Senegambian somewhere in the Cuban batpile where Senatorial lumber was seasoned."

Following integration, the more farsighted owners began scouring the islands for prospects. Innovative maverick Bill Veeck, who tried to buy the ailing Philadelphia Phillies in 1942 so that he could stock them with Negro League talent, led the way. In 1951, his Chicago White Sox fielded a team starting Cuban Saturnino Orestes "Minnie" Miñoso in left field and Venezuelan Chico Carrasquel at shortstop. Miñoso led the league in stolen bases and triples that year, was second in batting and runs scored, and third in slugging average. The next season, the Senators dipped into the brimming Cuban market and brought three pitchers north, Connie Marrero, Sandy Consuegra, and Jamie Moreno.

The Pirates, meanwhile, settled on a lithe young Puerto Rican, Roberto Clemente, as their right fielder in 1955, while the White Sox added Venezuelan Luis Aparicio at shortstop the next season. Aparicio won Rookie-of-the-Year honors in the American League that season, and both he and Clemente ended up in Cooperstown.

The club playing the most Latins, as well as the most Dominicans, was the Giants. Puerto Rican pitcher Rubén Gomez debuted in 1953, with Dominican Ozzie Virgil following in 1956. Rookie-of-the-Year Orlando Cepeda became their first baseman in 1958, and José Pagan and Felipe Alou joined him in 1959, followed by Juan Marichal and Mateo Alou (1960), Manuel Mota (1962), and Jésus Alou (1963).

The 1962 Giants, with Marichal winning 18 games, and Cepeda, Pagan, and Felipe Alou in the lineup almost every day, was the first heavily Latin ball club to make it to the World Series. Their vanquishers, the New York Yankees, had two Latin ballplayers of their own, Panamanian Hector Lopez and Puerto Rican Luis "Yo-Yo" Arroyo.

The Latin contingent shined during the 1960s, bringing more to the game than a medley of mellifluous names. Cuban Tony Oliva and Puerto Rican Roberto Clemente won back-to-back batting titles in the American and National Leagues in 1964 and 1965, and players from the Dominican Republic and Panama would earn theirs soon after. In 1966, four of the top five batters in the National League were Latins, with brothers Mateo and Felipe Alou first and second. Latins took nine of a possible twenty batting championships during the decade and won honors in almost every possible pitching and batting category but home runs and strikeouts.

By the end of the 1960s, no fan of the game could have doubted the impact that the Caribbean basin was making on major league ball. Finally, the 1971 Pirates, a team with players from Puerto Rico, Cuba, Panama, and Venezuela, won the World Series. Led by the incomparable Roberto Clemente, this truly Pan-American club overcame a two games to none deficit against Earl Weaver's Baltimore Orioles to win in seven games. Along the way, Clemente's play burned itself into the collective baseball consciousness of the United States and the basin. He became the first truly Caribbean-wide baseball hero since Martín Dihigo, the versatile Cuban ballplayer who wound up in the Hall of Fame in Cuba, Mexico, and the United States.

The flow of talent was hardly a one-way phenomenon. For almost every Latin American who traveled to the United States to play, a North American trekked southward during the winter. White major leaguers, in addition to Negro Leaguers, had played winter ball in Cuba since the turn of the century. Pro salaries were far lower then, and ballplayers welcomed the opportunity to supplement their incomes. Team owners saw island-hopping tours as a way to pick up additional revenue in the off-season and get a jump on spring training.

The Dominican Republic attracted Negro Leaguers and Cubans along with a smattering of Venezuelans and Puerto Ricans during their professional seasons in the 1920s and 1930s. And a few Puerto Rican, Venezuelan, and U.S. minor league teams played there in the 1930s. Finally, major league ball arrived in the presence of Kiki Cuyler, Johnny Mize, and the Cincinnati Reds, who won a pair of games against *Escogido* and *Licey* in 1936.

But the Dominican Republic was, even by Caribbean standards, a bush league until pro ball resumed in 1951. The best Dominicans, such as Horacio Martínez, Tetelo Vargas, and the Grillo brothers, played abroad, in the Negro Leagues, Cuba, or Venezuela.

Nineteen forty-eight was the pivotal year in Dominican baseball's renaissance. It began in tragedy as the plane carrying the *Caballeros,* the team representing the Cibao, crashed by the *Río Verde* on January 11, 1948 on the way back from the national tournament. That afternoon, Bombo Ramos had pitched the *Caballeros* to a 9–2 victory in the championship game in Barahona, a city on the island's southwestern coast. Afterwards, Ramos and the cream of the Cibao's baseball talent boarded a prop plane that smashed into the mountains by the *Río Verde*. The entire championship squad, except for catcher Enrique Lantigua, died.

"Lantigua had a premonition," Julito Martínez tells me during batting practice one night. "He refused to get on the plane after the *Caballeros* won and insisted on taking a car back to Santiago, instead. He lived, but everyone else on the team died." Martínez, whose godfather was Martín Dihigo, lost two brothers on that flight. As the club's mascot, Julio would have been on the flight except for a game his own team had scheduled. Only he and the legendary Horacio survive of the baseball-playing Martínez brothers.

Horacio Martínez, 77, is confined to a wheelchair in his Santo Domingo home. The victim of Parkinson's disease, the once-graceful shortstop now can hardly speak. While struggling to describe his career to me on an earlier trip, Horacio Martínez's eyes had filled with tears, brought on by frustration. I make the mistake of telling Julio about his brother's efforts and the *Aguilas* coach excuses himself. He walks down the first base line into the right field corner where he sheds tears of his own.

Dominican baseball was shattered by the tragedy of *Río Verde,* as it subsequently became known, yet the team the nation sent to the *Mundiales* in Managua later that year somehow came back with the world title. Older Dominicans still savor this sporting turnaround.

Almost as exciting as the victory in the world amateur championships was a visit that March by the Brooklyn Dodgers, only the second time that a major league club had come to the island. Accompanied by their Montreal Royals farm club, the Dodgers spent March training in Santo Domingo.

Frank Hatton, Director General of the nation's sports program, presented Dodger manager Leo Durocher and his wife, actress Laraine Day, with the key to the city at an airport arrival that featured the upper echelons of the Dominican armed forces. Even *"El excelentísimo Señor Presidente de la Republica, Generalísimo Dr.* Rafael L. Trujillo Molina" made the scene, tossing the ceremonial first ball at an International Series of the Dodgers, the Royals, and a Dominican Selection team. Afterwards, the dictator autographed a ball for Dodger president Branch Rickey.

For the next month, the 1947 National League pennant winners spent their days playing ball and their nights at the Hotel *Jaragua* along the *malecón,* where the casino stayed open till dawn. Pee Wee Reese, Gil Hodges, Duke Snider, Cookie Lavagetto, Carl Furillo and the other boys of summer attracted crowds wherever they went, but the most celebrated Dodger of all was Jackie Robinson, National League Rookie-of-the-Year in 1947 and the new inspiration to ballplayers across the Caribbean basin.

The following year, winter leagues in Cuba, Puerto Rico, Panama, and Venezuela inaugurated a Caribbean Series of their respective pennant winners. The first stage of this international competition lasted through 1960, and the Dominican Republic, shut out of the competition, gazed with more than a little envy at this new development in Caribbean play.

The series illustrated the ascent of winter ball. Monte Irvin, Willie Mays, Vic Power Pellot, Minnie Miñoso, Jim Bunning, and Norm Cash were but some of the better players to compete. Puerto Rico's *Santurce* club, champions of the 1954 Series, featured Willie Mays, Roberto

Clemente, Rubén Gomez, Don Zimmer, Sam Jones, and former Homestead Gray Bob Thurman. Such a squad could have held its own in any league.

Chafing at their inability to join this increasingly spectacular action, Dominican players and *fanáticos* plotted the resurrection of their own game. A group of sportswriters and players, led by Enrique Lantigua, organized a Barcelo Rum-sponsored competition between two teams called the Reds and the Blues. The colors evoked the almost primal memories of *Escogido* and *Licey,* and in the wake of this series the four traditional clubs reconstituted themselves.

Pro ball resumed in the summer of 1951, with *Licey* and *Escogido* in *Ciudad Trujillo,* the *Aguilas* in Santiago, and the *Estrellas Orientales* in San Pedro de Macoris. Many of the men associated with these clubs when they had last played, during the 1936 and 1937 championships, reclaimed their teams' directorships. Just as in the 1930s, these men were well-connected politically and socially.

For the next five summers, the Dominican league relied on the services of the better native players as well as a few Cubans and North Americans. Some ex-Negro Leaguers, for whom integration had come too late, and a sprinkling of former major leaguers like Joe Page, who was trying to pitch his way back into the majors, labored alongside them during the torpor of the Dominican summer. During *Aguilas'* first year, their roster of twenty included five Cubans, and four players from Puerto Rico, Venezuela, and the United States, skippered by Martín Dihigo.

Finally, in 1956, the Dominican game came of age and switched to winter play. It was the result of a mutually beneficial accommodation with major league baseball, which in the late 1940s and early 1950s, resolved its competition with Caribbean baseball by coopting the Latin leagues.

Caribbean leagues offered a summer alternative to both white and black ballplayers from the United States during the 1930s and 1940s. Latin ball frequently meant better pay and a different, usually less racist, atmosphere. From 1939 until the demise of independent black baseball a decade later, Venezuelan and Mexican franchises vied for Negro League talent, enticing Josh Gibson, Ray Dandridge, and other stars to jump their Negro League teams.

The major leagues were less vulnerable than the Negro Leagues to Latin competition but even they blanched when Mexican liquor mogul Jorge Pasquel sought to strengthen the six-team Mexican summer league in 1946. Pasquel convinced Mickey Owens, Sal Maglie, and Max Lanier to jump their major league clubs, and made a play for the Cardinals' future Hall-of-Famer, Stan Musial. Major league baseball took up the gauntlet, banishing the contract jumpers in retaliation. When the Mexican league faded after the 1948 season, due mostly to its own logistical and financial problems, major league baseball began to sign accords with Caribbean leagues that regulated player movement and institutionalized winter play.

The final factor propelling the Dominican Republic to the top of the Caribbean baseball world was the Cuban Revolution. Long the powerhouse of basin baseball, Cuba even had a AAA minor league team, the Havana Sugar Kings, which was affiliated with the Cincinnati Reds. The Sugar Kings were on their way to the Little World Series of AAA minor leagues in 1959, just months after Fidel Castro marched into Havana on New Years' Day of that year. The revolutionary government offered to underwrite the Sugar Kings' debts as Castro sought to keep the franchise there, "even if I have to pitch," but the International League shipped the club to Jersey City during the 1960 season.

Cuba soon fell out of organized baseball's orbit. After the United States blockaded the island, movement of players and equipment halted. Cuba developed its own sporting goods industry and relied on the repatriated Martín Dihigo to take charge of baseball. A political exile during the 1950s, Dihigo had lent money to Che Guevara in Mexico City for Fidel's return to Cuba in 1956. After the revolution, he returned to help teach the game. Cuban baseball shed its commercial skin and sought instead to advance the social and political aims of the revolution via sport. Although the island has remained the powerhouse of world amateur baseball ever since, the island stopped exporting major leaguers. After the Zoilo Versalles, Tony Oliva, Tony Pérez generations passed out of the game, the next set of Cubans to reach the majors were those who, while born on the island, had grown up in the United States.

The fulcrum of baseball power, meanwhile, shifted to the east, to Puerto Rico and the Dominican Republic.

Nineteen fifty-six was the Dominican league's first season of winter play. "At that point," Pedro Julio Santana explains, "we earned our long pants. We had come of age. We could start bringing in reinforcements from North America during their off-season and start thinking about night baseball. The winter game had begun."

And with time out for revolution in the 1960s, that's been the Dominican game ever since.

And Tony Peña is playing it that evening in Santiago. Although he has driven back and forth to Palo Verde that day on only a few hours of sleep, Peña seems fresh as he shoves Kevin Mitchell aside and steps into the batting cage. His warm-up jersey is torn to his nipple, and his muscles ripple visibly as he jerks three consecutive pitches into the same spot in the left field stands. By the third blast, the fans already in the park are on their feet screaming.

"Tony's got that big ass thunderstick tonight," Mitchell screams, referring to the 37-inch-long bat that Pena is using. "I guarantee you he'll get jammed tonight."

Six-year-old Tony Peña Jr. (a.k.a. TJ), dressed in a Pirate uniform, glances at the commotion from the visitors' dugout, where he is wrestling with José DeLeon, the former Pirate pitcher. After his 2–19 win-loss record during the 1985 season, the Pirates gave up on DeLeon and his once promising career. Two trades later, the still young right-hander was reunited with Peña on the Cardinals. When DeLeon was first called up to the show as a rookie with the Pirates, he (like Cecilio Guante, Rafael Belliard, and the other Dominicans on the Pirates when Peña played there) lived with Tony and his family in Pittsburgh. Peña insists that he only did for them what Panamanian catcher Manny Sanguillen once did for him.

"Besides," he argues, "your teammates are your family. You spend seven months of the year with them. They are your closest friends and I was the Dominican who had been there the longest."

Rafaelito, the clubhouse attendant, fixes the batting gloves in six-year-old TJ's pockets to look like his father's. TJ then jumps on center fielder Stanley Javier, son of former Cardinal second baseman Julian Javier, who bites TJ's tummy before handing him over the railing to Amaris Peña. With an entire ballpark his daycare center, TJ emanates security.

A man in a flower-print shirt dances with *mariachis* and makes tuba-like sounds with his mouth atop the dugout. Another performer, Cuchirimba, a young black man with a large golden spot on his Afro, soon replaces him. This conjurer in high-top Keds sticks four-inch-long nails up his nostrils and pokes wicked-looking needles through his cheeks and biceps without drawing blood.

Half the *Aguilas* squad stands in front of the dugout fascinated with the bizarre show. One player looks away in disgust, muttering *"Vudú,"* to himself. Peña watches for a moment before playfully taking a bat to the players' shins. *"Vamos, coño!* Let's play some ball."

Winston Llenas leans against the screen protecting the box seats near the dugout, talking with his boyhood friend, Tito Hernández. Once they played ball together on the streets of their neighborhood near the center of Santiago. Now Hernández is president of the *Aguilas* ball club and Llenas is its manager.

The last few years of winter ball have been difficult ones. Inflation ran at almost a 60 percent rate in 1988 and will probably go higher in 1989. While moderate by Mexican or Argentine standards of the late 1980s, the loss in buying power has hurt. The contrast with previous years, such as 1986 when the inflation rate was less than seven percent, is felt almost daily. Moreover, the devaluation of the Dominican *peso* vis-à-vis the U.S. dollar has meant that it is costing the Dominican teams almost twice as much to import North American minor leaguers as it did a few years ago.

"We tried lowering the number of Americans that each team could have," Hernández says in fluent English, "but that didn't help too much because the fans expect and want to see Americans playing here. They always have." The most recent threat to winter ball comes from the island's chronic power shortages. Blackouts are daily occurrences and a Santo Domingo politician has called into question the very existence of winter ball, arguing that the nation cannot afford to light the stadiums during the power crisis.

But Hernández, who grew up with the *Aguilas* ball club, is not deterred. "We'll play next season," he assures me the next day in his office. His suite offers a panorama of the mountains ringing the valley of Santiago, where Hernández operates a real estate and construction company and a handful of cattle farms.

While his secretary brings in the customary demitasses of sweetened espresso, Hernández traces his antecedents in the Lebanese and Spanish migrations to the island. Like San Pedro de Macoris, Santiago has a substantial Lebanese population. In both cities, these Middle Eastern migrants assumed leadership positions in the ball clubs.

"When I was seven, in 1951, the *Aguilas* team was renewed. My uncle was president of the club its second year and my grandfather had a hotel where we lived that the Cuban and American players stayed in during the season. I remember Martín Dihigo and the others well."

The directors of the *Aguilas* club came from the rum, tobacco, beer, and retail sectors of the Cibao economy. Several were active politically, too. "At that time, you needed a relationship with the Trujillo family to get things done. That's how things were handled."

Hernández studied in New York City before returning to help his father with the family's department store. He was only twenty but possessed a financial acumen that led the club to tap him for a directorship in 1964 and its vice-presidency in 1966.

As is the case with most of the men owning shares of the Dominican teams, baseball is his avocation. The *Aguilas,* Hernández says, have lost money or broken even more often than they have turned a profit. Annual government subsidies help cover the losses, but the directors often make up the additional deficits out of their own pockets. Hernández is quick to acknowledge, however, that there are indirect financial benefits from his association with the club.

"Financial considerations are secondary for most of us. We try to be profitable, but baseball is really a matter of pride. When pro ball resumed here in the 1950s, baseball was like a fever. We were fighting against Santo Domingo, the capital."

Regional identity is still fierce in the Dominican Republic. Trujillo's championing of the city that bore his name intensified the rivalries among the capital, Santiago, and San Pedro de Macoris. Historically, baseball provided a safe outlet for the residents of these second cities to express allegiance to their hometown and displeasure with the often overbearing capital.

"When we talked to people from the capital, they acted as if they were more important than we were. You know what answer we give to them since Trujillo's death? We say 'Well, you are important but we in the Cibao have given presidents to you.' In the last twenty-five years, all the presidents of the country have been from the Cibao.

"We hate the people, I mean the ball club, from Santo Domingo. We especially hate *Escogido*."

Ask any *Aguilas* adherent who recalls the 1950s and he will link the *Escogido* ball club with Trujillo. Rafael Trujillo's son, Ramfis, and brother-in-law, Paquito Martínez, took special interest in the team, even though the dictator himself showed more interest in women and horses. During a play-off game in 1957, Bahamanian-born, New York Giant shortstop Andre Rodgers committed an error in a game already made tense by a fight between Felipe Alou and the opposing pitcher. Petan Trujillo left his seat, walked onto the field, and began to berate Rodgers. He ended his tirade by slapping the startled player. When the North American players threatened to leave the island, Rafael Trujillo appeared at the park the next evening to insure order. But other than opening day, Trujillo rarely appeared at the ballpark.

His presence was felt nonetheless. "The Trujillo clan was synonomous with *Escogido* when I was a boy," Winston Llenas recalls later that evening in his Santiago home. A light rain falls as Llenas sits in a rocker on his front porch and savors a rare winter night away from the ballpark.

Born in 1943, a few months before Hernández, Llenas matured quickly as a ballplayer but never escaped his boyhood nickname of *"Chilote,"* a derivative of *chi chi lote* or chubby baby. "There was only one season for baseball here, but it went all year long. We kept playing and playing. My first organized team was sponsored by a rice factory, but my brothers and I would play all over the Cibao."

Winston's father and uncles played baseball, too. One of his uncles, Rafael Llenas, caught for the Santiago club during the 1937 championships.

"I have been a subversive for a long time," Llenas says, only half in jest. "For me, to be for *Aguilas* was also to be against Trujillo.

"In the 1950s, *Aviación* served as a farm club for *Escogido* and the Trujillos would make sure their team got the best players. They made it tough for the *Aguilas* and the *Estrellas*. . . .

"I'll tell you, in those days, even the air that we breathed belonged to Trujillo. He had it all."

But not Llenas's heart or mind. When Winston was seventeen, he and his brother were recruited by the team in Mao to play against *Aviación*. "Right after we came home, a jeep with Major Ubiera from the Air Force pulled up in front of our house. The major told my father that he wanted to take me and my brother, Nelson, to the *Aviación* team, because he liked the way we played. He got Nelson, but I had already signed with Kansas City.

"After they took my brother, I started proceedings to get my passport and visa. They denied my passport because somebody in my family was on a list of people against Trujillo. One of my uncles knew some people in Santo Domingo and they talked with Major Ubiera and he said 'He's the brother of a guy that is playing for us. Give him the passport.' I got it the day before I was supposed to leave."

Passport denials were only part of the restrictive Trujillo style. "We lived for 31 years in total darkness. I was only a high school kid in 1961 when I left, but my eyes were open. Trujillo was a sadistic dictator living a masquerade. We should treat Trujillo like the Holocaust and never let him be forgotten.

"You couldn't go anywhere from here without passing checkpoints where you had to identify yourself and show your identity card. You couldn't even listen to a radio broadcast from abroad without fear. In those days, one person was a group, two people a conspiracy, and three people a revolution!

"People filled the stadiums because that was the only place they could really get smashed and let it all hang out. The ballparks were the lungs that allowed us to breathe freely, if only for a few hours. And even at the ballpark, you had to put up with his people shouting '*Viva Trujillo!*' after the national anthem. They say here '*Al pueblo hay que darle pan y circo.*' To the people you must give bread and circus. Baseball has been the fucking circus! Trujillo used baseball to buy peace. When we were playing, it deflected attention away from politics. But for me, rooting against *Escogido* was the closest you could get to rooting against Trujillo."

After the league switched to winter play, Trujillo built stadiums in Santo Domingo, Santiago, and San Pedro. Just in case anyone doubted whose country this was, the parks were named *Estadio* Trujillo, *Estadio* Rhadames Trujillo, and *Estadio* Ramfis Trujillo. Equipped with lights, the new parks allowed night baseball to come to the island. The Caribbean Series, meanwhile, ceased after the Cuban Revolution. When they were revived in 1970, the Dominican Republic took part in the games, along with Puerto Rico, Venezuela, and Mexico.

Soon after Winston Llenas left the island in 1961, Trujillo fell. "When I went away, I had to decide between the book and the bat. I chose the bat." In the years that followed, Llenas played parts of six summers with the California Angels. For eighteen winters, he returned to his homeland to play winter ball. Only Rafael Batista came to the plate more times in Dominican league play, and few put their at-bats to better use. When he left the lineup in 1982, Llenas ranked second in career home runs (to Rico Carty) and RBIs (to Rafael Batista), and among the leaders in several other hitting categories. Near the end of his playing days, Llenas began to manage *Aguilas*, too, and holds the record for longevity among Dominican managers.

"After I left the majors, I played in Japan for a year and then was a player/manager in Mexico City. That was an experience. But I'll tell you, I am under more pressure here than I was in Mexico or when I managed AAA ball in the States. It means so much to the people here. That's something that's hard to explain to the young Americans who come here for winter ball."

Llenas is not alone in his frustrations with minor and major leaguers from the United States who balk at the cultural transition winter ball requires. The reinforcements, as they are called, often leave during the season. More than a few go home at Christmas each year and do not return.

On the bus ride back from San Pedro several nights before, the team stopped at a Chinese restaurant in Santo Domingo for a late dinner. While their teammates ordered, Tony Peña and Kevin Mitchell argued in the foyer. Mitchell, then a minor leaguer with the Mets, had come to winter ball to show New York that he could hit with power. He did, and earned a spot on the Mets roster their 1986 World Series season. Two trades and three seasons later, he would verge on stardom with the Giants.

But at the moment, Mitchell was more concerned with going home and resting before spring training. The last thing that he wanted was to extend his winter season by winning the league championship and going with the squad to Maracaibo, Venezuela for the Caribbean Series. He was tired, homesick, and fed up with culture shock. Peña was trying to persuade Mitchell to honor his contract and stick with the team until season's end, but the muscular minor leaguer from San Diego saw Peña's remonstrations as little more than "guilt-tripping."

The conflict is a recurring one for winter ball. The reinforcements' primary loyalties are to themselves and thus their major league clubs. The needs of their winter teams are secondary. But for most Dominican fans, and for someone like Tony Peña, these distinctions are difficult to make. Even Mitchell shakes his head in wonderment at Peña's consistently hard play. "Some guys will come down here and pull a Marvin Miller," Mitchell says, referring to the former director of the players' association. "You know, kind of wave at a hard hit ball and not put their body in front of it. Not Peña. He plays as hard here as in the States."

Aguilas was then in the midst of a run for first place after spending much of the season in the cellar. Mitchell's bat and the play of the other reinforcements had been instrumental in the team's turnaround. They would go on to win the postseason play-offs and represent the Dominican Republic in the Caribbean Series, but by the time they got to Maracaibo, most of their reinforcements were long gone. Although they picked up some other Dominican players to complete their roster, *Aguilas* lost the cohesiveness that got them there and failed to win the series.

"For American clubs," Tito Hernández argues, "sending their players here is like sending them to a university. In three months, they learn what would take two years in the minors. And then these players insult us by leaving. I know that we have the longest bus rides in the league and I realize that they need to rest up for spring training, but still!"

North American imports have profited immensely from winter ball and in return, they've given Dominican fans the benefit of their considerable talents and made them feel more connected to major league ball. *Aguilas* fans can follow Kevin Mitchell's exploits in the States and tell themselves that they saw his promise when he was still a minor leaguer. *Licey* adherents can track the work of their former winter star, Orel Hershiser, while *Escogidistas* take pleasure in the play of Tim Raines.

The imports not only earn far more in a few winter months than they do during their minor league seasons, but often stay at beachfront resorts and bask in the warmth of adoring fans. Most of all, these baseball hopefuls get the chance to play against competition often as good as they would face in the major leagues. More than a few will use this opportunity to gain the edge they need to make it in the major leagues. Tommy Lasorda, Bill Mazeroski, Willie Stargell, Frank Howard, and Steve Garvey, for example, each has Dominican winter ball somewhere on his resume.

For Bennie Distefano, Mickey Weston, and scores of minor leaguers from the States, winter ball has been a wonderfully exotic, if sometimes trying, experience. Few can quibble with the restaurants, and only the *Aguilas* reinforcements do not live on the beach. And for them, the ocean is only an hour away. "It's good money," says Distefano, who has played in Colombia, Venezuela, and the Dominican Republic. "And it's a heckuva lot nicer here right now than in Brooklyn. And the ladies!" he concludes with an aside to the joys of winter ball. "Some of them don't only stop traffic, they could give a city gridlock."

But other reinforcements never adapt. Only some have more than rudimentary Spanish and only a few have ever seen such unrelenting poverty. "It's been a real experience," pitcher Mickey Weston offers in the dugout, "but one I'm glad to have had. I'll come back next year if they want me. But I've seen guys down here just two or three weeks and they're ready to snap." The Flint, Michigan native has spent his career in the minors, trapped in the pitching-rich Mets organization. A minor league free agent, he will sign with Baltimore before the 1989 season and make his debut in June that year with a shutout stint of relief work to earn his first major league save.

"I've learned a lot here, and not just about baseball," Weston remarks. "I see how tough these people have it and know why someone like Tony Peña plays so hard all the time."

Some of the allure of Dominican baseball has diminished in recent years as more and more of the established native players sit out the campaign and too many of the reinforcements fail to last the season. Attendance is down and the country's economic crisis has intruded at the parks. Part of the problem was the expansion of the league to six teams for the 1983–84 season. The addition of the *Caimanes* in San Cristobal and the *Azucareros* in La Romana diluted the level of talent and increased costs without bringing in enough extra revenue. "It was ill-advised," Winston Llenas explains. "They did it for political reasons, but when it comes to baseball here, we are traditionalists."

But the young boys who cluster at the entrance to the locker rooms and watch batting practice have lost little of their idolatry for their demigod ballplayers. "All those kids in the cane fields and the *barrios* in Santo Domingo know that their only hope in getting out is becoming a Tony Peña or Joaquín Andújar," Winston Llenas observes. "If the players with big names get big heads and don't play, it's just going to create chances for some kids who will use that opportunity to make it big."

One boy hoping against the odds to follow these Dominicans to baseball's promised land is Junior, a parentless (and once seemingly nameless) child who former Detroit pitcher Milt Wilcox befriended several winter seasons ago. Wilcox was trying to show a major league team he still had it after rotator cuff surgery and his release by the Tigers. On the basis of his winter outings, he would pitch his way back into the majors. Junior became friends with Milt's son, Brian, and accompanied the Wilcox family during their winter stay. He lost touch with Wilcox after the player went home, but still has the wardrobe, glove, and name he received that season. After losing his patron, Junior insinuated himself into the dugout and now takes his directions from Rafaelito, the locker room manger. Now 12, he brings the *Aguilas* pitcher a jacket and a cup of water at the end of each inning. Before the game, he shags flies alongside the pitchers in the outfield and is always willing to warm a player up.

While Llenas speaks, Junior, with Miguel Diloné's bat, whacks huge flying insects that plop in the dirt in front of the dugout. Diloné recoils in mock horror at the desecration of his sacred stick and grabs the bat from Junior, who promptly finds another.

While Diloné practices his swings, Luis Polonia and Stanley Javier stretch on the grass nearby. Teammates on *Aguilas,* they also shared the outfield for the Oakland Athletics in the 1988 World Series. The speedy Cibao-born, West Coast-sophisticated tandem are Diloné's hares apparent in the Dominican running game and could be among the Dominican stars of the 1990s. Javier grew up in the United States, where his father, Julian, played second base for over a decade with the Cardinals and bears the name of Julian's revered teammate, Stan Musial. Polonia did not have the benefits of Stanley's crosscultural upbringing, but his Jheri-curled hair and obligatory golden chains suggest he's been playing catch-up ball. Javier has won two winter batting titles and Hernández fears that soon *Aguilas* will lose his services and that of Polonia. What these players make in a winter season simply pales in comparison with their major league salaries.

Batting practice ends and the players return to the locker room to change into their game jerseys. Kevin Mitchell strips off a tee-shirt that says "If you want to talk to me, call my agent," revealing a heavily-muscled torso. Most of the Dominicans, by comparison, are lean. At six feet, 180 pounds, Tony Peña is among the larger native players on the *Aguilas.*

Ramón Peña is a smaller left-handed version of his brother. "He may not have the size to make it in the majors," Winston Llenas once said of the *Aguilas* reliever, "but he's got the *cojones*—the balls." Signed and released by the Pirates, Ramón was picked up by the Tigers but remained mired in their farm system through the 1988 season.

During the 1988–89 winter season, Ramón Peña broke the league record for saves and Tony toasted his success with a *fiesta*. Peña's

Santiago home, which he bought from Tito Hernández nine years ago, is surrounded by palm trees and *bougainvillea*. While his house fills with teammates and the club's entourage, Peña collapses in a rocker on the patio and sips coffee. He is soon rousted by TJ, who plunks him in the side with a rubber-tipped dart. Dressed in camouflage pants, a cut-off Pirates tee-shirt, and a Mickey Mouse watch, TJ pours corn flakes into his sister's hair and generally adds to the growing commotion.

Amaris Peña, like Tony, the child of a banana worker, takes off a high heel and chases her son through the house before rescuing her daughter, Jennifer. Tall, trim, and athletic-looking, Amaris played softball in Palo Verde and helped with Tony's workouts during his minor league years. She chats with her guests while Octaviano, Tony's father, sits quietly by the side, entertaining his grandchildren. He is clearly less comfortable here than in Palo Verde, where he still works the land.

Tropical plants ascend through the skylight in the family room. Photos of Roberto Clemente and Ramón Lora flank a picture of Jesus Christ. A blackboard on which Tony practices English conceals a score of trophies. A princess in a Palo Verde fairy tale, Amaris echos words her husband had used the day we rode to his hometown. "I have my riches, my fine clothes, and this palace to live in, but I am the same person now that I was in Palo Verde."

The celebration is held in the style of the Line, the border with Haiti, and the scent of goat cooked with piquant spices wafts over the backyard. Players heap platters with cassava and *moro,* the popular rice-and-red-beans staple. Ramón Peña accepts the accolades for his record-breaking performance graciously. The following season, the Tigers will call Ramón up to the big leagues, and at least for a few weeks, he will join his brother in the box scores.

Little remains constant in the tropics. Composition and decomposition accelerate due to the abundant sun and rain. Winter baseball is not immune to that dynamic. The faces in the dugout change more rapidly than those in the major leagues and the vicissitudes of the Third World frequently invade the sanctity of the ballpark. Only the ambience, a rum-soaked, *merengue*-pounding fever, stays the same. That, and the game between the lines.

7

Three Kings Day in Consuelo

William Joseph and Roberto Caines sit under a grapefruit tree in Guachupita, in the shadow of *Ingenio* Consuelo's smokestacks. While the sugar mill's plume of smoke signals the beginning of another grinding season in the Dominican Republic, these men reflect upon the making of their community. It's a story that says much about why San Pedro de Macoris has become baseball's Mecca in recent years. Yet their tale begins at the turn of the century in the British West Indies and is as much about cricket as baseball.

Only a few hours before and ten kilometers away, Alfredo Griffin stood in the driveway of his home in San Pedro as several hundred young boys swarmed the compound's walls, chanting "*Reyes!* (Kings!) *Reyes!* (Kings!) Griffin! Griffin!" It's the morning of January 6th—Three Kings Day—the traditional Dominican day of holiday gift giving and a time when politicos and other notables dispense toys. The children had been outside his house since dawn, spilling over from neighbor Joaquín Andújar's annual sporting goods giveaway. And the sight of Los Angeles Dodger shortstop Griffin heading down the driveway in this tan BMW 635CSi sets off a stampede that blocks his exit.

No one had stood chanting outside William Joseph's or Roberto Caines' concrete block homes in Consuelo that morning. For 76-year-old Joseph, a blacksmith pensioned after fifty-one years in the *ingenio,* and 60-year-old Caines, who tends to the sugar mill's recalcitrant water pumps, already gave their gifts to the youth of Consuelo and the surrounding sugar estates, boys like Rico Carty, Pepé Frias, Rafael Batista, Julio César Franco, and Alfredo Griffin. And Griffin, hands on hips, wants badly to get back to Consuelo so that he can give his.

"How can you come over and ask for a gift when Joaquín has already given you a bat, a shirt, or a glove and other children haven't yet got anything?" Griffin implores in Spanish. Relenting, he hands gloves to a score of boys who seemed so far to have missed out and seizes the moment to ease his vehicle on to the streets of the town that currently sends more of its native sons to the major leagues on a per capita basis than any other town ever has.

Driving past Rico Carty's house, Griffin stops near that of his friend, George Bell, to pull out gloves for a trio of shoeshine boys. As Alfredo drives away, the boys run after his car, holding their prizes aloft. Weaving his car through San Pedro's traffic, a helter-skelter swirl of motor scooters, pedicabs and the occasional Mercedes Benz, Griffin passes Tetelo Vargas Stadium, home of the *Estrellas Orientales,* his winter ball club, and heads north on the two-lane blacktop to Consuelo, the largest of the six sugar mill towns that have made San Pedro the center of the Dominican Republic's sugar industry since late last century.

Griffin overtakes a boy astride a horse-drawn cart loaded with cane cut into four-foot sections. Haitian women balance jerrycans of water on their head as they walk through the cane fields to their *batey,* a cluster of company-owned shacks. Their husbands and sons cut and stack cane in the fields that stretch as far as one can see on both sides of the road from sunup until sundown for about a dollar a ton. A decent day's work is three tons.

Griffin slows to cross the tracks by the cemetery where Pirate prospect Alberto Lois lost a race with a train as he drove home from the ballpark one night. Lois's career ended on the spot, along with the lives of six of his passengers. In Consuelo, Griffin drives past the stadium where several youths practice under the watchful eyes of Red Sox scout Rafael Batista to the home of his mother, Mary Griffin, and unloads several mitts and pairs of running shoes from the trunk of his car.

Mary Griffin lives in the house on Carty Street her son bought for her when he won Rookie-of-the-Year honors in the American League in 1979. Although it was Rico Carty, the boy from Guachupita, who helped put Consuelo on the sporting firmament's map, it is his mother, Oliva, once the town's midwife, for whom the street is named. Carty Street stretches from Santa Ana Church to the *ingenio,* a century-old congeries of shops, giant grinding wheels, and centrifuges, that makes sugar out of the cane. Behind the mill lie Guachupita, La Habana, La Loma, Barrio Hato Mayor and the other neighborhoods of company-owned housing.

Just as Carty Street ties Consuelo together, Rico Carty is the ballplayer who links Joseph's and Caines' generation with Griffin's. "My mother wanted me to be a doctor," Rico Carty recalled earlier as he stretched across the rattan furniture in his San Pedro home, "but I didn't like that. My mother wouldn't let me go to the ball field, but I used to steal time to play. I tell my mother I going to school but I used to go the river and swim and play ball instead. I would have ended up in the mill but for baseball."

In 1960, Rico Carty joined the wave of Dominicans surging northward. His United States debut at the 1959 Pan American Games in Chicago so impressed U. S. clubs that nine of them made him offers to play professionally. Carty accepted them all.

Rico signed with all four Dominican winter clubs, too, and only the intervention of the president of the minor leagues saved him from permanent exile from the game. After Rico, whose .366 batting average led the majors in 1970, came his Guachupita *compañero* and Pan Am teammate, Pepé Frias, and then Rafael Batista, Griffin, Nelson Norman, Alberto Lois, Julio César Franco, Juan Samuel, and several score others who signed pro contracts. Other sugar mill town boys, like Rafael Ramírez, Rafael Santana, Tony Fernández, and Mariano Duncan, adopted a "have glove—will travel" approach and played for the *Ingenio* Consuelo "amateur" team, which sent five shortstops in a row to the majors.

An idol to a generation of San Pedro youth, Carty retired in 1983, never having missed a winter season. "I feel a real obligation to play here 'cause I owe my country a lot . . . because they pushed me so much here." Carty's debt is to men like William Joseph, Roberto Caines, his uncle Luis Carty, Austin Jacobo, and a score of sporting elders who nurtured baseball during its early years in Consuelo.

These men were the sons of migrants of African descent who arrived here at the turn of the century from St. Martin, Nevis, Tortola, Montserrat, and the other, mostly British, islands whose sugar industries were collapsing at the moment that the Dominican cane fields were expanding. "They were brought to cut cane on the estates," Roberto Caines explains in English with a West Indian lilt, "but they were scorned. It was a great trial to go to another country. We lived in barracks, four families to a house, with plenty bugs, plenty sickness, and vermin."

Sipping wine served by Joseph's niece, Caines continues. "They called us *Cocolos,* because many of the first English people here were from Tortola and the Dominicans had trouble saying that. They meant it as an insult and when a Dominican called an Englishman *Cocolo* it cause many a fight."

But this racial epithet subsequently became a term of pride as the English people forged their own cultural definition of *Cocolo.* That definition emphasized discipline and self-organization, at work and at play. Without these English-speaking, cricket-playing sojourners, Dominican baseball would never have become the best in the Caribbean.

"It's sugar that makes San Pedro baseball so sweet," Rafael Avila says one night before a game at Tetelo Vargas Stadium. "Just like in Cuba, but more so." Sugar cane came first, but baseball almost inevitably followed it on the islands of Cuba, Hispaniola, and Puerto Rico. And though the sugar industry is now in decline throughout the Caribbean, baseball remains on the ascent.

Christopher Colombus first brought cane to the western hemisphere, on his return voyage to Hispaniola in 1493. He planted it in La Isabela, a settlement on the northern side of the island. Small plantations proliferated and slaves were imported from Africa to tend the fields. The first *trapiche,* a small animal- or human-powered mill for grinding the cane, was built in Santo Domingo on a site called La Fé. Four and a half centuries later, Rafael Trujillo would build the capital's baseball stadium there.

But cane cultivation languished by 1600, due to shortages of capital and labor (especially after the epidemics of the 1580s decimated the slave population) and increasing competition, particularly from Portugal's Brazilian colony. What little cane was grown until its reintroduction in the 1870s was largely for making *aguardiente,* a raw, fiery rum.

In the 1870s, about four or five thousand Cubans fleeing their island's Ten Years' War for independence from Spain came eastward to the Dominican Republic. The conflict laid waste to enough fields and mills to reduce Cuban capacity to meet the growing international demand for sugar, which had gone from an elite delicacy to a European working class addiction, and thus encourage the Dominican Republic to reenter the market.

The Cuban exiles brought with them baseball and the expertise that had made Cuba the largest sugar producer in the Caribbean. Many settled in the southeastern plains around San Pedro de Macoris and La Romana. Coming at a time when the Dominican government was embracing foreign investment and development, these Cubans helped change the Republic from a former colonial backwater to the basin's second largest sugar producer and one increasingly coveted by United States interests.

Along with a few North Americans and the Italian entrepreneur, Juan Bautista Vicini, the Cubans began erecting steam-powered mills in the sparsely settled lowlands around San Pedro de Macoris, a small port about seventy kilometers east of Santo Domingo. Juan Amechazzura built the first, *Angelina,* in 1875; North American Santiago Mellor followed with *Porvenir* in 1879; and the most modern *ingenio* of all, *Consuelo*, fired up its boilers in 1882. Not long after-wards, the *Santa Fe, Quisqueya*, and *Cristóbal Colón* mills also began spewing their tiny cinders and sweet fumes into the air.

During the 1890s, San Pedro claimed center stage in the Domin-ican sugar industry, which, given its capital outlay, was already a larger entity than the Dominican government. Virtually isolated from the rest of the Dominican economy, the sugar industry formed an enclave looking outward to the world market. Only the better capitalized, mechanized mills could make a go of it, and increasingly, these enter-prises got their capital and equipment from the United States, which had become the largest consumer of Dominican sugar. An 1891 trade agreement slashed U. S. tariffs on Dominican sugar in exchange for reciprocal cuts on U. S. exports to the Republic.

World War I-induced demand for sugar sent prices soaring and brought about a tripling of the land under cultivation. It also spurred the U.S. takeover of the industry. By the end of the Marines' 1916–1924 occupation, U.S. interests owned more than 80 percent of the cane fields and most of the key mills. Control over the Dominican sugar industry was no longer on Hispaniola, but on another, much smaller island, that of Manhattan.

Sugar transformed the Dominican Republic as it became the is-land's key money-making export during the early twentieth century, but it has had a bitter, often pernicious impact. Its colonial legacy included slavery; its contemporary influence monocultural dependence on the vagaries of world market conditions (over which Dominicans exert little control), domination by foreign capital and management, and a lack of alternative development. It also has meant the wholesale migration of workers to cut the cane and labor in the mills.

The impetus for the industry was Cuban, the capital and tech-nology North American, and the hands that held the machetes and worked the grinding wheels and centrifuges inside the mill from the British, Dutch, Danish, and French West Indies. Only the land was Dominican. "Dominicans wouldn't cut no cane," William Joseph laughs. "Not then, not now! To get cutters, they went to the little islands, like Antigua, where my father was from, or St. Thomas, where Roberto's father was born."

The least densely populated of the Antilles, the Dominican Re-public numbered less than a quarter of a million people in the 1870s. Dominicans had easy access to land and thus little incentive to work for the *ingenios*. Most rural inhabitants preferred farming their *conuco*, a small plot of land on which they grew staple crops, to becoming cane cutters or mill workers. Moreover, Dominicans stigmatized working in the cane fields as Haitian, or slave work. The companies, meanwhile, felt it would be cheaper to import workers from abroad than to raise wages enough to lure the native born.

Later that day, we join Roberto's mother, 98-year-old Ina Caines, and her longtime friend Prince Thomas, in the shade of the Caines compound. Roberto and his wife, Alicia, have lived there since 1954, and currently share the concrete block, company-owned house with his mother and seven of their children. Like almost everything else in Consuelo, the house belongs to the now state-owned sugar mill. The company provides free electricity, but as is often the case, the power is out. A goat lies nearby, her litter sucking greedily at her teats, while Ina Caines and Prince Thomas recount their family genealogies.

Their parents were proletarian globetrotters who joined the unprecedented wave of people leaving the land for work in urban and industrial centers early this century. Thousands of these migrants came from overpopulated Caribbean islands and wound up in San Pedro and its mill towns. Ina Caines, a cousin of soul singer James Brown, is dressed in a white floral housecoat and light blue sneakers. She rocks slowly as she speaks of her parents bringing her to the Dominican Republic. "I am a St. Kitts woman," she says, "but I was only a girl when I came to Consuelo. None of this was built then," she adds, pointing to the surrounding *barrio* of Guachupita. "Not when Prince and I were children."

Prince Thomas, a tall man clad in a white shirt, blue pants, and gray wool cap, smiles his assent. The gold caps on his teeth flash as he leans forward into the sun. A veteran of fifty-five years in the bag room, where the sugar was poured into 50-kilo burlap bags, Thomas talks fondly of his boyhood on Tortola in the Virgin Islands before sailing for the Dominican Republic. "If you want to know about us, about the *Cocolos,* that's where you must go. To Tortola and the down islands."

Fortunately, I had been there and needed little encourgement to return. On Tortola, where many of Consuelo's *Cocolos* originated, a sharper picture of the forces that brought them to the Dominican Republic came into focus.

In recent years, Dominicans from Consuelo have been returning to Tortola and claiming citizenship on the basis of ancestry. It's easy to see why. The largest of the British Virgin Islands, Tortola itself is not much larger than the Consuelo sugar estate and with 15,000 residents, has about the same population. But while Consuelo and much of the Dominican Republic remain stuck in squalor, Tortola approximates tropical paradise. Its verdant volcanic hillsides are rimmed by secluded coves and coral reefs. And with the U.S. dollar the standard currency,

Tortola's economy remains buoyant, while the Dominican Republic's has sunk into crisis.

Most of the island's inhabitants are black descendants of the slaves that the Dutch and the British brought there in the seventeenth and eighteenth centuries. A few white-skinned refugees from European metropolitan life have joined them since the island's recent discovery by pleasure boaters. Catering to the needs of increasing numbers of sailors and tourists, Tortolans have achieved a standard of living that complements an already enviable quality of life. With Consuelo suffering amidst the decline of the Dominican sugar industry, more and more Dominicans are embarking on a reverse migration.

"The Dominicans are coming here now," H. R. Penn says from a chair in his haberdashery in Roadtown, Tortola. "On Sunday mornings they play their baseball on the cricket pitch." A tall, thin, light-skinned mulatto 86 years old, H. R. Penn sits surrounded by the men's furnishings he sells. His father, a boat builder by trade, was part of the *Cocolo* migration to San Pedro late last century.

"Almost all the able-bodied men went to Santo Domingo then," Penn explains, calling the Dominican Republic by its older, popular name. "They'd go in September or November and cut cane and return after the harvest. Then they'd come back here for the summer and go again the next fall. There just wasn't much of a way to make a living here at that time."

There hadn't been since the early nineteenth century when Tortola, St. Kitts, Antigua, Montserrat, and the other West Indian islands lost their competitive edge in the sugar industry. "It was becoming unprofitable to grow cane here," Penn observes, "and partially because of that, they emancipated the slaves. After emancipation, this country went right down." Complicating the Leeward Islands' plight was the wall of tariffs that European countries were erecting to protect their own sugar beet industry. Excluded from the lucrative European markets, sugar production in the British, French, Danish, and Dutch islands virtually ceased and thousands were left without work.

But for ten dollars, an islander could board the two-masted *Fancy May,* the *Warspite,* or the *Sea Hawk* for the week-long passage to the Dominican sugar fields. "The labor contractors would pick the men up on the other islands and then stop here along the way," Penn recalls. "You had to bring your own food with you. It was dangerous and crowded, and there was much loss of life."

But hundreds of Tortolans made the trip each year. The Dominicans called them *las golondrinas,* the swallows, because their migrations followed a seasonal pattern. There was little more than subsistence agriculture on Tortola at the time, and work in San Pedro offered the chance to accumulate a little cash. "But not much," Penn cautions. "They couldn't get much out of migration work in Santo Domingo as that was subsistence, too. They would come back to their plot of land here after cropping season there."

But not all came back. Although almost ninety percent of the early migrants stayed only for the cutting and grinding season, as was the agreement between the Dominican government and the British consulate, more and more of them began to remain year-round in the Republic. Although these *Cocolos* could be found scattered across the island, the heaviest concentrations were in San Pedro de Marcoris and nearby La Romana.

The passengers boarding these sailing ships for the cane fields took more aboard than provisions for the voyage. "They carried the British colonial tradition with them," Penn reminds me. "They were born and bred in that."

That British tradition meant a certain degree of experience in benevolent societies and collective self-help. That, Penn explains, was something the Tortolans learned from Anegadans, St. Kittians, and Anguillans. "We have always been individualistic on Tortola. The slaves got their own land here after emancipation and we get our sense of independence from that. We rely on our own families and don't form societies like them from the down islands. But Tortolans learned from this admixture from St. Kitts and Nevis folks, who were accustomed to those societies back home.

"And they brought cricket with them," Penn adds. "That was my game."

One can trace British influence in the Caribbean by the prevalence of cricket. On Barbados, Trinidad, and Jamaica, it reigns supreme. On Tortola, despite the inroads of basketball among the younger generation, the game still provides the sporting *joie-de-vivre* for those over middle age. The gardener outside my bungalow keeps his transistor radio tuned to the West Indian team's test match in England and conveys updates to passersby. And the *BVI Beacon* advertises a cricket instructional video tape that seeks to revive the game among youth lured away by basketball.

Later that day in Roadtown, Tortola's capital, white-uniformed practitioners of this most English of sports are engaged in the second day of a three day match between a team from Nevis and one composed of U. S. and British Virgin Islanders. The contest is part of a tournament sponsored by the Leeward Islands Cricket Association to mark its 75th year. The masts of sailing ships and hillside villas are visible from the benches ringing the boundary, a large oval lined by flour and red flags.

Vendors sell johnny cakes and fish patés to the several hundred, mostly male, spectators.

"It's always been the only real sport here," argues Orvie Shirley, a 62-year-old player and organizer of the sport, as an inning ends. "We grew up playing bat and ball in the streets, without umpires, using a mango or lime for a ball and making our own wicket. But cricket is not a game that comes to you naturally. When our lads went to Nevis, St. Kitts, and Antigua for schooling, they brought cricket back with them. Then men like Mr. Penn, and Carlton de Castro formed teams and taught my generation."

Carlton de Castro's playing days are over. Behind windows shuttered to keep out the summer heat, the 73-year-old man sits in a wheelchair, his left leg amputated at the knee. Cricket, de Castro says, was played on Tortola as long ago as the 1890s, when teams from Roadtown and East End vied for bragging rights on the island. "Baugher's Bay, Cane Garden Bay, Carrot Bay, and all the villages had teams. After I and some friends had been to school in Antigua, we got together and formed our own club. We elected a committee to run it and sent to England and India for our equipment. Called it the Tortola Junior Cricket Club. H. R. Penn managed us and we were the best club on the island.

"But much better cricket was played down island," he observes, referring to the British islands to the south and east of Tortola. De Castro presided over the British Virgin Island Cricket Association that formed in the 1930s. "The cricket match was the centerpiece for the August Monday Fair, and during the season, from February to July, we'd play on Saturdays and Sundays. It was *the* entertainment of the community.

"When people started going to St. Thomas to work during the war, they got Americanized and stopped playing," de Castro complains, nodding at the Hollywood-made western playing soundlessly on his televison. "But it taught us discipline here, although we did have our outbursts. In cricket you find that the match starts on time and you never argue with the umpires on the field. I tell you what I know. Cricket has done in the Caribbean like no politician has done. You've got a West Indian team together that has beaten every team in the world. That's something we haven't been able to do politically or economically."

Disembarking in San Pedro, these mostly male migratory workers harvested the cane crop and turned it into sugar and molasses. The cane cutters lived in hastily-constructed barracks in the fields, while the somewhat better-off mill workers stayed in equally shabby dwellings surrounding the mills. A cluster of the migrants lived in the Miramar section of San Pedro, along the sea, while others lived and worked on the Consuelo, Porvenir, Angelina, Quisqueya, Colón, and Santa Fe estates. No matter where they lived, though, or from where they had come, they encountered dismal conditions and a hostile native populace.

And because of this, they shed their identities as Tortolans, St. Kittians, Antiguans, *et al.* and became *Cocolos* instead. Because more of them were from the British islands than anywhere else, and perhaps because the British cultural mold was stronger than the French, Dutch, or Danish imprints, the migrants began to refer to themselves collectively as the English. But defining a cultural identity was hardly their chief concern. Coping with life on twenty-five cents a day wages amidst a xenophobic populace was a more pressing matter.

"The black and colored subjects of Your Majesty in the West Indies," wrote a British consular official in 1899, "have to choose between death by hunger in their native islands and suffering and poor treatment in Santo Domingo, where many have looked for work under the circumstances that their native islands are just islands of Death." San Pedro may not have been an "island of Death" but that was the fate of many migrants, victims of industrial accidents, malnutrition, and horrible public health conditions.

Malaria, dysentery, and leprosy were frequent visitors to the mill town and *bateyes,* where the undernourished workforce labored eleven to twelve hours a day during the grinding season. Safety conditions were primitive in the mills, with little or no compensation paid to those who lost an arm, leg, or life to the monstrous grinding wheels. Cutters sometimes slashed themselves or their co-workers with an errant hack of the *machete* and then waited helplessly to see if infection would set in. Wages were paid partially in scrip good only at the company store, where prices were high.

Compounding the low wages was the industry's seasonality. While cane grows, it needs little care. During this six-month *tiempo muerto* (the dead season), the cutters had no work at all and fell into debt, which bound them to the company for the next *zafra* (harvest). A reduced force was kept on in the factories to repair and maintain machinery, but even these more skilled, better-off employees found each dead season a trial.

The *bateyes,* crowded with seasonal male employees, offered few amenities. Single men were jammed into windowless barracks without water, sanitation, or electricity. The estates, where more women and children could be found, were no better. Medical, educational, and recreational facilities did not exist.

The migrant also faced antagonism from the native Dominicans, in part because they were black and black was associated with the spectre of Haiti. The *Cocolos* also spoke a different language (or languages), practiced Protestantism in a largely Catholic society, and were better educated and more skilled than most of the natives. Merchants decried the *Cocolo* practice of repatriating funds to their homelands instead of spending it on the merchants' wares. Newspapers wrote of their "inferior ethics" and accused them of carrying disease as they arrived aboard "vessels of calamities." And Dominican workers protested that the aliens undercut the wage scale and thus lowered their standard of living.

A crescendo of openly racist hostility spurred passage of an immigration law in 1912 that attempted to "whiten" the population. Caucasians retained their right to open admissions, while all non-Caucasian migrants were required to seek prior permission to come to the Republic.

The law affirmed Dominicans' profound unease with their own racial makeup, for many who espoused the most virulently racist positions toward Haitians were themselves of some Haitian descent. Then, as now, the neighboring country loomed as a threatening boogeyman. Nevertheless, the sugar industry's needs for labor won out over anti-immigrant sentiments and the flow of workers from the other islands continued.

The mills considered the *Cocolos* a more docile workforce than the native Dominicans, because the migrants had few options other than working for the *ingenio* once in the Republic. The *Cocolos* were also better educated, more skilled, and spoke English, the language of the mills' supervisory personnel. By Dominican standards, they were a proletarianized workforce accustomed to the time and labor demands of industrial capitalism.

That greater industrial sophistication and education cut both ways. If their industrial acculturation made them more desirable employees, it also meant they better understood the efficacy of collective action and how to turn their role in production to some advantage. And their education made them willing disciples of Marcus Garvey, the first great Pan-Caribbean political leader.

"Life here was god-awful," Roberto Caines says with conviction as he walks down the dirt roads of Guachupita, his *barrio* in Consuelo. "After my father died, we came to Consuelo from San Pedro and lived in a house by the entrance to the estate. There were six children in our family and we shared that house with three other families. The mill owners treated us like animals. Many a child was lost at birth or soon thereafter. During the dead season, we had nothing to eat but the cane we could steal from the fields." The teeth missing from his mouth attest to the dead season's dietary deficiencies.

Caines is only sixty, but he has spent most of those years working to better Consuelo's lot. He knows almost everybody on the estate, and many invite us into their homes as he takes me on a walking tour of Consuelo that turns into a history lesson on the *Cocolos'* efforts to overcome the ill effects of the omnipresent *ingenio*.

There is a well-known Dominican poem by Pablo Mir that Robert Smith, a Canadian priest from the Scarboro Order, quoted to me during my first visit to Consuelo. Its refrain is *"son del ingenio,"* meaning that it belongs to the mill. Consuelo was long a living testament to the poem's accuracy, for virtually everything on the estate belonged to the mill. Just about everything still does, but Caines identifies the gains that would have otherwise remained hidden to me.

Caines points to houses almost a hundred years old, and then to more recently constructed dwellings. It is hard, I tell him, to see that much of a difference. He introduces me to countless men and women and has a story to tell about each one of them—about who helped form a community club or cooperative and whose families lost members during the 1946 strike or to Trujillo's repression. "We fought together to build these dwellings," he tells me, "and some lost their lives because of that.

"You see these people here?" Caines asks, his hands sweeping in an arc that takes in street after street of lime green and aquamarine painted wooden and concrete block houses. "They brought them and their parents here to cut cane, but they scorned us, the Dominicans did. The only protection they have was to unificate each other together."

That they did, by creating their own ethnic identity. Unlike many Dominicans, the migrants did not try to deny their African heritage. Instead, they embraced their negritude and made a positive cultural statement by doing so. Blending militant black nationalism with a decidedly British sense of organization and sport, they forged their own identity as "the English." It was a Pan-Caribbean identity that transcended the migrants' island of origin and provided a collective strategy for coping with their new surroundings.

As that identity emerged, the *Cocolos* lost some of the allure that had made them such attractive workers in the first place. In 1902, Consuelo superintendent William Bass argued that the migrants, accustomed to respecting authority and property, and with little recourse but to work for the mills, were unlikely to become politically disaffected. Despite a strike by migrants on the Santa Fe estate during the 1902 grinding season, Bass and the other mill owners enjoyed the fruits of this seemingly pliant, easily disciplined workforce until the banner of black nationalism was waved over the estates during World War I.

As the western world system cracked under the carnage of that conflict, the aura of invincibility claimed by the European powers dissipated. Third World thinkers and activists challenged the ideological underpinnings of the "White Man's Burden," advancing their own racial and cultural agendas. In the Caribbean, this development was driven by Marcus Garvey and his Universal Negro Improvement Association.

"He was the man who first raised the Negro consciousness of the people of all these islands," H. R. Penn told me on Tortola. "Marcus Garvey stirred the hopes of all Negro people."

"We never had no politics here," Roberto Caines adds in Consuelo. "But the message of Garvey we spoke about because we always tried to maintain pride and heritage. From all those little islands, they work with Garvey and join his movement. He tried to bring us together."

Jamaican-born Marcus Garvey never made it to Consuelo or the region's other sugar estates, but his message of black pride and consciousness swept over the cane fields after an organizer from the Universal Negro Improvement Association (UNIA) arrived in San Pedro in September 1919.

UNIA cadre David Hennessey carried little more than a copy of the *Negro World* newspaper with him as he proselytized for members among the *Cocolos*. Few in San Pedro had ever heard of the charismatic Garvey, who founded the Universal Negro Improvement Association in 1914, and advocated a mix of black nationalism, self-reliance, and the return to Africa. But conditions in San Pedro were so dismal that Hennessey's call for creating a unit of the UNIA was quickly answered.

Ten men swore their allegiance to the UNIA at a meeting in a house in the Miramar section of San Pedro soon after Hennessey arrived. By December, three hundred more joined its ranks and a building, named Emancipation Hall, was secured. Within a year, Garvey could count on over two thousand adherents on the island, with most in San Pedro.

Garvey called for the redemption of Africa by those of African descent no matter where they lived. While his movement was centered in the United States, where it became the nation's largest black organization ever, it was popular throughout the West Indies and Central America. Its vision of African redemption ultimately called for black people to return to Africa. Accordingly, the Garveyites began a black-owned, black-manned fleet called the Black Star Line that would inspire black enterprise and later become the vehicle for returning to the mother continent. The idea captured the imagination of black Americans like few other ventures and tens of thousands bought shares of Black Star Line stock at five dollars a share. The UNIA also offered a package of sickness and death benefits along with its black nationalist rhetoric.

"We were all members of the Black Star Society," Ina Caines recalls in Consuelo. "They say Marcus Garvey going to get a steamer and take all the English people around here to Africa. Every Sunday, they came and collected money from the people on the estate. Plenty folks join. Mark my words, it was a tremendous fight then."

But it was a fight that the *Cocolos* were going to lose. During the 1916–1924 United States occupation of the island, the marines encamped in the Miramar section of San Pedro and occupied the sugar estates. UNIA organizers protested the marines' intercessions on behalf of the mill owners, claiming that U.S. forces press-ganged people to work on the estates and confined "members of the race" in holding pens made to keep swine. The marines keep our people without food or water in "the heat of sun," inflict beatings, and generally terrorize us, a UNIA organizer wrote from San Pedro.

The Garveyites took to the streets in August, 1921. On the day commemorating England's abolition of slavery, they paraded behind a band and the red, black, and green colors of the black nationalist banner. The marchers carried the British flag upside down as they converged on the home of British Consul Archibald Beer. Her Majesty's Representative remonstrated with the demonstrators to place the flag right side up, but when the parade reached Emancipation Hall, the Union Jack was trampled and spit upon.

Under the direction of the U.S. occupation forces, Dominican authorities rapidly quashed this incipient rebellion. After San Pedro's police commissioner consulted with the U.S. Provost Marshal, the leadership of the Garvey movement was arrested and deported. The message was clear—force would be used to ensure law and order in San Pedro and uninterrupted production on the estates.

Defending his actions, the Provost Marshal wrote that the UNIA was "inciting . . . class hatred, and a defiance of law and order. . . . Such an organization, if allowed to grow, inculcating Bolshevistic ideas to the ignorant, would soon become a menace to the peace of the community." Denouncing the Garveyites' arrogance, the Provost Marshal concluded that "From appearances, it (the UNIA) is a society for the uplift of the negro, but its ulterior motive is to engender racial hatred with an idea to ultimate domination of the white race. While this would be impossible in the United States, it is not at all impossible here after the occupation ceases."

The island's Military Governor accepted his subordinate's judgments and passed them on as his own to the Secretary of the Navy to counter the allegations of mistreatment and persecution made by UNIA organizers. The reports were duly noted and then relegated to the National Archives in Washington, D.C., where they still gather dust. Ironically, the records documenting Garveyism in the Dominican Republic can be found more readily in Washington than on the island.

The UNIA, on the other hand, was bereft of its leadership after the arrests and deportations, and the rank and file in San Pedro all too aware that continued protest would bring repression. Demonstrations had always been more hazardous on the estates, but even there the *Cocolos* vented their anger by striking in the midst of the 1921 grinding season. Cane cutters threw their *machetes* to the ground and mill workers allowed their steam engines to fall silent soon after the start of the harvest. The Garveyites led the walkout, according to elder *Cocolos* on the Consuelo and Santa Fe estates. Some argue that the Garvey leaders lost their courage and absconded with the organization's funds in the midst of the strike, but the collective memory is hazy on this and other matters pertaining to the conflict. The only clear recollection is that the strike was lost and that Garveyism soon faded, or at least went underground, in San Pedro and on the estates.

"I cannot recall what happened to the Black Star Society and those that led the movement here," Ina Caines confesses with a smile, "but I still waiting for that ship to come. Yes, indeed. I am still waiting."

The Black Star Line ran aground on its own ineptitude and Garvey was indicted for mail fraud. Jailed in 1925, the fiery proponent of black nationalism was deported in 1927. But his legacy, in terms of a collective affirmation of blackness, remained alive in the minds of men like Roberto Caines.

And though cries for liberation became whispers during the occupation and soon ceased completely during the Trujillo years, a pride in Negritude lingered on the estates and became an essential component to the *Cocolos'* self-definition.

While Garveyism denounced British colonialism, the *Cocolo* zeal for organizing benevolent and sporting societies embraced a decidedly British heritage. In San Pedro and its sugar estates, the migrants built their own mutual aid societies, modeled after the self-help organizations of the British working class. As their bonds with British colonialism weakened, the *Cocolos* selected aspects of that British experience to make life in the Dominican Republic more bearable.

We must "work . . . for each other's protection in a strange country," the thirteen founders of the Young Men Trial Association stressed on January 1, 1913. Actually, the Dominican Republic was becoming less strange with each harvest. A *Cocolo* nucleus had grown into a sizable year-round English community by the 1920s. Many of the migrants had no intention of returning to their islands of origin. Their lives, and those of their children, would take place on Dominican soil.

While the mill bosses closely supervised their activities in the *ingenios,* the *Cocolos* were left to their own devices away from work. "They did nothing for us then," William Joseph explains. "A man would work until he died. The company didn't care if he took sick or hurt himself. They would do nothing for him. And we couldn't make it by ourselves. We needed to band together. Whatever we had we did for ourselves, by making our societies."

"The first school we had here was the one the English make in the yard under the big tree," Roberto Caines adds. "That is where I learned to read and write. And we make plenty societies to care for people when they are sick, and make ceremony and carry them to the burial when they die."

In Consuelo, the English organized the Young Men and Women Trial Association, the Excelsius Society, the Energetic Benevolence Society, and the St. Gabriel Benevolent Association. Comparable bodies emerged in San Pedro and on the other estates. For decades, these organizations made life more secure and more dignified for their members and served as the center of social life on the estates.

In more recent times, as the need for such organizations faded, the four societies on the Consuelo estate merged. Cecilio Vanterpool has presided over this United Body since 1970. Now pensioned from the mill, Vanterpool administers Consuelo's remaining mutual aid society and tends to a small garden of tropical delights behind his pink and yellow house in the Puerto Principe (a.k.a. Haititown) section of Consuelo.

An ox-drawn cart carrying cane lumbers along the dirt path in front of his home, while Vanterpool, a handsome mahogany-skinned man, hands fruit to a few children on their way to school. Vanterpool's parents came to Consuelo from Tortola in 1911. "My father came and worked in the factory and never returned. I have a son, Juan Esteban Vanterpool, who went back. He lives on Tortola now, but I have never been there. . . .

"We were not too well protected here and the English people got together to help succor one another. You know it is painful when someone dies, but being in an association, you can help your countryman. You get together according to the laws of the association and bury him decently. We sustained each other in that."

One of the first societies, Vanterpool remembers, "formed on the basis of a cricket club. Alfred Peterson, the captain of the Energetics, got sick. He was a boiler tender in the factory and his teammates helped care for him. Out of that, the Energetic Benevolent Association was created."

Each society carefully codified its bylaws in pocket-sized booklets. Vanterpool finds a few well-thumbed copies and goes over their rules with me. The organizations did more than care for sick members and provide for a proper burial. They prescribed a code of behavior for the *Cocolos*, one that emphasized sobriety, decorum, and a dignified bearing toward each other. Members could be fined for slander, abusive or contentious discourse, and falling asleep during a meeting.

"We would celebrate together, too," Vanterpool adds. "Each society selected a day to give thanks to God for keeping us during the year. On the Energetics' Thanksgiving Day, the second Sunday in June, and on our Anniversary Day, we would make a celebration with music, food, and plenty goodwill. Delegations from the other societies would come and join us."

The same impulse for building a system of self-help was channeled into cricket, and a generation later, to baseball.

"My father and those who came from the islands brought cricket here, and I and the boys born here learned the game from them," William Joseph recounts. "In this estate, we had two cricket clubs, the Ever Jolly and the Energetic, that began—whoooo!—long time ago. And there were a number of junior clubs, too, like the Rattlers and the Fox.

"We got together with our small amount of money and sent for our gear from India. It took months! We made our own uniforms—all white, of course—and wore white sneakers and a sash with the club's colors. . . . After a while, cricket was established in the Republic. Wherever there were English to be found, wherever there were *ingenios*, there was cricket.

"But the first cricket around here was not on the Consuelo estate, but in San Pedro. You should talk to Basilio. He will know about the roots of the game here."

Sebastian "Basilio" Ferdinand lives in Miramar, across the street from the Portworkers Syndicate Hall. One of the first unions in San Pedro, the portworkers' syndicate was formed by *Cocolo* workers on the docks in 1913. As in Consuelo, the language of the street is a mix of West Indian-accented English and Spanish, but only the older men and women seem to use English.

The door to Basilio's striped green and white wooden house on the other side of the rutted street is open in hopes of attracting a breeze. A *telenovela*, a Dominican soap opera, competes with *merengue* blaring over the top of the wall shared with the dwelling next door. A space between the top of the wall and the ceiling maximizes circulation. Two young boys fight over a spinning top on the sidewalk outside. A third, wearing only a diaper, plays inside.

Basilio, their grandfather, sits on a couch in the living room under a framed certificate from the Oddfellows society. That document and the shelf of books along one wall are staples in many an Englishman's home, where the stress on organization and education remains strong.

"You've come to talk to me about cricket, have you?" Basilio asks, as a smile spread across his small, round face. "I have been waiting for you, then. You don't know how glad I am to see you."

Born on St. Kitts, Basilio came to San Pedro as a boy and has spent the years since in Miramar. "I stayed off the estates, thank the Lord. I don't do any hard work to mash me up. I was a tailor."

Slipping a pair of rubber thongs off his feet, Basilio curls his legs underneath his body. He is a small man, not much over five feet tall, but still flexible despite his 86 years.

"This is where the English lived," Basilio begins, gesturing to the streets of Miramar. "The English Lodge was two blocks down the street, and the Black Star Line had its office around the corner. I myself was president of the Egyptian Melodrama Association for twenty-five years. And our cricket field was down by the sea, where the Hotel Macorix is now. . . .

"Cricket was already popular when I got here from St. Kitts. I learned it on the streets of Miramar. Cricket was more popular than baseball then. It was the sport of the English.

"Many of the players had learned the game on their native islands, especially the Antiguans. Here, they mixed together on the teams. In San Pedro, we had the San Pedro cricket team and the Etons. The Golden Arrow were men from the Porvenir estate, and the Energetics and two or three other clubs came from Consuelo. There was at least one club on each estate where there were English to be found, and even a few teams in the *bateyes*."

Grabbing his youngest grandchild as the infant makes a break for the door to the street, Basilio continues. "I played as a boy, but as I became a man, I learned to umpire. I umpired matches on all the estates around here, in La Romana, and even in Santo Domingo. Mr. Slaymaker, the English Consul, was in attendance at that match and told me afterwards that I was good enough to umpire in England."

The English played their games in the dead season, and on festival days such as Easter Monday, Whit Monday, and their Thanksgiving Day in June. "Cricket was the star game then. A thousand people and more would watch us play on the pitch by the sea. It was a wonderful scene, it looked like you were almost playing in the water."

Although some Dominicans learned the game, cricket remained a conduit for holding on to elements of an English culture. "Cricket taught people how to behave. It was in the English countries that you played cricket, and while the boys played here they never mixed in a word of Spanish. Cricket was played in English thoroughly. It was a way of retaining the old culture.

"The English have a more disciplined approach to the upbringing of their children," Basilio admonishes me. It is something I have heard from countless Dominicans. "Maybe that carries over to learning the game. I know we took our cricket very seriously."

The Dominican Republic, however, never contributed a player to one of the West Indian teams that propelled Caribbean cricket to the upper levels of the game. "We had good players that come out of San Pedro. Good, but not great. Great is W. G. Grace and Constantine, and when you are speaking of Grace, you are speaking of those Englishmen who bat for three and four days and achieves a century [by scoring a hundred runs]. These boys here played one-day matches, sometimes two innings if they could. But there were some players here! Charlie Brickwater from Consuelo, Ben Ryan at La Romana, and John Ramos here in San Pedro and Winston Richards from the Golden Arrow. Ramos still has the bats, and Richards is a young man yet. You'll find him working on the Cristóbal Colón estate. He was probably the best of the lot."

I find John Ramos first, living only a few streets away from Basilio. Not quite eighty years old, he seems much younger as he drags out a bag of cricket gear and demonstrates his batting style in the living room of his modest home. The bats might be the only ones remaining in San Pedro. "I used to mash the ball in the crease," Ramos exclaims as he pivots and slashes at an imaginary ball.

As a boy, Ramos was somewhat of an exception among the English in San Pedro because he played more baseball than cricket. "We played both at the ball field by the sea. The Americans made the field when they came here in 1916. That's where their encampment was. I was only six then, but as I grew older, I used to watch the marines play baseball there. They would give us balls and old gloves and sometimes we would play catch with them. Some of the older boys played with them in their games. That helped baseball plenty around here.

"I played cricket in the street as a boy. Actually, it was only bat and ball. We put an old pan on some sticks for a wicket and used anything we could for a bat or a ball. That's how we started to play. As I grew, I gave up baseball for cricket and joined the San Pedro Cricket Club." The club evolved from the Etons, which, like the Energetics in Consuelo, evolved from a cricket team into a benevolent society.

"Cricket got me my first mill job. I was employed by *Central Romana* so that I could play cricket for them. The *central* would give the players time off to play and we could ride their railroad engines to play on another estate. Hundreds would come with us then, bringing their food and drink, especially for the holiday matches. You know, we played every July 4th because that was celebrated, too, at the American-owned mills."

While fans used to bet "plenty money" on the matches, the players, Ramos attests, played "for the love of the game." Pooling their resources, players on the San Pedro Cricket Club contributed forty cents a week at a time when most were making only 75 cents for a day's wage. "This bat," he says, picking up a Herbert Sutcliffe autographed model called "The Cannon," "cost 20 or 25 dollars then."

As president of the cricket club, Ramos held onto the bats, the red leather balls, and the wicket keeper's pads. "I haven't had these out of this bag in twenty years," he laments. "In 1963, we make two teams between the men at the Santa Fe and Porvenir estates and played a few innings. Some of us were so old we could hardly move, but we liked to play. Now, it's all gone."

Winston Richards shares John Ramos' regrets at the passing of his game. Born in East End, Tortola, Winston Richards came with his parents to the Porvenir estate in 1920 when he was five years old. His father, a schoolmaster by training, became the mill's auditor and founded its cricket team, the Golden Arrows.

"We were the best club in the Republic," Richards remembers with conviction from his house near the Cristóbal Colón estate. "And they had no better batsman than me. It used to be a happy time when we played cricket. We would walk from Porvenir to Colón to play and the people on the estate would come with us."

Porvenir, like Consuelo, had a mostly *Cocolo* workforce. English was the languge of the mill, which was owned by the Kelly family from New York City. "We played baseball on the estate, too. I played for Porvenir, and even pitched for La Romana's team. They paid me for that. But I never was paid to play cricket. In fact, we used to pay fifty cents a week to maintain the team ourselves. But by playing cricket, we were keeping our English culture."

The Porvenir mill is in the city of San Pedro proper. Its cane arrives on railroad cars from the fields encircling the city. The estates further away from town, like Consuelo and Angelina, are generally more self-contained worlds. The Santa Fe estate falls somewhere in between, within walking distance of town, yet surrounded by cane fields.

The road to the Santa Fe *ingenios* passes a cockfighting arena and a cemetery. Piles of rubbish burn in the fields alongside the pitted road.

Two boys walking off a ball field carry their team's gloves strung like trophies from a bat that they hold by either end.

A huge century-old cast-iron grinding wheel stands upright in front of the Santa Fe mill, at the end of the *"calle de gringos,"* the street of *gringos,* with its more substantial housing. Coleridge Mayers lives a few blocks away in a house he earned by dint of his forty years working as a foreman in the mill. St. Louis Cardinal slugger Pedro Guerrero grew up in a house across the street; Toronto Blue Jay outfielder George Bell not far away. They are two of the reasons that Santa Fe has become a stop on baseball's scouting trail in the last decade, just the way it was a fixture on the cricket circuit in Coleridge Mayers' time.

"We played cricket right here," he shows me as we walk past the mill, silent due to the dead season, and arrive at the ball field, a splash of green next to a cluster of abandoned cane carts and the crisscross of railroad tracks. The Houston Astros run a baseball academy there, but practice is over and the hopefuls, mostly boys from Santa Fe and the other estates, have dispersed.

"Once you worked until you died," Coleridge says as we find grandstand seats shaded by a few orange *flamboyant* trees. "It was very, very tough. When my parents came from Antigua, their finances were so poor that they couldn't make it by themselves. You could get a little credit from the company during the *tiempo muerto* but it cost you plenty for that later on. You couldn't make it by yourself, and that is why they formed sickness and death societies."

Like most of the English people on the Santa Fe estate, Coleridge Mayers grew up a member of the Ever Live Society. "I was a follower of Marcus Garvey, too," he adds. Later, he digs through his personal papers until he uncovers a document espousing the principles of the Universal Negro Improvement Association. "But you couldn't talk much about that," he offers.

"When I was a boy, the marines rode through here every afternoon. They would come through on horseback with their guns and bayonets. They were supposed to be protecting the estate from the *gavilleros,* the guerrillas, but there was never much fighting here. That went on more in the countryside. They just letting us know that they around."

After the marines left, Trujillo soon arrived. "Trujillo dominated everything here. He was the boss and the English kept their silence. You didn't even talk much to one another about him. There were too many spies."

What did keep the English together in those years was cricket. "You'd have nothing to do in the *tiempo muerto* but play cricket. We would practice almost every day and play each weekend. It kept people in touch. It tied the English on the estates together."

Coleridge, the wickets keep for the Santa Fe team, was one of cricket's cadres. "We organized our own teams, making collections among ourselves and sending for the bats. We made our own pitch, exclusively." No league formally linked the estates together, but "If you wanted to play a team, you sent them a written challenge and if they agreed, they wrote back 'I accept the challenge.'

"It was a great sacrifice to collect the money for equipment and to maintain the team. Most of us had jobs in the mill—we were not cutting cane by then—but our wages were small. Yet cricket made us feel independent. It gave us a chance to socialize with the other estates."

Santa Fe was mostly English then, but *Cocolos* like Coleridge Mayers are a dwindling minority now. Many left after Trujillo enacted a statute in 1932 that called for at least 70 percent employment for native-born Dominicians in the sugar industry. Those that remained saw their children become Dominican.

Falling sugar prices in the 1920s and the depression of the 1930s led the mill industry to seek the cheapest possible workforce. The mill owners looked across their border to Haiti and began importing increasing numbers of its desperate citizens. The Haitians took the *Cocolos'* place at the bottom of the industry's labor hierarchy and became the cane cutters. There were nearly 50,000 in the country by 1935, and despite the slaughter of thousands in October 1937, Haitians have remained the cane cutting workforce ever since. The *Cocolos,* meanwhile, moved into the skilled positions in the mills, drove the trains in the countryside, and oversaw the Haitians.

"We are almost all gone now," Coleridge says, idly scratching a long scar on his leg. Like most men, he bears some physical mark from his tenure in the mill. "Cricket was *the* sport among the English people, but you could not make any personal gain at it. Now baseball, it has a livelihood."

Cecilio Vanterpool says almost the same thing as he describes the passing of cricket and the rise of baseball in Consuelo. "But we didn't play cricket for money. We did it for the competition and the sport.

"When my brother and I were working in the warehouse, we made a junior club. We were about twenty then. Our club was named Twentieth Century Fox. There was another club named Metro Goldwyn Mayer and we used to compete all the time."

The names came from the players' infatuation with Hollywood and the recently constructed Consuelo Theatre. "We viewed the movies and see those names at the beginning of them and name our clubs after them."

Some of their bats and pads were hand-me-downs from the Energetics and Rattlers, Consuelos' senior teams. The rest they bought by pooling their resources.

The cricket pitch was in a big field near the mill. "They abolish cricket many years ago and now they prepare it for baseball," Vanterpool sighs. "But you should have seen it the first day of the cricket season. We would parade to the ballpark down Main Street. All the children would be about, and each team would march in their white uniforms behind the queen of the club and a cornet player.

"We looked handsome," he recalls as he describes the Energetics' uniforms. A green and yellow stripe ran down the side of their pants, and each member had a rosette with the team's colors. The club's officers had a sash. "You could tell a man's team by his color then."

"We didn't have much then," Roberto Caines says later that day with a faint smile, as he eats his lunch during the two-hour midday break. "But though we were not Catholics, we had our trinity. It was Garvey, benevolence, and cricket.

"The children had sport crafted in them. They were exposed to sport and taught that they must try not to fail or that the color will fail, and the race will be beaten. My father was not only a Garveyite and a syndicalist, but a sportsman. He participated in every movement here to get contact with the people. I, too, study sports, but baseball was more my game than cricket.

"We took great pride from sport and when a black man did well, that meant that the race had done well. And not just in cricket and baseball, but in boxing, too."

Fighters with the boxing *nom de guerres*, Handsome Harris, Baby's Smile, and Carpio, represented the English in the ring. "Ruben Brooks was from right here in Guachupita," Caines exclaims. "He was, pound for pound, the greatest boxer in Latin America at that time. Hilary Carty, one of Rico's uncles, taught him to box in a ring that we built ourselves. The boys would rise early in the morning to study boxing because the ring was right out there in the hot sun. And they loved Joe Louis plenty here. He was a great fighter and he was black. He crossed the color line and reigned as the champion of the world. Yes, that meant something to us here.

"But cricket began to pass," Caines says with a shrug. "Those folks were getting old, their time was finishing, and no one concerned themselves with cricket anymore. It was a great loss that cricket died out. For many of us, it was our sport.

"But baseball becomes the English sport here and it almost teaches the same things as cricket did. The English gained acceptance by playing baseball and we found more benefit in it because in cricket we never were paid."

Cricket succumbed as the children of the migrants matured in a new society and became Dominicans with an English island heritage. Those born after 1920 grew up with baseball on the ascent.

Several of these sporting elders pointed to the 1936 and 1937 national championships that brought Cuban and Negro League players to the island as a turning point. Roberto Caines and Coleridge Mayers are but two of the many *Cocolos* who watched in fascination as the black-skinned North American athletes displayed their talents and crossed a social line previously impassable by blacks.

"In those two seasons," Basilio argues, "we didn't play much cricket. People cease coming to see us because the Great Dictator wanted baseball to prosper. He didn't tell nobody to stop, but we stopped. But I don't want you to write that. He still has those who like him around here and I don't want them to make trouble for me."

Basilio relents later in our discussion, adding that perhaps a more significant factor was the return of many of the *Cocolos* to their homelands in the 1930s. "That is one part of cricket's decline," John Ramos concurs. "The great demise of cricket was when the English people start to go back to their islands. Quite a few left."

Nobody can affix a date to cricket's death, but by the 1940s, it had lost its most favored sport status to baseball.

"Baseball overpowered cricket in Consuelo and the other estates," grieves William Joseph as he pushes his brown pork pie hat back on his head. "It just took over."

While Joseph, Leopoldo Carty, Albert Reed, Stanley Norman, Henry Conton, and their peers once donned white uniforms and played a game whose language was that of wickets, overs, and maidens, their sons, Rico Carty, Alfredo Griffin, Nelson Norman, Chico Conton, and their *compadres* grew up in the world of balls and strikes. Bridging the generational divide, sporting cadre like Roberto Caines, Luis Carty, and Austin Jacobo carried the impetus that had organized cricket into the Dominican pastime.

"All the great baseball players around here are English or their descendants," Joseph attests. "It has to do with cricket. It's got to be that." Not all the ballplayers emerging from San Pedro's sandlots are of English descent, but few question that historically the chief concentrations of baseball talent in San Pedro have been on the estates with the most English and the best cricket. Son Howell, Garabato Sackie, Chico Conton, and Clemente Hart (all of whom played cricket, too) starred in Dominican ball in the 1940s and '50s, while the third generation of Griffin, George Bell, Juan Samuel, Mariano Duncan, Manny Lee, and José Offerman leads the current crop of San Pedro ballplayers in the major leagues. All four Dominicans at the 1987 All-Star game, for example, were from San Pedro, with two the grandsons of English migrants.

Most San Pedro natives, of English or Dominican descent, acknowledge the hegemony of the sons of the cricketers. They suggest that their family discipline, approach to sport, and affinity for organizing their lives amidst the deprivation of the *bateyes* and *ingenios* are the reasons why. "The English approached baseball with the same discipline that they took to cricket," John Ramos attests.

"The adoption of cricket makes one more vigilant," Basilio argues, "and one could say that it is perhaps from the seed of cricket that baseball blossomed. The tradition coming down has made them better players."

"We are a bigger people, too," Roberto Caines reminds me. "Especially the Cartys. They are all big." Indeed, the descendants of these West Indian migrants are generally taller and heavier than most Dominicans. "But there is another reason why we become so good at baseball," Caines interjects. "That is because of Mauricio Báez and *Padre* José. Without them, we would not have had the chance."

8
Mauricio, Padre *José* and Rico

By the 1940s, the forces revitalizing Dominican baseball were coming into alignment. But despite forsaking cricket for baseball, the *Cocolos* were unable to enter the sporting mainstream. The reason was a simple one.

"We just could not play during the grinding season," Coleridge Mayers tells me with conviction. "A man would go to work at six in the morning and work until six at night. You could barely struggle back home again after your turn in the factory. And those in the fields! Whooooo! They worked as long as there was light in the day. Nobody wanted to play anything then. That's why we played in the dead season exclusively."

But twelve hour shifts abruptly ended during a brief post-World War II "democratic opening," as the sugar workers seized the moment to wage their first successful strike. The man who led them was not a *Cocolo,* but a tall, fiery dockworker from San Pedro named Mauricio Báez. And though Báez was no ballplayer, he made it possible for the *Cocolos* to play the Dominican pastime year-round.

Báez has been dead for over forty years, killed by Trujillo's agents in 1950, but the workers I meet as Roberto Caines escorts me through the Consuelo mill still revere him. An older man's voice cracks with emotion as he recalls the 1946 strike, and even those who were born after Báez's death can recite his legend. Almost to a man, they attribute the shorter workday to his leadership.

Actually, overwork does not seem like much of a problem on this day early in the grinding season. The air is redolent with vinegarish-smelling bagasse, the pulp that remains after the cane is ground. A few workers bang away in the machine shop, but men sit in repose elsewhere and five men are asleep in the bag room, sprawled on burlap bags of still-warm sugar. Another methodically slices off the top of a coconut with a *machete.*

The problem, I'm told, is that despite massive unemployment, the government has not been able to find enough cutters for the harvest. Turmoil in Haiti has interrupted that country's seemingly inexhaustible supply of the wretched of the earth. Without enough Haitians in the fields, the mill lacks cane to grind.

As a mechanic, Caines knows the mill intimately. It is composed of several huge hangars housing grinding gears, rollers, centrifuges, boilers, and machine shops. Accumulated industrial detritus lies abandoned in the yards between the sheds. Constructed in 1882 as the *Ingenio* Agua Dulce, the mill was named for the sweet-tasting stream that ran from there to the *Río Higuamo* and then on to San Pedro. A road did not yet connect the estate to San Pedro and the sugar was shipped out by barge.

Since being renamed the *Ingenio* Consuelo, the complex has been renovated in a piecemeal fashion over the last hundred years, with some of the machinery dating to late last century. A few of the workers look like they were there when the mill was built. Most are middle-aged or simply elderly. Layoffs have chased most of the younger workers from the mill; those who remain are there only because the government does not want to risk the political fallout of further unemployment.

In the United States, per capita sugar consumption has dropped by more than a third since 1971. Moreover, due to the enormous clout of the domestic sugar cane and sugar beets lobbies, the United States has maintained artificially high domestic sugar prices, at a cost to consumers estimated at perhaps three billion dollars a year. For most of the century, the sugar producing nations under U.S. sway profited by a quota system, under which importing nations were guaranteed a price set well above the free market price. The Dominican was a latecomer to the quota system, gaining a share in 1959, after the Cuban revolution. But in the 1980s, due to the domestic sugar cane and beets lobbies, the foreign quota share of the juicy U.S. market all but disappeared, and the Dominican Republic's sugar industry languished. Going naked into the oversupplied, underdemanded world market has been rough, especially when, as today, Dominican sugar sells for one half as much as it costs to produce. Little wonder Dominican sugar workers follow the price of their product on the world exchange the way ballplayers study batting averages.

The Dominican government has owned most of the mills since Trujillo's takeover of the industry after World War II. Trujillo owned the mills personally from 1956 to 1961; after his death, the government nationalized his holdings. Several were closed recently as the government reduced capacity and promoted "free zones" (tax free, light manufacturing enclaves for foreign investors) and tourism instead. More shutdowns are likely.

As my escort Caines introduces me to his mates, the saga of Mauricio Báez and the story of the 1946 strike emerges.

Báez was not an Englishman, one grizzled veteran of the mill tells me, but "He was a black man who called out to us on the estates. It did not matter to him if you were an Englishman, a Dominican, or a Congo," he says, using the oft-heard expression for a Haitian. "And when he spoke—whooo—people would walk in from the *bateyes* to hear him."

Born near an estate, Báez worked at the *Ingenio* Cristóbal Colón's company store as a youth. During the 1930s, he labored on the docks in San Pedro, then the most cosmopolitan and economically active city in the Republic. Báez began publishing a monthly newspaper dedicated to the defense of the working class and had some success agitating among the city's workers.

But the labor movement, never very strong in the Dominican Republic, had been paralyzed by the rise of Trujillo. And its focus on native-born craftsmen ignored the mostly foreign-born cane cutters and industrial workers on the sugar estates. The seasonality of the industry compounded the difficulties in organizing this workforce.

But World War II gave impetus to democratic impulses throughout the Caribbean basin. In Central America, dictators Maximiliano Hernández Martínez and Jorge Ubico were toppled in El Salvador and Guatemala. In the Dominican Republic, the new U.S. ambassador did not conceal his displeasure with Trujillo. Sensing the shift in hemispheric conditions, Trujillo opened the political process to allow some semblance of opposition. It was more appearance than reality, but Báez and his lieutenants in the labor movement sought to exploit the opening to organize the sugar workers.

Earlier efforts had been quashed with bloodshed. The army ended a walkout at *Central Romana* in 1942 and few doubted that any renewed activism would ultimately encounter the same force. But a new labor law in 1944 called for government intervention in wage disputes, creating a dynamic in which workers could seek Trujillo's intercession against the then privately-owned companies. Báez tried to finesse Trujillo as his organizers entered the estates. His newspaper featured Trujillo's visage on its front pages, although stopping short of the state-run labor paper which glorified him as the *"Maximo Protector"* of the working class.

Pushing his goggles back on to his forehead, Armando Carty stops work when Caines and I enter his domain, the pattern shop. Carty is chief of the five small shops that endeavor to keep the ancient works running. "We are the university of the estates in this land," he laughs.

"We cannot buy replacement parts for this mill. We must cast our own patterns and make them ourselves when something goes." Cane's sugar content decreases rapidly after it is cut and these master mechanics must cannibalize old machines and find ways to innovate in their ongoing skirmish against the obstacles impeding production.

Armando is one of the two hundred or more Cartys who live in Consuelo, descendants of St. Martin islanders who made the trek early this century. "There are more of our family than any other on the estate," he says. "We are all Catholics." And all big. Among them is Rico Carty, the first boy from Consuelo to make it to the major leagues. Two of Rico's brothers and two of his cousins who played minor league ball work elsewhere in the mill.

While proud of his younger cousin's success, Armando finds equal satisfaction in his clan's mastery of the mechanical arts. The mill is a craftsmen's empire, the kind that Frederick Winslowe Taylor and the apostles of Scientific Management attacked with their stopwatches and time studies during the dawn of corporate America. But the efficiency experts lost the battle in this mill. As Wobbly agitator Big Bill Haywood once remarked, "The manager's brains are under the workman's cap." Without the mill workers' expertise and input, production would not only cease, but would never resume. It was that power which Mauricio Báez helped them to realize.

"The workers at *La Romana* went out in December, 1945," Carty explains, "but they went back in again after Trujillo sent his people to talk with them. But a few weeks later, in January, after the grinding had begun, they went back out on strike."

The two crucial demands were higher wages and shorter hours. Unskilled cane cutters earned a mere 40 cents a day; the most skilled pocketed just $1.50. Shifts ran twelve hours. The workers called for a doubling of the wages, with a minimum of a dollar's pay per day, and a shortening of their hours to eight, with a third shift added.

"Mauricio then came here," Caines says as he picks up the story. "They had a meeting—him, Edwin Kilbourne, and someone from the government. They meet right over there in the mill office by the park and afterward, Mauricio come out and speak to the people."

Báez climbed atop a bridge under which the railroad cars bringing the cane into the mill ran. He told the workers what Kilbourne, the mill's superintendent, had promised. But while he was speaking to the gathering crowd about the negotiations, someone spotted a regiment of the *guardia* making its way toward the mill.

"Mauricio ran into the cane fields," Caines relates as most of the shop's workers gather round. "The *guardia* did not have a good sense of who he was. They just knew that he was a tall black man. They wound up grabbing Crazy Charles, thinking he was Mauricio, and beat him up plenty. But Mauricio fled through the fields to *La Romana* where the dock workers smuggled him out of the country, to Cuba."

That night, the workers who had entered the mill for the 6 P. M. shift walked out at two in the morning, voting with their feet for the eight-hour turn. The *guardia* kept people in their homes the next day but Trujillo's mediators soon validated the walkout. Wages were raised from 50 cents to a dollar a day, and three shifts of eight hours became the norm for mill workers.

As Cecilio Vanterpool explained, "That gave us more time for life and it meant that more people were working. Those were the objects that we fought for. Before Báez, we had a syndicate but it had too much touch with the government. It had no real strength or independence. There were workers here who wanted to fight, but they weren't united enough till Mauricio came. He focused the workers and gave us strength by linking us with unions elsewhere."

Looking back at the strike, Vanterpool and others wonder how they managed to get away with it. Trujillo, they argue, was not to be trifled with. That the companies were owned by foreigners probably was the key. In the wake of the strike, Trujillo began to acquire a monopoly over the sugar industry, and as he did, labor activism ceased. So did Mauricio Báez.

The labor activist sought asylum in the Mexican embassy after the strike and then went into exile. He returned to proselytize for the Popular Socialist Party during the late 1940s before resuming his exile in Cuba. On the night of December 10, 1950, three men went to his home in Havana and convinced him to go with them to meet an opposition congressman. Báez was never seen again, nor was his body ever found.

Nobody in Consuelo doubts his fate. "Trujillo had him killed," Caines says, as the men in the pattern shop nod in assent. "He chased him to Cuba and murdered him."

While the strike itself had been relatively peaceful, its leaders were victimized in the following months. Caines previously had introduced me to several older women who had lost brothers and fathers in the strike's aftermath. "They disappeared and their bodies were found later hanging in the trees or lying in the cane fields."

But the industry's workforce had won the critical battle for shorter hours. Though trade unionism fell dormant and would remain a company-inspired fraud until the death of Trujillo, the sugar mill workers would keep their eight-hour day.

"That gave us more time and energy to play baseball," Armando Carty recalls. "I myself had just about given up cricket by then. After the English people went home, cricket had fallen. So we took up baseball. I played with Bibi," he says, using Caines' nickname, "on *Padre* José's team, *Santa Ana.*"

Santa Ana became the booster rocket to baseball's amazing trajectory on the Consuelo estate, helping to push it into orbit around major league baseball. But *Santa Ana* did not burst full-blown onto Consuelo's playing fields, ready to mark the estate's placement in the sporting firmament. It resulted from the diversion of the *Cocolos'* sporting energies to baseball and the creation of an informal network of Dominican-born English players organized by the likes of Roberto Caines and Luis Carty. By the 1960s, Consuelo baseball was ready to send its native sons to the Dominican league. By the following decade, these migrant laborers would be tending fields from Candlestick Park to Yankee Stadium.

If there is a dean to Consuelo baseball, it might be Luis Carty. A tall, thin, Scatman Carrothers look-alike in sandals and brown polyester pants, Luis Carty is dozing in a straight-backed chair tilted against the wall of his concrete block home. He somehow manages to sleep through the crescendo of buses and motorcycles changing gears on the nearby road to the Santa Fe estate.

As I stand there deliberating whether to wake him or return another day, Carty opens his eyes and smiles. When I tell him why I am there, he invites me inside, saying, "You can't believe how happy I am to see you. Sit down, my friend, sit down."

His living room is crammed with a television, a refrigerator, an ancient Singer sewing machine, and rocking chairs. An eclectic set of photos and pictures cover the walls. Now in his seventies, Carty survives on a pension of 240 *pesos* a month (about $80 at the current rate of exchange but about to plummet due to high inflation and an adverse rate in the following year) and on money sent from family members working in New York. He is not alone in this. New York City has replaced San Pedro as the magnet attracting *Cocolo* migrants and many of the older men and women with whom I speak depend on these earnings from abroad. The six to eight hundred million dollars that Dominicans in the United States send home each year is the nation's second largest source of foreign exchange.

Carty was born on the Consuelo estate in 1917; his parents had come there from St. Martin. "Well, my dear, you cannot imagine how hard we had it in those days in Consuelo. I began work as a *peon* in a work gang, and oh! it was hard work. But I started going to school, the one that the English made for their children, and that's the way I get along."

Carty became a shopkeeper, running the company store on the Consuelo estate and later managing similar shops on the Boca Chica and Santa Fe *ingenios*. "But you know *Padre* José, if it wasn't for he, we would be living in a home with five or six families still! . . .

"When I was a boy, cricket was the game on the estates. My father used to play it—almost all the Cartys did—but I didn't like that sport. I never appreciate it much. Baseball was my game.

"I was a young man when I take up all of baseball in Consuelo and *Padre* José helped me a lot, because he is the man that came to Consuelo and helped us in baseball and everything else, too. Without him, I don't even want to think about what our life would have been like."

As a youth during the early 1930s, Carty played baseball with the boys he grew up with in "Baketown," a section of Consuelo near the path that led to San Pedro and so named because many of the estate's bakers lived there.

"You could live and work on the estate and never leave your entire life! Baseball is what got me off the estate, but at first we just forming our little clubs from the boys that we lived among. They that lived 'up the road' played on one team, those 'down the road' on another. There might have been five or six of these teams, but we were not so much organized then. Nobody had uniforms and most of the equipment was what we could make for ourselves.

"They had a golf course here then, did you know that? It was right behind the mill. The American people from Santa Fe, Quisqueya, Porvenir and those that worked here in the offices would play. It had nine holes and you would be twelve miles walking to play it. I know because we carried the Americans' clubs while they play and took the golf balls we find to make into baseballs when we could.

"When Joshua Gibson and Cool Papa Bell were here for the championships in, I believe it was 1937, they would come here and play. Only blacks who did that! They closed the course in 1957 after Trujillo bought the mill because Dominicans never interested in golf. No English either."

By the time that Dominican baseball held its 1936 and 1937 tournaments, Carty had helped form a club called *Paraiso* or Paradise. "That's the club that we started after we got to be about fifteen, sixteen years of age. We started clubbing up every week, each member paying 25 cents so that we can buy a ball and bat and get things together. To go to play a team on another estate we would have to go on horseback or walk and most days we had to do more walking than anything else. It wasn't easy, my dear boy, but we loved the game."

The mill contributed nothing to cricket and did not formally support a baseball club then. But there was a team associated with the mill called *Agua Dulce,* the mill's original name.

Carty explains, "Baseball was not flourishing then as it is nowadays. The company maintain a club then (in the 1930s) that play all the other estates. We make a serial against the workers on the other estates each year, but the company wasn't very much interested in that. We could go on their railroad cars to play, but no one make a livelihood out of baseball, no one at all."

Three children from the house next door politely interrupt Carty to ask him for ice, which he gets from his refrigerator. Power has been off for hours and the cubes he empties into their red plastic bowl are already fast disappearing.

Carty captained *Agua Dulce,* which counted on its roster a number of other Cartys from St. Martin. "But not Rico, my sister Oliva's son. He was not even a puppy then. And many that played for *Agua Dulce* still played cricket and had their heart more in that than baseball."

In the 1940s, as the state organized a series of regional tournaments culminating in a national championship, *Agua Dulce* became the Consuelo Baseball Club. Most of the players were workers on the estate. Meanwhile, a group of younger players, including Roberto Caines and his friends, were pursuing the game with the same sort of commitment that cricket had previously commanded on the estate.

"Those are the boys that *Padre* José worked with," Carty states. "He took those boys and made them *Santa Ana.* That is the start of real baseball on the estate, when *Padre* José came."

Like Luis Carty, Roberto Caines loved baseball more than any other sport. Born a decade after Carty, Caines was part of that 1920s generation that matured with baseball on the ascent, especially after the 1936 and 1937 championships and the repatriation of many English after the 1932 Dominicanization of Labor Law in the workplace took effect.

"My brother used to carry me to the ball field when Satchel Paige and the Cubans played here. I remember everything I see from that vantage point. And I'll tell you, Martín Dihigo was the greatest ballplayer that God ever gave the world.

"I played on the Up the Road All-Stars, a team that fourteen of us had here. We were all English except for Neftali Frias, the only Dominican on the club. His younger brother is Pepé, who played for Montreal. We were only boys, but we were already better than the men on the estate's team. It is from those boys that Luis Carty and *Padre* José form the Santa Ana club. Garabato Sackie, Clemente Hart, and my brother Dick Caines, played for us." Each would later star in Dominican league play. So would Severino Foy, Silvio Foy, and Rafael Gums (whose name would be Dominicanized to Gomez when he played professionally).

"*Padre* José made that team," Caines affirms. Scratching the Yassir Arafat stubble on his chin with a bandaged finger, he raises his hand in the air. "He was the one to open the eyes of the laborers here after they chased Mauricio Báez away. He made us see the way."

After listening to Consuelo practically canonize *Padre* José, it comes as something of a shock to find that the man is still alive, a day's drive north of my home in Pittsburgh. I visit him in Seeley's Bay, Ontario, late one August. Birds are rehearsing for their migration south over the spruce and birch trees behind his church, a small parish that Father Joseph Ainslie has tended for the past few years.

He has light blue eyes, graying hair, a ruddy complexion, and a pear-shaped body. My three-year-old son confuses him with the man fishing in a Norman Rockwell print on the kitchen wall in the rectory.

After mass on Sunday morning, we go to his lodge on a small island north of Kingston, and Ainslie traces the steps that took him to Consuelo.

"When I was in boarding school in Kingston, there was a fellow who ate at my table whose brother belonged to the Scarboro Foreign Mission. He would read letters from his brother in China and I was intrigued. I decided that that was what I was going to do and never changed my mind.

"The problem was that when they put all of the foreigners out of China, they put all the priests out, too. By then, I had finished studying as a priest. It would have been 1943. I was twenty-five years old at the time. For awhile they didn't know what to do with us, but then Archbishop Pittini responded to the Superior General of the Scarboros, who had written a number of dioceses in Latin America to see if they needed clergy.

"Pittini was a clever old duck. He was an Italian working in the Jesuit reduction missions in Paraguay and then learned English in the States before winding up down there. He was blind in his later years, but he saved the church in Santo Domingo."

The first contingent of Scarboro priests arrived in March of 1943. Joseph Ainslie was on the third trip, a year later.

"My first tour of duty was in Monte Plata, but I preferred to go to an old village further north in Boya, where the church is one of the four oldest in the Americas. I think it was left to the church by Enriquillo, the last of the Indian chiefs, although that could be myth. I was supposed to collect fifty cents a year from every household as part of the church's inheritance, but I never asked for it.

"The first meal that I ate in Monte Plata gave me amoebic dysentery. I lost forty pounds in about two weeks. After a year, I went to Yamasa, where they thought it would be a good place to start cooperatives. Then I became quite ill—from the dysentery, malaria, and a few other things—and came back home. I weighed 119 pounds" [at least 80 to 90 pounds below his current praying weight]. "When I returned a bit later, they sent me to Consuelo."

The Scarboro Foreign Mission was ahead of its times, advancing a social agenda as well as a spiritual one decades before parish radicals began building base communities in Latin America and shaking up orthodox Catholicism. "The words 'liberation theology' just started fifteen years ago. We were doing it without the terminology. You know some people have this ideal of the Catholic Church—that it's a monarchal system—that you get orders from the pope and everybody jumps to attention. That's nonsense! It doesn't seep down from the top, it percolates up from the bottom. After we were doing that, other priests, like the Maryknolls, began calling it liberation theology. But we didn't call it that then."

When Ainslie arrived in Consuelo in March, 1947 he found the Catholics in town holding mass in the home of *Doña* Alicia Guerrero, wife of a Dominican office worker. "There was no religion there. Everyone was a nominal Catholic, except for the *Cocolos,* but there had never been a priest or even a Protestant minister who had lived there. They had, however, just built a wonderful little church, *Santa Ana.*"

The mill built the church after Edwin Kilbourne's wife, Ana Rosa Santoni Kilbourne, had escaped injury in a crash of its twin engine Beechcraft. Kilbourne kept a plane on the estate so that he could travel to the other estates that he managed in the Caribbean. The story I've been told is that as the plane descended, the *Señora* negotiated with her lord, pledging to build a church for the people of Consuelo if she survived the plane's troubled landing. She did, and the result was a white stucco church with a mahogany-beamed ceiling and a tiled mosaic of the *Señora* of Altagracia on the wall.

Ainslie had been in the country long enough to understand Dominican poverty, but he was still unprepared for the unremitting horrors of the *bateyes* and *ingenios.*

"I encountered deplorable housing, poor wages, work for only four or five months a year, and money-lending at twenty percent per week. That was outrageous. The labor union was controlled by Kilbourne, and the people had no educational facilities whatsoever. There was absolutely nothing but suffering.

"I had to get a technique, to find a way to introduce myself to that melee. I kept thinking about how to get an entree with these people and saw the obvious—that they played baseball—that they loved the game.

"I thought that this would be how I would infiltrate the people.

"There was a field right across from the church where they played. I saw the kids using sticks and making balls from twine. Almost none of them had gloves. I also saw that they were hanging around my house when I showed interest in getting something for them.

"I would have taken up Kung Fu if it would have served my purpose. But instead I got them some boxing gloves and started to work with some of the older boys and men in helping them with a baseball team. Remember that with baseball you teach a lot of social skills. You need a leader and you need loyalty. While I would emphasize the word competition very slightly, I preferred the word cooperation. The fact that they would establish an association among themselves and were very proud of their team stimulated a great deal of interest in baseball in the other areas, too. But it wasn't my suggestion, so much as their own.

"But it allowed me to infiltrate the people and gain their trust. Then, we could attack the money-lending and go after better housing."

Although Ainslie was unfamiliar with the history of Garveyism, benevolent societies, and cricket in Consuelo, he noted the primacy of the *Cocolos* in the self-organized dynamics of the town. "The *Cocolos* were a great help to me—and they weren't even Catholics. They seemed to understand organization better than the Dominican people.

"One of the things that I noticed was that the Dominicans did not make good mechanics. They had been brought up for centuries using just a *machete,* while the English people were better trained and more accustomed to sophisticated machinery.

"I began to admire the English method of colonization although being an Irishman, I never thought much of the English. . . . The *Cocolo* old-timers had an upbringing. They dressed better, they lived better, and overall, they were decent, law-abiding citizens."

Most of all, Ainslie realized that social change in Consuelo would be impossible without them. It did not matter to him that most of the *Cocolos* were Anglicans or members of evangelical Protestant sects. His mission was to organize the community to seek better conditions. "We never made any distinctions between Catholics and non-Catholics. That word, religion, never came into what we were doing."

The genesis for the *Santa Ana* club came when Luis Carty proposed that Ainslie help sponsor a team. "I met *Padre* José soon after he came to Consuelo," Carty remembers, "and I talk with him. He liked baseball and he tell me what we have to do is get together and take a little contribution from each member, a weekly taxation of fifty cents.

Padre José was the club's president and treasurer. I was its manager, and men like Roberto Carty, Austin Jacobo, and Roberto Caines were helping to run it."

Doña Ana Rosa Kilbourne chipped in with a contribution and within six months, the club had purchased the equipment necessary to field a team. "We gave it the name of *Santa Ana* in honor of the *señora* and the church," Carty explains.

The club met twice weekly at Ainslie's house. "He did not mind the sweat and grime. He used to sit on the floor with the boys, even though he wearing his white silk robes." At these meetings, a set of rules for conduct and discipline were written.

"We were very strict. Yes, we were!" Carty remembers with pleasure, his rocker creaking faster as his enthusiasm builds. "The English people were well trained and you had to respect yourselves. You see a lot of music and such there now, but music and drinking? NOOOOOOOO! No-no-no-no-no! Not then. You had to be in your place, and on Sunday you had to go to church.

"The players had to respect the directors of the club. Nobody could use anything that belonged to the club unless there was a game or practice. Anybody who violated this rule was expelled."

When a team from San Pedro or another estate visited Consuelo, *Santa Ana* hosted them after the game. "What we used to do was this," Carty explains. "Some of the boys would go and ask for a little donation—five or ten cents—that was plenty money then. Six cents buy a pound of meat, an egg cost only a cent. Some of the *bodegas* would give us some food—everybody give us something. And then we have them to my house after the game for a little *fiesta.*"

Members of the community helped in a variety of ways. "My mother made the first uniforms," Dr. Fernando Guerrero Mark, one of the few non-English players on the club, recalls. "They were baggy, almost balloonlike, made out of gray flannel with *Santa Ana* written in blue on them." Men like Roberto Carty and Austin Jacobo helped train the boys and arrange for games. Others simply basked in its reflected camaraderie and success.

The ball club energized the community in a fashion similar to the cricket clubs of earlier years. But by bringing the English into the Dominican mainstream, it also created an institution that would raise the collective self-image of Consuelo and its standing in the region. Soon, even aficionados of the game hundreds of kilometers away in the *Cibao* would hear of *Padre* José's club.

Much of *Santa Ana*'s legacy flowed from its success on the field. The club soon became the best amateur squad in the area. In its dozen or so years, the team fielded a handful of players who would go on to star in Dominican league play and even sent a few, like Rico Carty, Pepé Frias, and Severino Foy, into pro ball in the United States. And when the club lost its identity as *Padre* José's team and merged with the *ingenio*'s team, the latter appropriated the name *Santa Ana*. From that second generation *Santa Ana* team, scores would sign contracts with pro clubs, making *Consuelo* a veritable lodestone of baseball talent.

Before Ainslie arrived in town, mass was said at the home of Fernando Guerrero Mark's parents. Guerrero did his medical internship in Canada because of Ainslie and is now a surgeon in Santo Domingo. A former *Santa Ana* ballplayer, he returns regularly to Consuelo to treat his old neighbors free of charge.

"He had an incredible impact on us," Guerrero remembers some forty years later. "I was finishing high school about the time he arrived and took him to the different *bateyes* by horseback and helped him with mass. He got to Consuelo at the moment when a man like that was necessary.

"I suppose he did infiltrate us. At that time, I didn't know what he was doing, but I do now. He got himself into the heart of the people, especially the youth. He did it by helping us with baseball and taking us to the beach. He even put on boxing gloves and instructed us in how to fight. And then he starts attacking the moneylenders and arguing with Kilbourne for better housing.

"There had been a good deal of cultural and religious segregation in the town, but sports brought people together. That's one of the things that Consuelo owes Joseph Ainslie. He used sport to bring people together.

"That's why he's remembered in Consuelo. He'll be remembered there forever."

Ainslie is bemused, and a bit surprised that the church's team had such sporting consequence. His goal had not been to turn out big league prospects, but to build ties that would allow him to work on other projects.

"I must admit that I enjoyed the ball club," Ainslie remarks as we walk through the woods. "It was not a chore for me. Other things were, but the team was a pleasure and a satisfaction.

"After I had established myself, the first thing I wanted to do was attack the money-lending at twenty percent a week. So I started a credit union and if the moneylenders did not disappear, at least they went underground. Then, I wanted individual houses with a little front lawn and a back yard. I wanted to help them develop compost heap gardening, and have some chickens and rabbits. Let them have their privacy, and become more self-sufficient, especially during the dead season."

Within a year of his arrival in Consuelo, Ainslie was shaking the estate out of the political quiescence it had settled into after the strike. "I remember Father Ainslie on top of his jeep with a loudspeaker in the park next to the mill every Saturday evening when the workers were paid," Dr. Guerrero recalls. "I remember it well. He told the people that they should ask for better housing and for better salaries. That they should at least own a cat. That horses lived better than they did.

"You must remember that people in Consuelo kept silent. Those were the days of the Great Dictator. When Mauricio Báez organized the strike there, nobody had wanted to even take a leaflet from him because everyone was so afraid of Trujillo.

"Then Father Ainslie came. This priest from Canada was not afraid. But people would hear him talking with his loudspeaker and they would listen and then run away.

"Nobody was up there on the jeep with him. Anyone could have shot him up there, but his religion was respected and that is what kept him from harm."

Soon more people would stay and listen, and a claque of Ainslie's supporters responded to the priest's orations. "I had them organized so that if I touched my left ear, they would cheer and if I touched my right one, they would boo," Ainslie recalls. He began to get results. Cooperatives were formed and the mill responded to his pressures by building two new neighborhoods, Guachupita and Pueblo Nuevo, which were decided improvements on most of the housing stock.

"Now I know that he was saying the truth," Dr. Guerrero says. "But then I thought that he was crazy. In those days, if he spoke on Saturday night about the standard of living, we were afraid to go to church the next day."

The fears had foundation. Edwin Kilbourne and Ainslie were on reasonable terms the first few months of the father's residency, but relations deteriorated rapidly.

Edwin I. Kilbourne arrived on the island on the heels of the U.S. occupation during World War I, Hugh Kelly III, former manager of the Porvenir mill, explained during an interview in a hotel along the *malecón* in Santo Domingo. "I think he came down with the marines and stayed on. He went to Annapolis, one of those ninety-day wonders like they had in World War II, but washed out on account of his eyes. But he wanted something to do here and was a graduate of Cornell and my grandfather helped him get a job in the sugar business.

"The rumor is that he came here in his uniform and they called him Skipper the rest of his life. He became one of the biggest men in the sugar industry in the world. He was general manager of mills here, in Haiti, and in Cuba. Until Trujillo forced him out, Kilbourne was a powerful man."

But not, say men like Caines, Vanterpool, and Joseph, a respected or liked one.

"My good relations with Kilbourne ended rather abruptly," Ainslie explains. "He knew what I was doing and that I wasn't going to change to suit him. You see, everything belonged to the *ingenio*. They had built the church and the beautiful house that I lived in. They gave me money to buy a jeep and even gave me a monthly check. Even the priest belonged to the *ingenio!*

"Kilbourne was using it as a sales pitch. Any time any of the big shots came from the States or any other country to visit, they were always brought to meet the priest. But it must have irritated Kilbourne that they had given me all of this stuff and I didn't show appreciation.

"Reverend Beard, the old Anglican minister in San Pedro, told me that Kilbourne was a man who mounted his way to the top on many fallen heads. I've heard stories, but it's not my business to investigate the truth of them. I just know that he wanted me out."

Military men and government officials began to visit Ainslie, cautioning him to show restraint. When he failed to censor himself, allegations were made that Ainslie was a communist. His meetings in the park next to the mill were banned, and the *guardia* increased its visibility in town. Those who aligned themselves with the priest sometimes found themselves out of work and under greater scrutiny themselves. "I had friends who said I was crazy to be seen talking with Father Ainslie," Dr. Guerrero remembers. "They say that someone will see me with him and they will say I was against Trujillo."

"The thought never entered my mind that I was in danger," Ainslie says with hindsight. "I wasn't as far as I was concerned. But I did a lot of stupid things that if I was older and more mature, I wouldn't have had the guts to do."

Ainslie has no regrets that he confronted Kilbourne and the government on an individual basis, laughing deeply as he remembers appearing uninvited at a soiree at Kilbourne's house and proceeding to use the evening as a forum to advance his causes. He does, however, recall that he sometimes feared his actions might lead to the mill's shutdown or acts of violence, either on the part of the government or by the workers in his defense.

"The communists have the right idea," he says with a smile. "You need noise because people don't listen to a whisper.

"People say did you make any Catholics? I wasn't there to make Catholics, but I took a very simple note from St. Thomas Aquinas. He said a 'modicum of comfort is necessary for the practice of ritual. Without that modicum of comfort, there isn't any morality.' There's another Spanish refrain, 'You can't fill a man's heart with the love of God on an empty belly.' So let's fill bellies and then fill a man's heart with dignity."

Ainslie's very presence in Consuelo led to mounting annoyance on the part of Kilbourne and the government. Unable to eliminate a foreign priest without risking international fallout, the government contrived to remove him from the country by working through Archbishop Pittini. Pittini arranged for Ainslie to be appointed head of an agency raising funds for children of the third world. It wasn't until afterwards that Ainslie found he would not be allowed to return.

"I had been willing to stay forever as far as I was concerned. But the church is usually pretty smooth in difficult situations. You'll find that they have a system. It's Italian; a way of managing to avoid confrontations and scandal. It's true that sometimes they sacrifice the individual for the cause. In our case, they defended me to save face, not mine, but the church's. Eventually, I found that I was appointed to that position in Canada to get me out. When I tried to get back into Santo Domingo, it dawned on me that I had been thrown out of the place to smooth things over. I wasn't angry about it. It was a good way of handling the situation. I was not really of any more use to Consuelo by this time. . . .

"I was a catalyst. I didn't contribute anything substantial moneywise. But I helped people to organize themselves, which was something they had shown they could do. That's the whole thing. I carry these words by Lao-tse with me all the time. He says that a leader is best when people barely know that he exists; not so good when people obey and acclaim him. His aim is fulfilled when the people say we did it ourselves. That's the way I operated.

"I wasn't allowed back into the country until after they murdered Trujillo. If I had stayed, I might have ended up like Arthur MacKinnon, a Scarboro priest who was taken out on a highway and shot by army officers (during the 1965 revolution)."

Dr. Guerrero agrees. "If they did not take him out of the country, something would have happened. Trujillo didn't kill you directly, but you might be on the road and a truck would hit you and they say it's an accident. There were lots of accidents."

After Ainslie left, his followers were watched and his letters from Canada were opened. But the Scarboro Order continues to maintain a presence in the town and remains committed to the social agenda that Ainslie helped motivate in the late 1940s.

Forty years after his arrival in Consuelo, *Padre* José returned for a week of celebrations commemorating his work in the town. Accompanied by delegations from Canada and New York City, Ainslie met old friends as well as children born long after his departure who grew up being told that they owed a debt to the man called *Padre* José.

Ainslie himself shrugs off such notions as he stands by a lake in eastern Ontario, reminiscing about his three years in Consuelo. "If I had stayed any longer, I would have made myself redundant within a very short time. That was the objective of my mission."

"Maybe if he wasn't sent back to Canada, he wouldn't have been such a hero to us," Dr. Guerrero reasons. "But when he was kicked out, the people got mad and he became a legend. People opened their eyes more about the dictator. The people had more consciousness and sugar cane fields would sometimes be burned at night."

The people not only had more consciousness, a commodity of questionable safety in the age of the Great Dictator, they had more baseball. Workers stopped on the way home to watch their sons play, and throughout the region, the goal for the other amateur teams became beating Consuelo.

A dispute among players led to the formation of a second church-related club called *Santa Rosa*. Over the next decade, these teams played across the country.

Eventually, Luis Carty explains, the *Santa Ana* team was taken over by the estate team. "The estate said that I would be the man to take care of the club and get everything in shape and I did so." With the union contract deducting 20 cents a worker every payday, baseball on the estates gained solid footing.

"When the championships start on the estates, all the people could think about was baseball. The company give players time off to practice and play, and you'd still make your pay."

In 1957, Carty managed the club to the regional championship. "We then made a selection and took the best players from Santa Fe and Porvenir, like Amado Samuel from Santa Fe who played for Milwaukee and then the Mets, and Monkey Huggins from Quisqueya. We beat Manzanillo and *Aviación* and won the national championship."

After Carty managed for four seasons, Roberto Caines took his place. Under his tutelage, the club won four more regional championships. After Caines, former New York Yankee and Atlanta Brave infielder Pedro González took over. And the beat went on, with more and more boys on the Consuelo team playing their way into professional baseball.

Thousands flood the *malecón* in San Pedro for the beginning of *Patronales*, the annual, week-long festivities celebrating St. Peter, the patron saint of Macoris. Flashes of lightning illuminate the throng, adding electricity to the release that comes each summer at the end of the grinding season in the mills. No one seems to mind an occasional rain shower as children climb aboard rickety-looking carnival rides, and kiosks dispense enough rum and beer to give the town a colossal hangover.

The next day, Rico Carty, the leading member of Consuelo's "first family," sinks deep in the floral cushions of the furniture in his den and kicks off his sandals. A painting of Jesus and enough photos, plaques, and commendations to start a small museum cover the walls.

While his wife and daughters watch soap operas in an adjoining room, the first ballplayer from San Pedro to make a lasting impression in the major leagues talks of his baseball odyssey. Scores have followed in his wake, but this immense black man with a beard has kept his status as San Pedro's sporting icon.

"My dad, Leopoldo, worked in the Consuelo mill for sixty years. He played cricket, was a wickets keep, but what he really loved was boxing. My mother, Oliva, was a midwife. You see the street they name after her? It runs right by the *Santa Ana* church. Alfredo's mama, Mary Griffin, lives on it, and so does *El Gallo,* Rafael Batista. . . .

"We Cartys are from St. Martin, from the French side. They spell our name C-a-r-t-i but they change it here. My grandmother and grand-father would speak French and English, my parents English and Spanish. When we comes up in the school, we speaking Spanish and going to school in Spanish.

"When I went to the States, I thought I knew English but I didn't know anything. I speak one word in English and three in Spanish."

Carty has long since overcome the linguistic barrier and speaks easily in English with a decidedly French accent.

"When I go to Davenport, Iowa in 1960, I eat chicken for three months and then after that I eat hamburger for three months cuz I didn't understand anything in English. I feel frustrated, but my teammates start teaching me how to speak the words."

Born in 1941, Rico was still a boy when his family received housing in Guachupita, a *barrio* built behind the mill because of *Padre* José's persistence. "We played in the streets. The ball field that is there now, across from the church, was planted in cane then. Trujillo thought he could make so much money with cane that he planted every foot he could find with it after he buy the mill.

"We had to pick our spots in the streets to play. You had to hit it straight down the street. You hit it over the house, you is out. That is why I think that mostly all the Latin hitters is such good up the middle hitters. We had to conduct ourselves that way."

As a youth, Rico played with the boys from Guachupita as they took on rival teams from La Loma, La Habana, and Pueblo Nuevo. "You never see a fastball then. We didn't have no Wilson balls, ours made out of threads and cloth and all that stuff. From time you small, you accustomed to off-speed stuff that breaks all over the place. They say Latin players is better off-speed batters. I think it's because you playing that off speed since you small."

Sometimes the boys pooled their change and placed bets on the games. "It more exciting that way. You really put all that you got into it if everyone's money down on it. . . .

"My mother wouldn't let me go to the ball field. I used to steal time to play. She used to fight so much with me to go to school. I end up school in 8th grade because I didn't pass my grades after that. I tell my mother I going to school but I didn't go. I used to go to the river, the *Agua Dulce,* to swim, or play baseball. About fifteen or twenty of us used to hide our books and take off. We just start being bad kids and we don't pass in school. . . .

"My mother wanted me to be a doctor, and she took me to a hospital where there was this doctor who was a good friend of hers, but I didn't like it. What I liked was boxing when I was coming up.

"You always stick to mostly what your mother wants you to do. In this country, we have a great respect for our mother and are closer to her than our father. In the States, when you make eighteen, you can do what you want, but here, you could be 62 and you still be under your mother's wings. It's very seldom that you see a kid blast out at his mother. In my day, you could not even raise your voice to your mother. I guess that comes from the English upbringing."

But if medical school seemed unlikely, there was always a place for another Carty in the mill. "I was to learn a trade with my uncle in the mill where you cut logs and wood to make homes. But he worked me too hard and I say one day, 'This is for animals, it's not for me,' and he hit me with a saw on my back and I run from there and never go back. I keep on going to school, sort of, but I don't know what I want to be. And then I start picking up baseball and it gets in my blood."

By then, Carty had played some ball for *Arena,* a team organized by a man who worked in the sand yard, and spent many an afternoon and weekend insinuating himself into games with the older boys on the *Santa Ana* club. Always tall, he had yet to fill his six-foot-three-inch frame to his almost 200 pound playing weight. But with brother Juan Carty, uncle Luis Carty, and neighbor Roberto Caines schooling him, he was beginning to display a glimpse of his prodigious talents.

In the late 1950s, amateur baseball in Consuelo came of age, and *Santa Ana,* by then more of an *ingenio-* than church-sponsored squad, set the standard for baseball in the cane fields. It also sent Rico to the national squad for the 1959 Pan American Games in Chicago.

At the 1955 games in Mexico, with future major leaguers Julian Javier and Felipe Alou in the lineup, the Dominican Republic won the gold medal. Hopes were high for the 1959 squad, which was managed by Horacio Martínez, supervised by Pedro Julio Santana, and under the surveillance of Trujillo's secret service agents. But the team played poorly and finished out of the running.

Despite its lacklustre team play, individual Dominican players held up well under the scrutiny of major league scouts and several wound up playing pro ball.

"I had a fantastic series at the Pan Am Games," Carty says as he stretches and seems to fill the entire room. "They start to really like me when I hit one into the bleachers in left center. And then there is a ball hit into right center with a man on second base. I'm playing right field and I get the ball off the fence and throw the ball to home plate about this high off the ground and get the runner at the plate. They go wild in Comiskey Park when that happen."

The scouts went wild, too, and went into a feeding frenzy that overwhelmed Carty. "I wasn't hungry for the money, never ever been that in my life, but at the end of the session, they coming up to me with contracts and saying 'Sign, Rico, sign.' So I start signing. I just go ahead and sign 'cause all I want to do is play baseball. I get the baseball in my blood and I keep on signing. When I got over there, I thought I could defend myself in English, but I find I don't really know English. They is telling me I can sign and I keep on signing. Most of the teams want to give me bonuses, but that's what save me because I don't take any money."

By the time Carty had left Chicago, he had signed contracts with nine different major league organizations as well as all four Dominican teams.

"Trujillo was going to suspend me because I wasn't going to play for *Escogido*. He was going to suspend me for life. He was going to really give it to me. But what happened is that Rafael Antun and him were *compadres*, very good friends. They stand for each other's sons. They start arguing on the phone with Trujillo saying if he don't play for *Escogido*, he not going to play, and Antun saying he from San Pedro and he going to play for San Pedro."

The dispute wound up in the Dominican courts. For fifteen days, Carty accompanied Antun on the road to Santo Domingo where the tribunal was ready to suspend him. But on the sixteenth day, George Trautman, the president of the association of minor leagues, intervened.

"He called at nine o'clock at night and told them they couldn't do that because I was innocent. He say I innocent because I don't take no money. He say I was an innocent boy away from home who don't speak

English and sign all those contracts just because I wanted to play. They told me that he said that one day I was gonna be a super star and represent my home town. I just laugh cuz I never think I'm gonna be that great in baseball. But it became true."

Rico wound up with San Pedro's *Estrellas Orientales* on the island and with the Milwaukee Braves in the States. He came to the plate only once during the 1959–60 winter season before going to spring training with the Braves.

At the Braves' camp, he fell in with *Santa Ana* alum Severino Foy, and Consuelo native Chico Conton, who, like Rico, had a father who starred on the estate's cricket teams. Neither made it to the majors but each starred in Dominican play. Jompy Jiménez from the Santa Fe estate was there too, as well as a number of Puerto Rican and black players.

"Relations between Latin and black players were regular. After I start getting to the big leagues is where things start turning around because we hear black players say that white players treating us better than them.

"I didn't understand this racialness. I go to a restaurant that is away from the training camp and I look at a lady who was serving and I say please, but I cannot ask for what I want to eat. But this is my luck. There's a guy who had just left the Dominican Republic two weeks ago and he heard me and he says to me that when I heard you I knew you were from the Dominican and he asked me what I wanted and he tells her. He also tells her I not from here, but from the Dominican and you can see the tension went off.

"I say to myself, 'What the hell is going on?' But the people are smiling at me now, and I eat, and pay, and go out and walk the streets. I don't see no black people. I didn't know nothing about racialness and after I got back to the camp the other ballplayers ask, 'Rico, where was you?'

"I say 'I go over there. That place is clean. I'm not going to eat over here anymore, but back there.' They say 'Rico! What you doing? Man, you lucky they didn't lynch you over there. You got to start learning this country. Black people can't eat over there!'

"I say 'I'm not black. I'm Spanish. When I want to eat, I'll go over there.'

"I get frustrated. If I can't eat where I want, I just as soon leave this country. But the players tell John McMullen, who is general manager of the minor league camp, and he say to me 'You can't do what you do at home. You might get hurt.' And I start thinking and going with the other players, but it was tough."

In 1963, Rico crossed the .300 batting threshold in Dominican play, the first of six consecutive seasons he kept his average over that plateau. He would win batting championships and lead the league in RBIs, total bases, slugging percentage, walks and home runs. When he retired after fifteen winter seasons, Carty was the all-time leader in round-trippers (nobody was even a close second), and among the leaders in other batting categories.

In the course of his career, Carty played for all four traditional Dominican teams and made a brief appearance in the uniform of the expansion *Azucareros* from La Romana. "I never missed a season. I didn't really need the money to play and much of the money that I made here I used to donate to buy things for the kids. I feel a real obligation to play here 'cause I owe my country a lot. They pushed me so hard here."

Rico, meanwhile, pushed himself hard in the States. He broke into the majors with a bang in 1964, hitting .330 with 22 home runs and 88 RBIs. He hit over three hundred for five of his first six seasons en route to a lifetime .303 batting average. In 1970, the right-handed outfielder hit an astronomical .366 to lead the National League.

In fourteen seasons in the show, Carty played for six different teams. With his thundering bat and broad smiling face, Carty won fans over easily, especially in Atlanta. In 1970, Carty's name was left off the All-Star Game ballot, but he became the first player ever elected on the basis of write-in votes.

During his first few years in the majors, Rico returned to Consuelo each winter and played ball for the *Estrellas* in San Pedro. In 1967, he moved to town and became the cornerstone of what has become the ballplayers' ghetto in Macoris. He has lived there ever since.

"Everyone wanted to follow Rico's footsteps in San Pedro," he says matter-of-factly. Eventually, Joaquín Andújar, Alfredo Griffin, George Bell, and Mariano Duncan would move on to nearby streets. Carty retired before the explosion of salaries made millionaires out of even journeymen ballplayers, but he lives comfortably.

"I ain't working. I living off income. I hope that I never need to work. Maybe one of these days, I'll get a job with one of the clubs in the States as a batting instructor. That my best area."

Carty served a stint as president of the Dominican players' association and has stayed involved with youth programs in Consuelo. He has kept active as a player, too, leading the Dominican entry to several international over-forty baseball tournaments.

"He can still play!" Roberto Caines had said in Consuelo. "He come out here and play on Sundays. He manage that team, too, but he got no patience. No patience at all."

There had been other players from San Pedro to make it to the majors before Rico, but Carty was the best until the Macoris pipeline

opened in the 1970s. And even then, he remained the idol of a generation of San Pedro *peloteros.*

Alfredo Griffin is one of them.

A half century ago, mill superintendent Edwin Kilbourne handed out
the toys and sweets on Three Kings Day in Consuelo. Now, it's Alfredo
Griffin, clad in white from his polo shirt to his half-laced high-top
Reeboks, and with his close-cropped black hair and beard, reminiscent
of an earlier, sporting era when cricket was king.

Griffin's grandparents migrated from the Caribbean island of Nevis
to Consuelo and then to Angelina, the neighboring estate, where his
father, Alberto Reed, was born. "He was not that much a sportsman,"
Griffin says in English, "but he could surely play the guitar! And he
could dance."

Alfredo began life in Villa Francisca in Santo Domingo in 1957.
Alberto Reed worked at the port and played *soneros,* an older style of
Cuban music, at the *Borojol,* a nearby nightspot, and sometimes appeared on Dominican television. Alfredo played the conga drum and
sang in a band as a teenager and can still be found dancing late into the
night at San Pedro's discos.

His introduction to baseball came on the streets of Santo Domingo,
playing endless variations of the game with his brothers and neighbors.
But when he was eight, the revolution broke out as junior military
officers sought to restore Juan Bosch to the presidency.

"I remember when the American soldiers came. They brought a lot
of food in cans and we always used to hang around with them. But there
was fighting, too. I was a kid, running up and down the streets. I wasn't
scared of anything, but my mother wanted to get me out of there."

Mary Griffin left Santo Domingo and Alberto Reed, to whom she
had never been wed, and returned to her family in Consuelo. More than
twenty years later, Alfredo stands in front of his mother's home, the one
he bought for her after he won Rookie-of-the-Year honors in 1979, and
pulls running shoes and baseball gear out of his car for the children of
Consuelo.

Afterwards, he stands in the shade, chatting with two youths in
floral shirts. One has recently signed with the California Angels and he
questions Alfredo about rookie camp. They now look to Griffin as their
role model in the way Alfredo once looked to Rico.

The street they are standing by is named Carty Street, for Oliva
Carty, Consuelo's midwife. Like an umbilical cord, it stretches from the
Santa Ana church through the neighborhoods of Pueblo Nuevo, La
Loma, and La Habana to Guachupita, where the Cartys and the Griffins
once lived. Since the time of *Padre* José, *Santa Ana* has pumped life

into these *barrios.* Griffin caught on to the tail-end of the *Santa Ana* phenomenon and grew up idolizing Rico.

"Everybody when I was coming up was fond of Rico. He was a big influence on me. When I played in Cleveland, Rico was there. I went to Toronto and Rico was there. Rico was a big help for me. He helped me all around, with hitting and with discipline.

"Everybody says Rico was a troublemaker. He wasn't a troublemaker! He was a guy who'd stick up for whoever needed help and didn't know how to handle himself. He was telling us, me and Dámaso García (the Moca-born second baseman then with the Toronto Blue Jays), what to do. We didn't know. We were young, but he was a veteran. He had some problems with Toronto because he was telling us what to do. They got upset about that. But I thank him for that. He was a big influence on me."

So much so that Alfredo bought a home in San Pedro around the corner from Rico after he established himself in the majors. Although both are tall and dark, Alfredo is slender, with a dancer's body, and has earned his All-Star status mostly because of his slick defensive play. Carty, never all that proficient with a glove, gained his with the bat.

Later, we talk at Griffin's house. A dish parabola sits atop his red tiled roof like some ancient Taino Indian stele. Pink rockers with floral patterned cushions adorn a front porch, while a lone boy stands with his hands clutching the pink grillwork fence, looking for some sight of one of San Pedro's chosen people. The buzzer at the front gate is broken and Griffin looks at me in astonishment when I ask him if he intends to fix it.

Seated in his den with a sunken floor and dressed in black shorts, thongs, and a gold pendant of a diamond-studded number four, Griffin connects himself to Consuelo's sporting continuum. He is, despite his effervescent persona on the field, an intensely private, almost shy, man off it.

"We played in the streets, in backyards, in the cane fields. After we played, we'd go and cut a piece of cane and peel it with our teeth.

"Consuelo to me is everything. If I stay in Santo Domingo, maybe I wouldn't be talking to you right now, maybe I would have taken another road. It wasn't nice in the capital for kids. Lots of bad influence. I can tell because when I go back there to see my friends, they're doing nothing. When I say 'Where's Monchin?' they say he's in jail."

But on the tightly-disciplined estate, Alfredo had little choice but to behave himself. "If I don't listen, my grandmother go upside my head a few times. Then, I listen good. The English were very strict and the kids respected their elders. That was for me, the main thing. If the men running the team say we gonna leave at 8 o'clock to go to Angelina, the kids be there at 7 o'clock. You late or disrespectful, they sit you on the bench or wouldn't let you make the trip. I never remember kids talking back to their parents or the men running the team in those days. I do remember listening to them talk about *Padre* José a lot when I was growing up. A lot of people ask me why so many players from Consuelo. For me, that's one of the answers."

His uncle, Clemente Hart, played cricket and later starred for the *Estrellas Orientales*. Alfredo played for an amateur team in the Consuelo equivalent of Little League, and then moved on to the *Ingenio* Consuelo team. Because a veteran player was ensconced at shortstop, he saw only a little action for the estate team before signing with Cleveland when he was sixteen years old.

But he was a well-schooled sixteen-year-old, having studied under the men who made *Santa Ana* a sporting institution. "Austin Jacobo and Roberto Caines were working in the community, helping kids to play. Bibi (Caines) handled me for awhile when I was a second baseman. He was a big influence. Right now, he's one of the guys running my little league in Consuelo. . . . And Austin Jacobo would look at a kid and know when he was ready to play on a higher level.

"When I was a kid, I didn't see how important these men were or what it was about the English and sport. But when I grew up, I realized that most of the kids from Consuelo that are professional ballplayers now are probably there because of him and the other men who worked and fought hard to have sport in Consuelo."

The transition from Consuelo to minor league ball in Reno, Nevada was not easy for Griffin. "I had a lot of bad times my first year. I was away from my mother and my friends for the first time. I didn't know enough English and it was cold. They took my passport away and said if I tried to go home without it, they'd put me in jail. There was a Puerto Rican guy on the team and the manager was Cuban, but I was the only Dominican."

Griffin joined the *Estrellas* after signing with Cleveland, but sat on the San Pedro bench for several seasons before winning Rookie-of-the-Year honors in the States and replacing Guachupita-bred Pepé Frias at shortstop. He's been a fixture in the *Estrellas* infield ever since.

After Cleveland traded Griffin to Toronto, he combined with Dámaso García to give the Blue Jays an all-star, all-Dominican combination at shortstop and second base. He spent six years in Toronto and then three with the Oakland Athletics. Before the 1988 season, the Dodgers traded for him to stabilize one of the shakier infields in baseball. Stretched ligaments in his left thumb forced Griffin to sit out the winter season, the first time in over a decade he did not play. His brilliant smile and artistry in the field, which personify the dazzle of winter ball, were missed.

"This last year has been a rough one for me. My dad died, my godmother died, and then my brother was killed in a motorcycle accident the day before Christmas. I get injured last year and it's tough to sit out. I don't like to remember it.

"I always say that for me, I owe playing here to the fans. When I come back as rookie of the year, they were going crazy here. They follow me on the radio and TV, and they know the game. I think we owe this playing here to them because it's the only chance they get to see you play in this country. If I am healthy, I'll play next season."

That's a promise he keeps. And when his playing days are over, says *Estrellas* president Eddie Antun, he can manage the team.

While he waits for his thumb to heal, Griffin quietly works on projects that he and his friend and neighbor, Toronto slugger George Bell, are undertaking in Consuelo. Griffin has donated money for the completion of a high school there and delivers over a hundred baskets of food every Christmas to some of the poorer families in town. He and Bell, a native of the Santa Fe estate, have begun construction of an orphanage. They sponsor an annual golf tournament at the nearby *Casa de Campo* resort to fund their efforts.

"It's bad when you're by yourself, but if we, a bunch of guys that live here and have the power to do so, stick together, we could do a lot of things in Consuelo. Not only in Consuelo, but here in San Pedro. I don't want to get involved in so many things at the same time. I'm only one person. But if the other players join us, we got the power to do something. . . .

"I wanted to go to Consuelo this morning for *Reyes,* because nobody is there to donate anything anymore. Here you have businessmen, but in Consuelo, you don't have too many people who got anything. For me, they need more than anybody else. And that is where I am from."

Thoughts of Dodger Stadium and playing with his friend Pedro Guerrero on the Dodgers bring some relief to what has been an uncharacteristically somber winter for Griffin. "That's the best gift to me, when I come to the stadium and see forty or fifty thousand people. Then, I'm a happy man."

Although Guerrero would be traded in mid-season, Griffin found himself in the World Series at season's end. And as he ran from the shortstop position to hug Orel Hershiser after the final out in the Dodgers' surprising championship season, Griffin's joy was shared by Luis Carty, Roberto Caines, and throughout the estates.

If there is a secret to the remarkable baseball success story of Macoris, it is a tale of how an informal network of *Cocolos* built a sporting life as part of the larger quest to fashion a community in their new land. Putting aside cricket for baseball, their sons and grandsons Dominicanized both this passion for sport and themselves as they moved into the vanguard of baseball, both in the Caribbean and in the United States.

Back in Guachupita, William Joseph scratches the head of a ten-day-old goat as Roberto Caines carries the wooden chairs they had been sitting on back to the kitchen. Arm-in-arm, they set off through the streets of the community they helped build into a place to live and a place to play.

9

The City of Shortstops

Pedro González stands behind first base, hands on hips, as three runners take staggered leads off first base. It's ten in the morning and the runners shimmer in the heat rising from the baked infield dirt of Tetelo Vargas Stadium. A hundred or so onlookers sit in the shade of the stadium's canopy. Most are male, many of school age, but the only students taking their lessons seriously this dead season morning are those on the field, under the scrutiny of San Pedro professor Pedro González.

The pitcher, a 17-year-old left-hander from the Quisqueya estate, nods at the catcher before stepping off the rubber and firing the ball to the first baseman. Two of the three runners have anticipated the pick-off attempt, but the third finds himself leaning the wrong way. Caught in a rundown, he breaks back and forth between the bases until the second baseman tags him out. González calls the youth over, places his hands on the boy's shoulders, and patiently reminds him to watch the pitcher's feet for telltale signs as to whether he's going to pitch the ball or throw to first. When he feels the lesson has registered, González sends the boy back to first base where he and the two other students repeat the exercise again and again.

Elsewhere on the field, a coach hits fungos to a quartet of out-fielders while another instructor slaps grounders to a group of infielders between second and third base. In the stands, an old man in a black "Spys R Us" tee-shirt and a green *Estrellas Orientales* cap sweeps plastic cups and debris into a pile. Two boys lay atop the dugout, peer down into the players' sanctuary, and futilely plead for a baseball from still another coach.

González runs the infielders through simulations with runners on base and zero, one, or two outs. The language of instruction is Spanish, but when the players shout to each other during the play, they often yell "I got it! I got it!" or name the base at which the play should be made in English. González then has each pitcher take several turns covering first on balls fielded by the first baseman. Glancing at his watch, he calls his squad, the Atlanta Braves' Dominican rookie team, to the sidelines.

167

Most of the boys are teenagers from the surrounding estates, but a few come from elsewhere in the Republic, and two from the adjoining island of Puerto Rico. González lectures them on the team's signals, going through the cryptically spastic motions of a third base coach until an assistant calls *"Jefe,"* and points to a group of young men in Houston Astros uniforms filing onto the field, led by a short, round man in a blue nylon Mizuno sweat suit and orange wraparound sunglasses.

González claps his large hands together and shouts, "OK! *Vamos.* Let's play some baseball."

As his players separate into two groups, one that takes to the field and another that retires to the dugout, Gonzáles greets Bell Arias, the Houston rookie team's manager, and deftly nabs the latter's orange shades and tries them on. When play begins, the two men sit on folding chairs near the backstop where they watch their charges and take notes, while their assistants run the two teams through a summer league rookie game.

These contests are daily occurrences in San Pedro, where almost a dozen major league clubs maintain a year-round presence. González and Arias, both former Dominican pros, are but two of San Pedro's native sons who have joined its sporting professoriate in recent years as the city has become one large prep school for the baseball world.

Bell Arias, the senior of the two, played for San Pedro during the 1937 championships. Then a slender reserve center fielder, he picked up his nickname, Bell, for his purported resemblance to Cool Papa Bell, *Ciudad Trujillo's* center fielder that season. He has since bulked up to 195 pounds spread over a five-feet-eight-inch frame and now more resembles the Liberty Bell than the svelte Hall-of-Famer. Arias played for the legendary *Papagayo,* the La Romana estate ball club, and then for the *Estrellas.* He ended his career in 1957, the same year Pedro González broke into Dominican league play.

Seventeen years Arias's junior, González was born in the Miramar section of San Pedro in 1938. His father was Puerto Rican, his mother Dominican-born to St. Martin islanders. When his parents separated, González moved with his mother to the Angelina estate, where he lived until baseball beckoned him away.

"I had about six uniforms as a boy," González chortles in the distinct West Indian-accented English of the *Cocolos.* "I just want to be sure I can play somewhere. It didn't matter much to me what team I play for as long as I was in the lineup."

And in the lineup he was, for *San Rafael, Aurora,* and even Consuelo's *Santa Ana* club. One year, he, and future pros Elvio Jiménez and Amado Samuel from the Santa Fe estate played for a team run by the Haitian vice-consul in San Pedro called *Fraternidad Dominicana de Hayti.* By the time González was eighteen, *Aviación* drafted him and Ricardo Joseph, another Santa Fe *Cocolo,* to play for Ramfis Trujillo's team, along with Marichal, Mota, and the two Jiménez brothers from Santa Fe. By 1957, González was defending second base for *Licey* in winter play, the first of his seventeen seasons in Dominican ball. And in 1963, González debuted in Yankee Stadium.

After five seasons with the Yankees and the Cleveland Indians, González asked for his release when faced with demotion to the minors. He wound up managing Tampico in the Mexican League and then became a scout for Atlanta. He now directs scouting for the Braves in the Caribbean, runs their rookie team in San Pedro, and for several seasons, also managed the *Estrellas Orientales* in winter play.

Six feet tall, González has the height and musculature that only the Dominican ballplayers of English descent seem to possess. An articulate, thoughtful man whose children attend medical school in San Pedro, González speaks to the forces that have made Macoris the most fecund source of baseball talent anywhere, anytime.

"I think we've always been better," González says like a true *Macorisano,* "but lately, there's never been anything like it." Of the hundred plus Dominicans to have played in the majors by 1988, over a third came via San Pedro. And while the *Cibao* offered Ozzie Virgil, Juan Marichal, and Diomedes Olivo to the pros in the late 1950s and Santo Domingo sent its progeny during the 1960s, since the 1970s, San Pedro de Macoris has provided the most bountiful harvests.

"The people from the estates never had anything to do," González comments. "You go there when the cropping season is over and you see the old men playing dominos and younger people playing baseball. Once the season is over, what you gonna do, sit on your butt? NO! You play ball, that's what you gonna do."

Perhaps half of San Pedro's baseball paladins have had, like González, English antecedents. And many of the non-English *Macorisano* ballplayers grew up in the estates alongside them, influenced by the *Cocolos'* approach to sport.

"The English have a very organized, very disciplined community here," González argues. "They don't steal; they don't drink. They grow up with manners. If the father says nine o'clock in bed, it don't mean ten after nine. That carries over to baseball."

And González concludes, "We are a big people. Look at Rico Carty, George Bell, Pedro Guerrero, myself. We all have English blood and we are each bigger than most Dominicans."

Heritage is of less and less consequence these days, González explains, because the highly competitive baseball culture in San Pedro has been stamped in the English mold. Discipline has become internalized as an item of faith. Thus, the distinction between English and Dominican has waned. "We are all born here now. When I managed the Consuelo team in the 1970s, it didn't matter if a boy was born to English or Dominican parents. They all Dominicans."

When González managed the Consuelo team, he fielded a club that had Alfredo Griffin and Nelson Norman in the infield and Rafael Ramírez in right field. Rafael Santana and Julio César Franco joined the team a year later. Each would make it to the majors and all but Norman are still there. And although each played shortstop in the big leagues, the position generally considered to require the best infielder on the team, that did not mean each was good enough to do so for the Consuelo team.

"These boys are hungry," González declares with a gesture that encompasses the players and the growing number of spectators. "There's not a lot of work in San Pedro these days. And what job here could pay what they can make in the majors?

"We did almost everything on our own when I was coming up. Now, the government and the mills sponsor baseball. That's a big difference. You should see what La Romana does for baseball. Here in San Pedro, there are hundreds of teams. Every boy grows up with a bat and a ball—it's the first present a male baby gets in his crib—and every one that wants the chance to play gets it.

"The other big difference is that the major league teams are here now. There's a team at each of the estates. Toronto has Epy Guerrero's camp, the Dodgers have Las Palmas. This stadium is in use from morning to night almost every day of the year. Everywhere you look you find scouts. They don't miss a boy. And these boys are better prepared than we were. We don't only teach them how to play, but we give them lessons in English and try to make the adjustment easier for them when they go to the United States."

Since Rico Carty, San Pedro has sent César Cedeño, Joaquín Andújar, Alfredo Griffin, Pedro Guerrero, Juan Samuel, Tony Fernandez, Julio César Franco, George Bell, and Rafael Ramírez to all-star careers. Hundreds of other *Macorisanos* have played minor league ball, and thousands more are in training for a baseball career. The town of 80,000 remains perhaps the only one in the world that could form a credible major league franchise solely with local talent.

There are no comparable alternatives to a baseball career, at least no legal ones, and the boys know it. Ask them what they would do if not playing baseball and most answer with little enthusiasm that they would try to find work in the mills, the free zone, or in the growing hotel corridor on the coast west of town. Some look blankly and mumble, *"Nada. No hay trabajo aqui."* ("Nothing. There is no work here.")

Despite the frequent charge that these youths are being exploited, most are not forsaking more realistic vocational or educational options by devoting themselves to the sport. Few options exist in San Pedro and this is hardly the fault of baseball. Moreover, the decision to play ball is often made with family considerations in mind. If a boy signs a contract, his bonus usually goes to the family, frequently to buy a house. If he makes it to the minors, he stands the chance of making enough to start a business of his own upon returning. If he makes it to the majors, his life will be transformed.

But even if they make it, almost all of them will return to San Pedro each winter and after their playing days are over. These elder role models give the youth of this town a tangible sense of the possibility of making it. And it gives them a core of talented advisors who can frequently be found at the ballpark or on the local sandlot.

Every boy who leaves the island and returns to San Pedro a major leaguer raises the town's fever for the game. Baseball is an ever-present preoccupation that shows no signs of abating soon. Ask any kid on any *calle* where Joaquín Andújar or Alfredo Griffin lives and they will escort you there personally. Go to a ball field and wait during the winter, and chances are that a major or minor leaguer will soon appear and play alongside the boys who wish to join him in baseball's promised land.

As a result, baseball in the Dominican Republic has remained much closer to the way the game was in the United States before television, corporate ownership, and megabucks deepened the divide between players and fans. In San Pedro, that gap has yet to become a chasm. Though undeniably revered, the players have not become remote idols watched from afar, but men who put some of their time and money back into their town's sporting life. They are seen and heard, not just on the satellite transmissions of games from the United States, but in person, on the street, and on the field.

"Come back later and Joaquín will be here," González suggests, referring to the then St. Louis Cardinal pitcher who lives next door to Griffin. "He comes and works out and helps the boys some. I managed Joaquín when he was a boy in amateur ball. He had a temper then, too. I will never forget the day I had to take him out of a game. Joaquín ripped off his shirt and threw it and his glove into the stands. I had to toss him off the team. But you know, he's not what he seems to be in the United States."

A gust of wind lifts a pile of debris into the air, and before González can explain just what sort of *hombre* Joaquín Andújar is, a sheet of rain sweeps across the field. Nobody needs to officially call this game as the summer rains quickly turn the infield into a quagmire. González and Arias slap hands and make for their respective dugouts. They'll meet again tomorrow.

I decide to push on for La Romana, despite streets so flooded that cars hydroplane or stall. A boy *merengues* in the rain by the roadside; another dodges the splashes of each passing car, waving his shirt *toreador* style.

Maybe it's the sugar that makes this such a hyperkinetic society. It's in the air, in the food, absorbed through every pore and orifice. It could explain the superquick reflexes that Dominicans exhibit in every aspect of their lives, from the rapidity of their speech, to the *merengue,* to their driving where motorists honk at the car in front of them simultaneously with the light's change. And the quick hands of San Pedro's infielders. (The only hands faster that I've seen were those of the Santo Domingo black market moneychanger who somehow slipped single *peso* notes into the wad of money he was giving me instead of the promised twenties.)

Soon the rains cease and a rainbow appears, one end touching down in the cane fields, the other disappearing into the Caribbean, and I arrive in La Romana.

La Romana hugs the coast thirty-five kilometers east of San Pedro de Macoris. Originally built around a sugar factory, the town of 80,000 has diversified its economic base in recent years, adding a free zone and a swank tourist enclave, *Casa de Campo.* La Romana has broadened its sporting focus, too, but without losing its emphasis on baseball. And while Santo Domingo represents Dominican baseball's early romantic epoch, the *Cibao* its breakthrough to the major leagues, and San Pedro the flowering of the tropical game, La Romana might very well be its future.

The South Porto (sic) Rico Sugar Company cultivated the first cane around La Romana *circa* 1910 and shipped it to Puerto Rico for grinding. In 1917, the company dispensed with this cumbersome transshipment and built a mill by the sea, which, seventy-odd years later, grinds more sugar than any other single *ingenio* in the world. Its cane comes from fields that extend in a forty kilometer arc around the town, stretching as far as the arches of the shrine of the Virgin of Altagracia in Higüey. For most of the century, its holdings dwarfed those of every other estate in the country. Unlike most Dominican sugar concerns, La Romana escaped Trujillo's transparent takeover of the industry in the 1950s. It remained in private hands, passing from the South Porto Rico Sugar Company to Gulf and Western to its current owners, the Cuban-American Fanjul family.

The entrance to the mill is near a bust of Cuban independence leader José Marti, an incongruity in that the mill has long represented the sort of foreign power with whom Marti once jousted. Although the mill's former president, Carlos Morales, is now Vice-President of the

Republic, the town recently elected candidates of Juan Bosch's leftist *Partido Liberacíon Dominicana* as mayor and senator.

Better capitalized than the state-run mills, *Central Romana*, as it is now called, is also cleaner and more modern-looking than the other mills I have visited. Mill workers in San Pedro and La Romana tell me that from an employee's perspective, the company compares favorably to the state-run industry. Housing is visibly better around the mill than on San Pedro's estates, and the company operates mobile medical units that attend to those who live in its *bateyes*. The workers are paid more, too, and enjoy an unusually diversified sporting program.

In a well air-conditioned office where he directs public relations for the company, Francisco Micheli II sits behind his desk and tosses a small burlap bag of sugar with a red, green, and blue parrot painted on it into my lap. The parrot on the bag, he tells me, is a *papagayo*, once found in abundance in the region.

"*Papagayo* is also the name of the baseball team that the mill began many years ago. It was the first team sponsored by an *ingenio* in the Dominican Republic. And it was once the best. When my father, who worked for the company for fifty years, was in charge of it, there was a great rivalry with *Los Caballeros* of Santiago, which was the best team in all the Republic. *Papagayo* disputed their position of supremacy until the *Caballeros* were killed in a plane crash in 1948.

"Practically all the players then were workers for the company who at the same time were very dedicated to baseball. I have absolutely no doubt that, if at that time, there had been the openness there is now in the United States for players of color, many players that never went beyond being amateur players for *La Romana* would have made it to your big leagues."

Most of those who remember the beginnings of the team are dead but there is one man, I am told, who might be able to help me. He is called *"Buenas Noches."*

Danilo Troncoso, a third-generation mill worker who is Micheli's assistant director of public relations as well as a former *Papagayo* manager, helps me track him down.

"Buenas Noches" is standing barefooted in a pile of wood shavings, dressed in a white sleeveless tee-shirt, stained brown pants, and an *Azucareros* hat. He chisels a bat out of a block of wood turning on a lathe in an open-air workshop behind his modest home. Now 71, Rafael *"Buenas Noches"* Santana was the youngest member of the *Papagayo* team when it was formed in 1934.

"Cricket was played in times past around here even more than baseball, but Mr. Lawrence Martarell, a Cuban who was raised in the United States, where he had gone as a child, decided to start a team for the *ingenio.* He was crazy for baseball. When I was a boy, the police used to bother us when we played ball in the streets. I got taken to jail twice for that, but now they were going to make a team for us!"

With the help of North American engineer Enoch Corby Pratt, who managed the club, *Papagayo* melded Dominican and *Cocolo* sportsmen into the best team in the cane fields. Roberto Caines told me that they had a saying in Consuelo then that "You might as well pick up your bats and go home before *Papagayo* came," because they were going to beat you. Santana is happy to confirm its accuracy.

"I was born and raised here and started working for the mill for 25 *centavos* a day in 1934. I started playing for the team at the same time. I was a pitcher then, but you see this?" he says, pointing to a large scar on his right arm. "There was an accident in the mill and I could only bat and play second base afterwards."

In the beginning, the club was composed solely of mill workers who qualified for amateur status. "*No dinero! Nada!* Whoooo! All they gave me was a glove. But we were good!" he says, punctuating his remarks with the smack of a baseball bat against a block of wood.

In 1936, Santana went to San Pedro to play for the *Estrellas* in the championships. "Afterwards, I came back to *Papagayo* and got my job back in the mill."

The team began to change as the distinction between amateur and professional, never all that clear-cut, further eroded. With recruits like Tetelo Vargas, Loro Escalante, and the three Lucas brothers, each of whom played professionally elsewhere in the Caribbean, *Papagayo* became the scourge of the cane fields.

"This park," he says with a gesture to the ball field that virtually abuts his house, "*Buena Vista,* was filled with thousands of fans, so many that the police would have to come when teams visited to play us. And the fans would bet—on anything. And whenever I would get a hit—whooooo!—they would throw money at me. Once I made thirty *pesos* (then worth $30 U.S.) on a home run. They would stuff the money through the fence and I would send the batboy to collect for me.

"I could hit!" Santana declares as he smacks his bat down again. "I was dangerous at the plate. The good pitchers hated me."

For thirty seasons, Santana worked as a locomotive conductor on the estate's railways. Each day after work, "I went home, drank a *cafecito,* changed into my uniform, and headed for the field."

When he surrendered his spot on the *Papagayo* roster to a younger player, Santana switched to softball, a sport introduced to the Republic by Francisco Micheli's father. He also managed and coached the *Papagayo* team and could be found daily at the *Buena Vista* field next to his house, showing boys how to lay down a bunt or make the pivot on the double play.

Despite his 71 years, Santana looks like he could still hold his own in the batter's box. A far younger cousin of Santana's, also named Rafael Santana, played shortstop for the New York Mets in their 1986 championship season and now plays for the Indians. During the winter season, the younger Santana plays for the *Azucareros*, La Romana's team in the Dominican league for which *"Buenas Noches"* coaches.

The elder Santana, concentrating on his current craft, corrects me when I compliment his workmanship. "This is not a bat," he laughs, swinging what I had thought was a bat for a young boy. "It's a *macana*—a club—that some guy asked me to make to keep in his truck. But I made all my own bats when I played. I would not use a foreign one."

Before leaving, I ask how he came to be called *"Buenas Noches."* Santana cheerfully obliges me. "When I was eight, I used to play marbles all the time. We would make a circle on the ground and shoot these glass balls into it. Because of that, I would come to school with my school uniform all dirty. *Don* Leopoldo, my teacher, asked my father why I was the grimiest boy every day, despite my mother, may God have her in his glory always, who was very meticulous about cleaning my uniform.

"Well, the next day I was engrossed in my game of marbles and had the bad luck of having my back turned when my father appeared. It was already an hour past the start of school and he snuck up behind me and hit me so hard that it clouded my vision. His hand was harder than this hammer here! When I got to school, seeing that it was as dark as if it was night time, I said '*buenas noches, maestro*' and when I came back from that haze, all the kids started calling me that. And even when I played, that was how they knew me."

After we leave Santana ankle-deep in wood chips, Danilo Troncoso takes me to lunch at the company's seaside *Club de la Costa*, a place to which his father and grandfather, who both worked for the mill, would never have been admitted. Troncoso, 43, has worked for the company since he was a teenager and now directs its sporting program. He managed the *Papagayo* team for fifteen years and now scouts for the Texas Rangers. Eleven former *Papagayo* players, including Rafael Santana and Julio Solano, have made it to the pros, and over a half dozen boys Troncoso signed play in the minors.

Sitting under a thatched canopy by the pool, Troncoso sips a club soda and speaks of the country's need for diversification. Like many Dominicans, he recognizes sugar's dire consequences. "The crop has not yielded the kind of fruits that it once did. I do not see prices recovering to that level again anytime soon. The country needs to break its dependency on one crop."

But not, he responds to my prompting, on baseball. "It is good that we play other sports, too, but baseball is in our blood."

After lunch, we return to Francisco Micheli's office and talk about the reasons for *Central Romana*'s commitment to sport. A photo of the newly-constructed La Romana ballpark, named for his father, hangs next to one of the mill.

"Over the years, the *Central Romana* has given its support to amateur baseball. I believe that we contributed to enlarging the participation of the humble classes in the game of baseball. In the last few decades, that support has continued not only with *Papagayo* but extended itself to other teams in our region. We have about 100 *bateyes* and each has a team. Last year, there were perhaps 1500 boys on these teams. Now, our sporting program has diversified. In every *batey,* there is a multipurpose field for basketball and volleyball. We have programs in softball for older workers, swimming, track and field, and boxing for their children. We even have *fútbol* (soccer) and chess!

"We spend thousands and thousands of *pesos* each year on these programs. We have brought in coaches from New York to give clinics in basketball and even sent a boxing team to an amateur tournament in Madison Square Garden."

While no one seems to be able to provide an exact accounting, a 1980 article in *El Papagayo,* a magazine for La Romana's employees, spoke of over ten million *pesos* having been invested in the company's sporting infrastructure. That would have been over three million dollars at the 1980 rate of exchange.

"The *Central Romana* makes such an important economic investment of funds in the support of sport in general and baseball in particular because it understands that this is a way to contribute to the future of the youth. It is a business policy of ours to give the biggest backing possible not only to sports but to all areas of social life, here in La Romana, and throughout the whole region."

The mill employs between fifteen and twenty thousand workers, depending on the number of harvest hires. It also controls the duty-free manufacturing zone in town, cattle, citrus, and vegetable ranches elsewhere on the island, and the *Casa de Campo* complex.

A night at *Casa de Campo* would cost a mill worker several months' pay. Make it past the vigilant guards at the tourist enclave's entrance and one enters a rarefied world whose ambience was selected by Dominican designer Oscar de la Renta.

The mostly foreign guests enjoying the white-stuccoed, orange-tiled villas that dot its 7,000 acres of countryside eschew baseball for polo and golf. The resort boasts two courses designed by Pete Dye, including the world-renowned Teeth of the Dog links whose fairways are bounded by the volcanic coastline. Although in close physical proximity to each other, *Casa de Campo* is as far away from the *bateyes* as one can get.

As for the *bateyes,* Micheli argues, "The firm has concerned itself that this situation called the *tiempo muerto* should not exist. After the *zafra,* employment doesn't go down like in years past. We try to find ways to keep the larger portion of our employees working during the time when there is no grinding of sugar cane. This personnel is maintained in the job of repair, in field work, in one way or another. People don't have to go back to their houses and wait for four to five months. What used to be called the *tiempo muerto* I would daresay does not exist anymore. That is a great accomplishment of the *Central Romana.*"

On another trip to La Romana, I meet Danilo Troncoso at an AA amateur contest between *Papagayo* and a team from *Batey* Higüeral at Francisco Micheli Stadium. Higüeral was once a village of small independent farmers, but during the marines' occupation, the mill expelled its residents and burnt their *bohíos* down. The company then claimed the land for the mill, an expropriation which the courts subsequently ratified. Now Higüeral's workers labor for the *ingenio.*

Troncoso exchanges elaborate handshakes and greetings with many of the fans, listens to a few grievances, and counsels Manny José, a minor leaguer whose career has been interrupted by torn ligaments. José stands on crutches, nodding as Troncoso discusses his rehabilitation and future prospects.

The stadium is both the newest and the nicest park in the country, with reddish dirt base paths and a blue-green Bermuda grass outfield. Season ticket holders for winter league games have their names painted on their seats. The stadium clock even works.

It's a Sunday morning and female fans must be worshipping elsewhere, for the spectators are overwhelmingly male. The *Papagayo* players range from 18 to 30 years old, and all are employed at the factory. Rafael, who was born on *Central Romana* property, pitched for a *batey* club at 15 and was recruited by the *La Policía* team three years later to play in Santo Domingo. "I pitched for them, and they paid me as if I were a cop." He then returned to La Romana where he cuts the stadium grass, cares for the field, and plays baseball. "It's easy," he grins, "but I don't want to do this forever." Other players are watchmen or have comparably taxing work.

When he can, Rafael attends classes in mechanical engineering at UCE, the *Universidad Central del Este* in San Pedro, a school founded by José Hazim, one of the original backers of the *Estrellas*. He asks about the job market for mechanics in Detroit and Pittsburgh and months later, he writes to ask if I can help with his tuition payments.

Only a few of these players still think about pro ball. Most Dominican prospects are already signed by the time they are eighteen or nineteen, and once a player has been signed and released, he is ineligible for amateur ball. The emphasis that the backers of AA teams place on winning means that they often field older players at the expense of younger ones. "That's why amateur baseball here is so weak," Troncoso argues.

"But watch the shortstop, Johnny Hernández," he urges. "His brother, Manuel, is in the Houston organization. This kid can pick it."

In the stands, fans discuss the AA teams from Boca Chica and San Pedro the way college basketball fans evaluate the personnel on their rivals' squads. A cluster of boys aged eight to eleven sits behind the first base dugout, betting as feverishly as traders on the commodities exchanges. Each bet is a *peseta,* less than a nickel, but the boys wager with gusto. One, a mocha-skinned boy wearing laceless sneakers, cutoffs, and a large Afro pick in his hair, performs a little *merengue* on the dugout roof each time he wins.

The play on the field is almost as good as the spectacle in the stands. At the end of the AA season, La Romana will select a squad composed of its best AA players to compete in a regional competition. By September, the regional selections will play for the national championships.

I had come to La Romana with a certain degree of suspicion regarding the company's role in the community. After all, Gulf & Western seemed to personify the multinational corporation running amok in the Third World. I thought about my session with Francisco Micheli II, and while I realized that his profession was public relations, my visual impressions and the testimony of many workers seemed to corroborate his claims. Even union activists I talked with confirmed that La Romana was a preferred employer.

But one former *Papagayo* player who still works for the company reminds me that the motive behind its support of baseball was not altogether altruistic. "They wanted to win our hearts and minds," he tells me as we chat outside the factory. "It is good promotion for them, and gives something to the workers that everybody likes. That makes us think more kindly of them."

Juan Villali, who worked as an office manager for the company for decades and helped Francisco Micheli run *Papagayo,* adds that "The motive of the company, I should say, was to give all the hands the opportunity of having baseball so that they are satisfied. It keeps up morale, reduces absenteeism, and keeps turnover down. It helps maintain the community, because the *central* is the basis of the community."

A red-haired anthropologist from Notre Dame further illuminates the question during a blackout-plagued evening in Santo Domingo later that summer. Martin Murphy might have walked out of a course with Margaret Mead after 45 minutes, but he has stuck around the Dominican cane fields longer than most social scientists. He married a Dominican woman and heads the department of anthropology at *El Museo del Hombre Dominicano,* for which he pulls down the princely sum of $56 a month at the current rate of exchange.

Somehow managing to look cool despite the incredible heat, Murphy sips beer and reviews the considerable study of the Dominican sugar industry and its labor practices that he wrote for his dissertation at Columbia University.

When I ask what he thinks about La Romana's sporting and social welfare program, Murphy places their largesse in a broader, historical context. The keys, he argues, are the takeover of La Romana by Gulf & Western in 1967 and the way that the corporation responded to Dominican law.

"Gulf & Western had an amazing corporate growth as it went from being a small company with 200 employees in Grand Rapids, Michigan in the 1950s to one of the major United States-based multinationals in 1967 when it took over the South Porto Rico Sugar Company. Much of G & W's success is due to its Swiss-born founder and president, Charles Bluhdorn. The man pulled off some truly hair-raising corporate capers."

Gulf & Western arrived in 1967, after the commotion from the 1965 revolution and the subsequent military invasion by the United States had subsided. Its original investment of $62 million had exceeded $300 million by 1978. With sugar prices high, G & W was making substantial profits. "But," Murphy explains, "there was also a Dominican law that indirectly mandated further investment by foreign corporations operating here by putting a ceiling of 18 percent on the profits which could be repatriated."

Pausing to light a cigarette, Murphy continues. "This law is a good example of an ideologically liberal piece of legislation which backfired. It attempted to curb excess profits being sent out of the country with no benefits to the nation. The 82 percent of the profits not repatriated to Gulf & Western in the U.S. would have to either be turned over to the Dominican government, given to charity, or be reinvested in the economy. Gulf & Western chose to give it to charity or reinvest."

Some of this profit went toward purchasing other businesses, including the country's largest cattle ranch. Some of it went into making *Casa de Campo* a jet-setter's haven.

Bluhdorn, who took a special interest in G & W's Dominican holdings, spent millions constructing a replica of a 16th century European village called *Altos de Chavón*. Perched on a hillside above the slow-moving Chavón river and descending layers of royal palms, *Altos de Chavón* projects a timeless quality at odds with the trendy boutiques it houses.

Other revenue was contributed to the *Universidad Central del Este* in San Pedro, which in turn provided the company with better-trained employees. Still more, Murphy explains, funded the elaborate sporting and social welfare activities in La Romana and its outlying *bateyes*.

"Obviously, these programs had social merit, but G & W also was wise enough to directly or indirectly benefit from them. They allowed the corporation to maintain a high public relations profile. These sporting programs generally diverted demands for better working conditions and higher pay, and in that respect, they were consciously run to the company's benefit, and they still are, even though G & W is gone.

"Understand that Charles Bluhdorn thought of G & W's Dominican operations as a special project. He stated that he would show what multinational capital and modern technology and administration could do for a developing country. On the other hand, other board members said that the tourist side of their holdings here were losing money and that the bad publicity created by the living and working conditions of the Haitian plantation workers wasn't worth the profits that the sugar operations made."

In 1983, as he was flying back to the United States from *Casa de Campo,* an already gravely ill Charles Bluhdorn succumbed. G & W sold its Dominican holdings to Alfonso and José Pepé Fanjul shortly afterwards. But the new owners maintained the extensive sporting program that Danilo Troncoso and Rafael Santana believe will someday allow La Romana to rival San Pedro as the island's mother lode of baseball players. Murphy, a font of knowledge about the island, talks until the supply of beer is exhausted and I'm ready to return to my hotel room. The power goes off, and as I make my way down the darkened stairway, I hear Murphy sigh and say, "Damn! I wanted to take a shower."

The "miracle of Macoris," as San Pedro's pipeline to the majors has been dubbed, is a hybrid of the *Cocolos'* sporting offspring grafted to Dominican stock. The resulting progeny have flourished in the network of teams, leagues, and instruction that has taken hold in and around

San Pedro. Now based in the sugar estates and their *bateyes* and backed by the government and the sugar workers' syndicate, Macoris baseball has widened baseball's traditional sources of talent and will shape its future on the field as much as any town in the world.

In Consuelo, boys play baseball day in and day out, in the blazing sun and in the rain, on the complex of fields across from the *Santa Ana* church. I don't recall ever passing the fields when some sort of game is not underway.

On this early January day in 1987, I find a handful of boys at play with 28-year-old Julio César Franco sitting in the stands, kibitzing their game. Franco, in stocking feet and jock, wrings the moisture out of his sweat-soaked baseball pants and tugs on a *Presidente* beer.

Then an infielder with Cleveland, Consuelo-born Franco was sitting out the 1987 winter season. "I got hurt playing last year in winter ball. I'm a free agent next year and it's just too big a chance for me to play," he says with an apologetic smile.

A youth tosses Franco a towel and he rubs it through his black Jheri-curled hair. "I'm just working out with these boys and trying to get into shape for spring training."

In his first six full years with Cleveland, Franco averaged close to .300 at the plate with over seventy RBIs per season. He also led the Indians in AWOL disappearances when homesickness and unhappiness struck. The Indians traded him to the Texas Rangers before the 1989 season; two thirds of the way through that campaign, Franco was leading the league in RBIs and hitting well over .300, while his image had undergone a makeover from erratic malcontent to solid team player and confidant to the Rangers' younger Latin players.

Keeping one eye on the field while we talk, Franco yells instruction and some encouragement to the players. "I grew up right here in *Pueblo Nuevo,* with Alfredo (Griffin) and Nelson (Norman) and played with them on the Consuelo amateur team. Rafael Ramírez would come from Angelina and Rafael Santana all the way from La Romana to play with us. Some team, huh?"

When he returns to the island each winter, Franco stays with his family in Consuelo. He doesn't know yet if he will build a home in the ballplayers' ghetto in San Pedro, but realizes that the sort of dwelling he can now afford would dwarf anything Consuelo has ever known.

Although Franco had taken a beating in the Cleveland press, it was nothing compared to what Blue Jay George Bell suffered in Toronto. The 1987 American League MVP and home run champ, who hails from the Santa Fe estate, was excoriated by the press for his accusations that the umpires were unfair to Latins and for his unwillingness to switch to designated hitter for the Blue Jays. In 1989, Bell was so rankled by

Toronto fans that he was moved to taunt "They can kiss my Dominican ass."

Other Dominicans have encountered criticism, including Rico Carty who was sometimes perceived as a malcontent, and Alberto Lois, a Consuelan the Pirates once thought might help fill some of the void created by Roberto Clemente's tragic death.

Lois had both tremendous natural abilities and an instinct for the game. "Lois could flat out play," I had been told once by Branch B. Rickey, then the Pirates' minor league director. But he had little discipline. Nelson Norman, who grew up with Lois there and played with him in the Pittsburgh farm system, told me that Lois was so good he could come to the park drunk (which he sometimes did) and still get two or three hits. "It was such a waste," Nelson told me before a game in San Pedro one evening. "He had as much potential as anyone I've seen."

After breaking into the majors at the end of the 1979 season, Lois looked as if he would stay there for years. But as fleet of foot as Lois was, he could not outrun the train that smashed into his pickup truck as he crossed the railroad tracks by the cemetery outside Consuelo late one night as he was returning from the ballpark. Six died, three others were hurt, and Lois lost enough sight in one eye to end his playing days forever.

I find him sitting wrapped in a brown towel in La Loma, a *barrio* in Consuelo. A Rico Carty baseball card is tacked to the wall next to a photo of Lois in his Pirate uniform. He doesn't work; he no longer plays. His future lies trapped in his past.

Of all the Dominican major leaguers, none has built a more outrageous public persona for himself than Joaquín Andújar. (Pasqual Pérez, the histrionic Montreal Expo pitcher, who was arrested in Santiago in 1984 for possession of cocaine and once failed to make it to the ballpark in time to pitch because he became hopelessly lost on the Atlanta beltway, may yet rival him, but he still has a way to go.)

A twenty-game winner in 1984 and 1985, Andújar came across as a hotdog and a hothead to fans in the States, mostly because of his tempestuous exits in the seventh game of both the 1982 and 1985 World Series. In 1982, Andújar was pitching St. Louis to victory in the final game and closed the seventh inning by fielding Milwaukee Brewer second baseman Jim Gantner's comebacker. After he held the ball until the last possible moment before throwing to first, he and Gantner exchanged words. Umpire Lee Weyer intervened and pulled Andújar off the field with help from Cardinal pitching coach Hup Kittle, who had once managed Andújar on the *Estrellas*. Cardinal manager Whitey Herzog did not let Andújar stay in to finish the game.

Three years later, the sight of Andújar, screaming and ready to fight anybody on the field, charging off the mound in the seventh game of the 1985 World Series after the Cardinals had totally self-destructed, is an even harder image to erase. Andújar had lost his composure again before a worldwide audience. Joaquín's earlier eccentricities, such as showering in his uniform and pouring milk over his head after losses, only added to his public portrait.

But if you ask most *Macorisanos* about Andújar, their answers will usually approximate that of Modesto Nivar, a former AA player who works at the *Costa Linda* hotel at *Playa* Juan Dolio, near San Pedro. *"Joaquín es un poco loco,"* Modesto says as he taps his head, *"pero tiene un grande corazon."* The kids waiting outside his house for gifts the morning of Three Kings Day each year would probably agree.

While boys and girls come running from blocks away, afraid that they will miss out, others sit on the curb clutching their bats or gloves as if they will vanish if they loosen their grips. When I ask if ballplayers other than Andújar and Griffin give gifts for *Reyes,* one boy says *"No, son duros"* (No, they are hard.) and hits his fingers against his elbow for emphasis. In fact, some other players, including the oft-maligned Bell, help out in one way or another. No one, however, matches Andújar's generosity.

Whatever the truth in the allegations regarding San Pedro's players, there is also the reality that these men are performing in an alien cultural milieu that understands little about their background. There is little appreciation outside the Caribbean that so many of the Dominican ballplayers have a distinct, *Cocolo* heritage about which they are fiercely possessive. And too many North American whites seem to see only color, and vent their frequent hostility toward Afro-Americans on Latin Americans. While racism is a problem in the Dominican Republic, it manifests itself quite differently than in the United States. Rico Carty's arrest in 1971 suggests why some Dominican players have become angry and distant while in the United States.

Two white policemen had been killed in a black Atlanta neighborhood that summer and the city was edgy. Coming back from a restaurant, Carty and his brother, Carlos, stopped at a light on Peachtree Avenue alongside two white plainclothes policemen talking abusively to a black man in the back seat of their car.

"They calling this guy 'nigger' and Carlos asks me in Spanish what's going on," Rico recounts. "I say you in a different country now and one of the white guys say 'What the hell you laughing about, nigger?' I say 'Hey! Wait a minute. You is more nigger than me because you is American and I'm not!'

"When the light change, he just take his car and go bam! Bash right into my car. I had just taken the cast off my leg and the doctor said I had to be real careful so I just got out of the car when I see a police car coming. You see, I didn't know they were cops dressed as civilians.

"But the other guy says Carlos and me the cop-killing niggers! He took his gun out and I raise my hands and look for Carlos. He's already in the police car with his head busted open. Then, I'm on the ground and they is beating the hell out of me. I never seen anything like it. I hear sirens coming from all over and the guy puts his knee on my stomach and slaps handcuffs on me.

"I say what the hell you all trying to do, mess up my career? And this detective says 'Goddamn! This is Rico! What you doing here?' He gets me up and says 'Goddamn, Rico, you! These s-o-b muthafuckers!' He was blowing like a crazy man and he hit the cops."

After a court appearance, Carty was cleared of any allegations of wrongdoing and the policemen involved were suspended without pay. "But I stay on the disabled list the rest of the season, and was hurt for part of the next one, too. I remember this letter that I got. Most of them were supporting me, but this one said, 'Rico, you is a Dominican, but you still is a nigger to me.' "

While such problems are generally not as severe as they once were, the cultural discord lingers and is not likely to totally abate any time soon.

As I watch Franco standing in his socks, showing a young boy how to position himself to field a ball, and I look behind the field to the neighborhood from which he came, I wonder if the stereotype of the temperamental Latin would change if more North American fans were to share this tableau.

Postscript:
Season's End

The lights are going out in Santo Domingo, and like so many aspects of the Dominican Republic's recent descent into economic chaos, it's affecting baseball. As I bluff my way through traffic made even more anarchic than usual by the lack of streetlights, I wonder if there will even be a game this evening. Or, for that matter, whether winter ball will survive much longer.

The streets outside *Estadio Quisqueya* are dark; a few motorbikes and cars lurch out of swirling clouds of black exhaust fumes. I park across the street, pay a few *pesos* to the man who will watch over my vehicle, and join the 200 or so fans circulating outside the ballpark. The crowd, the smallest I've ever seen, is relatively subdued. So is the contingent of soldiers that stands at ease behind the screened entrance to the stadium.

The players, from the *Licey* and *Aguilas* ball clubs, recline in clusters on the grass inside. A couple take a form of batting practice, hitting balls tossed laterally from a few feet away into a net. Soon, as darkness becomes nearly complete, they hit off a tee. Then even that becomes impossible.

A lone player runs sprints from foul pole to foul pole. Boys sitting on the fence hoot and whistle at him; a few streak across left field. Only a crescent moon and Venus cast any light on this early December evening. Gradually, the Big Dipper becomes visible, standing straight up to form a celestial question mark that might as well be asking if tonight's game will be played.

It's too dark to make out any of the players and I wander in the outfield until I find a spot to my liking in center field. I sit and wonder if I am witnessing winter ball's end.

In the years I have been investigating winter ball's past, its very future has come into question. Attendance in the Dominican Republic and on neighboring Puerto Rico has been halved in recent years, knocking one Dominican franchise out of action and threatening several Puerto Rican clubs. Similar crises have been brewing in the Venezuelan and Mexican leagues. Those close to the game are asking what it will take to ensure winter baseball's survival in the 1990s.

The causes of winter ball's woes are complex, both economic and cultural in nature. Some of the problems lie within the winter game, others are a result of the region's overall decline.

The Dominican Republic's economic collapse in the late 1980s is part of a slide that has seen much of Latin America regress to a level last seen during the 1930s. Nearly two years into an economic downturn in which inflation and the exchange rate for the *peso* with the U.S. dollar have soared and living standards have fallen, the country suffers from severe electrical shortages, a lack of potable water, and a transportation system in suspended motion. The ballparks, once a beacon of light in the evening sky, now often remain dark until shortly before game time.

Just when I think that tonight's game will be called, the generator deep within the bowels of the stadium kicks in and bulbs pop on in the light stanchions with a fireworks-like flourish. At first, nobody moves, then gradually bodies rise stiffly from the grass and walk onto the field.

I find Winston Llenas, now general manager for the *Aguilas*, standing not far from the dugout he skippered for most of the 1980s, and ask for his assessment of the winter game.

"Dominicans haven't lost their love of the game," Llenas attests, "but this society is in trouble, serious trouble. It's living dangerously now. Stress was never a word used in Spanish here. We didn't even know the word. Now, it's very common."

While only a few games have actually been canceled due to power outages, many fans are staying home at night. "They're becoming afraid to go out in the dark," Llenas notes. "And when the game is over, it's past midnight and they can't get taxis or buses home. . . .

"But perhaps our biggest problem," Llenas offers, "is the lack of desire on the part of the established players to play." Indeed, as salaries have spiraled upward since the players won free agency and major league baseball embarked upon its most profitable epoch ever, the incentive for the better-known Latins to play winter ball has all but disappeared.

Winter ball, which rarely pays even its top players more than $7,000 a month, offers little to a player who has signed a multimillion-dollar contract. And it does offer the risk of a career-ending injury, as well as the long bus rides and the cold water showers.

Just five years ago, players such as Pedro Guerrero, Tony Fernández, Juan Samuel, Julio Franco, Pascual Pérez, Tony Peña, and Alfredo Griffin were in the winter lineup. The Dominican winter league could have fielded a credible major league franchise with its native sons alone. Now, only a few established major leaguers play, and most of them suit up only late in the season.

"They lose face if they play from Day One," Llenas explains.

Most winter-ball players are now minor leaguers, increasingly from the lower levels. Juan Marichal, who joins the conversation, considers this the root cause of winter ball's crisis.

"We are accustomed to seeing real quality baseball in this country," Marichal says. "The fans want at least Triple-A prospects out there. They've had better than that in the past.

"When I go to the United States, I tell the people there that we can sometimes see five major league games a day. Dominican fans have been spoiled by television, especially by cable and dish antennas."

Marichal, who pitched for *Escogido* during most of his tenure with the Giants, dates the problem to the late 1970s. "Before then, we made very little money in the States and the salary here was attractive. Then, the Alous, Manny Mota, Rico Carty, Julian Javier, and many others would play." They were joined by scores of major leaguers from the States who supplemented their pre-free agency income with winter ball.

Moreover, television, discos, and other sports have made inroads during the 1980s. It's particularly evident in Santo Domingo, where young Dominicans prowl the *malecón* on weekend nights, every other car radio blasting *merengue*. This generation has strayed from the church of baseball, perhaps never to return.

I think for a moment of the basketball court by the track at the *Universidad Católica Madre y Maestra* in Santiago. While Santiago will never rival Chapel Hill for basketball, the action on the court there gets better each year.

I recall sitting one evening after a run at the track there, watching the players weave into fast breaks on the court. I asked some of the guys waiting for winners whether the Dominican game's recent improvement had something to do with the Dominican Yorks, natives who have lived in New York and brought basketball, the city game, back with them. They didn't think so. I then ask whether contact with Puerto Rico, where basketball is supplanting baseball as *el rey de deportes,* might have had something to do with it. They nix that thought, too. Finally, one of them points skywards. "We pick it up on the dish," he says. "We learn our moves by watching Magic and Michael on television."

When I ask why they prefer basketball to baseball, they smile and refer to themselves as the *nueva gente,* literally the new people of the city, as distinguished from the traditional rural folk. I guess once you've skyed with Air Jordan, you never want to come down.

But not all of winter ball's problems are the result of cultural change and economic collapse. Rafael Avila, who runs the Dodgers' academy at Las Palmas, argues that "For too long, the owners have felt that the people had an obligation to come to the game. That it was tradition. But they haven't given them clean facilities. And they don't realize that professional baseball is also a business. To make money they have to invest money.

"In the past, nobody put any attention to these things. But in the past, there were no alternatives to baseball. Now there are."

Another factor, specific to the Dominican Republic, was the league's expansion from four to six teams for the 1983–84 season. "Expansion," says Llenas, "has been good for the players, but bad for the fans and the teams. We are traditionalists here. The people want to see the four original clubs."

Expansion diluted the talent pool, but a more critical factor was the failure of the San Cristobal *Caimanes* franchise. That left the league with a lopsided five-team schedule for two of the past five years. Even when they played, the *Caimanes* drew poorly, both at home and on the road. The other expansion club, the *Azucareros* of La Romana, has done better. Still, Dominicans prefer to see the almost century-long rivalries of *Licey* versus *Escogido,* and San Pedro against Santiago.

The week before, I had found that winter ball's malaise was even more profound in Puerto Rico. If the Dominican Republic embodies third world underdevelopment, Puerto Rico personifies the cultural dislocation of a society undergoing the transition from a sleepy agricultural island to a society as fast-paced as its unofficial capital, New York. And all in a matter of decades.

This season caps 52 years of Puerto Rican winter ball and the game is still strong at the grassroots. With the emergence of Benito Santiago, Rubén Sierra, Roberto and Sandy Alomar, Juan Nieves, and José Lind, Puerto Ricans are witnessing a contingent of stars not seen in some time. But the league verges on collapse.

Luis Rodriguez-Mayoral, a front-office administrator for the San Juan Metropolitans, chain-smokes Salems in an office adorned with photographs of Bart Giamatti and Fay Vincent. With his Texas Rangers jacket half zipped for protection against the air conditioner, he fingers his brush mustache and reflects on the devolution of the Puerto Rican game.

"Our decline began in the late 1970s. It is mostly due to the fact that before the 1980s, we were able to get real name players to come to Puerto Rico—be they natives or players from the United States. They were players, though, who had paid their dues."

In the 1950s and '60s, Roberto Clemente, Orlando Cepeda, Juan Pizzaro, and Vic Power were joined by Willie Mays, Tommy Davis, and Don Zimmer. One year, the Santurce *Cangrejeros* outfield was Clemente, Mays, and former Homestead Grays slugger Bob Thurman. Its current outfield consists of three minor leaguers.

"Shortly after free agency began to bloom," Rodriguez-Mayoral continues, "even journeymen players began to reap the monetary rewards. And then"—he throws up his hands as if to say what's the use.

"Once they get into the money, there's no hunger to play winter ball. Take Ruben Sierra. He's on the verge of getting his first million dollar contract and there is no way Texas will let him play. It's not necessary to tell players that they can't play. There's no way they will risk their futures."

Rodriguez-Mayoral accepts some of the responsibility for the league's problems. "I'm within the game, but the mentality of the front-office people here is such that they don't seek to learn from public relations people or about promotions in the States. Damn! If the Russians were number one in baseball, I'd go to Russia!

"There is a lack of business aptitude by the owners. And unlike the States," he emphasizes, jabbing his finger in the air, "owners don't work hand-in-hand. There is a market out there. There are corporate sponsors. But the owners have not gotten together to sell a product."

Would it be all that bad if professional baseball collapsed in the islands? If the sport reverted to its sandlot past?

I think it would be a profound loss. Not only would major league baseball lose a vital training grounds and several already poor countries a functioning business employing thousands, but these societies would be deprived of the professional level of the game which has become virtually a Pan-Caribbean art form and the one arena in which they have been able to compete with the North Americans on equal footing.

"Never forget," says Mayoral-Rodriguez, "that this game is a vehicle for bringing people together. Baseball has a social and a political aspect, too."

In the Dominican Republic, it is frequently said that given the game's potency for distracting Dominicans from their often grim economic and social realities, there will never be political trouble during the season—only afterwards. For that reason, governments from Trujillo on down have subsidized Dominican baseball. But these subsidies no longer seem adequate.

What, then, can be done? The most frequently heard prescriptions for winter ball's recovery include a strong dose of savvy marketing and promotions as well as direct subsidies from major league baseball.

"We need to start courting back the fans," Llenas argues. "We must promote our game better." Some of that is beginning. Llenas's club admits any boy wearing a baseball uniform for free, but giveaway items such as painters' caps or helmets, which have become regular features in the United States, are still a rarity in the Caribbean. And stadium amenities are few.

In the past, Dominican clubs split their gate fifty-fifty between the home and visiting clubs. "Next year," Llenas explains, "the league will not have a common fund. Each club will have to scratch for itself because it will be one hundred percent for the home club."

Puerto Rican baseball lacks that sense of marketing and promotion, too, says Rodriguez-Mayoral. He argues for better cooperation among clubs and finding corporate sponsors.

But greater business acumen might not be enough, given the depths of the Caribbean basin's slide. That's why many here argue that major league baseball should directly subsidize winter ball.

Llenas points to the benefits that have accrued to major league baseball from winter ball. "It's been a good partnership. Look at the resumes of players, managers, and even umpires in the United States. You have a saying there, 'What's good for General Motors is good for the USA.' Well, what's good for winter baseball is what's good for the major leagues.

"They should not let us die," he implores. "Not when we need their help."

Juan Marichal concurs. "They should pay subsidies. It's the only way Dominican baseball can survive."

But if the desire for subsidies is broadly based in the Caribbean, the idea has fewer adherents to the North.

"What I fear," admits Rodriguez-Mayoral, "is that one day baseball people in the United States are going to get pissed off and start their own winter league in the States."

That day might not be far away. According to Bill Murray, Director of Baseball Operations for the major leagues, "There appears to be growing sentiment for a United States winter league."

By competing for U.S. minor leaguers, such a league would further weaken winter ball in the Caribbean and make subsidies an unlikely possibility.

"Major league baseball has no position on subsidies," Murray contends. "The question hasn't been put to us. Right now, we are seeing what happens. They haven't come to us to seek support. If they did, I don't know if support would be voted by the major league clubs. I don't know that we should step up and take over everything down there."

Murray says that the major leagues understand that there have been financial difficulties "down below," and that some brief discussion with regard to promotion and moving the Caribbean Series to the mainland have occurred. "If they would specifically request it, we would try to get people together and create a task force to help review the area.

"These people," Murray acknowledges, "are people we've known for some time, and we hate to see friends in financial trouble."

But the initiative for subsidies will not be forthcoming from major league baseball in the near future.

The morning after the nearly-blacked-out game, I talk with Tom Reich, an attorney who has represented Latin ballplayers since 1971. He is not a disinterested observer of the tumultuous changes affecting baseball, given that he represents about thirty-five Latin ballplayers. Seated in the penthouse suite at the *Jaragua,* Santo Domingo's swankiest digs, Reich adds further perspective to the unmaking of the winter game.

"Remember that once there were three classes of citizenship in baseball and Latins were the third. It stayed that way into the '80s when the differential in salaries all but disappeared."

Reich, who also represents a significant number of black ball-players, was a major force in erasing racial bias in salaries. But increasing equity in pay, coming during the free agency era, has radically restructured the relative pay scales of the major leagues and winter baseball. The upshot is that the economic pressure for Latin stars to play winter ball has decreased.

"There are no stipulations in contracts that stop native players from playing," the curly-haired, fifty-year-old Reich explains. "But the club's influence is strong."

Moreover, a player who has attained free agency or arbitration, or who is negotiating a new contract, would place his economic future in jeopardy by risking injury in winter ball until his contract had been signed.

"I never tell a player not to play in front of his home aficionados," attests Reich, a Pittsburgh native who rarely hesitated when it came down to attending either Forbes Field or his classes at the University of Pittsburgh next door. "I do tell a player not to beat himself to death."

Reich agrees that winter ball needs to get a fix on itself and that subsidies are in order. But he goes further.

"I feel very strongly about this, that major league baseball as an entity, the teams that set up shop here, and the union, which is an affluent union, should be doing more for these people. It's very depressing. There's much more that should be done for the community, the league, and the state of baseball here.

"I am in favor of subsidies by the institutionalized elements as far as the sustenance of the league and the institution of baseball down here. And the local players have to be a big part of it. And it is, in part, the agents' responsibility to help—by bringing together those guys who want to be more vocal and influential—galvanizing their efforts."

Reich, who alludes frequently to Bart Giamatti during his remarks, argues a point that the late commissioner made. "I think that baseball should be a socially responsible institution."

He concludes by mixing metaphors that would have made the classicist-*cum*-commissioner groan, but his point is clear. "There's plenty of pie there and some of it should go to the game's roots."

That night, I return to San Pedro de Macoris. It still smells the same as it always has as I cross the *Río Higuamo* into San Pedro. A vinegarish smell of bagasse, the waste product of refining sugar cane, wafts across the darkening purple and orange sky. There is a new Mitsubishi power plant on one side of the bridge, but it's yet to come on line.

(Later, I discover that the Japanese, whose presence grows daily in the islands, are constructing a baseball academy on the road to Consuelo. The Hermit Kingdom has pursued baseball with singular devotion for over half a century and the Hiroshima Toyo Carp are building a facility that will rival the Dodgers' camp at Las Palmas. The Carp want to create a few Dominican ballplayers with a Japanese mindset for their island's professional league. That they have turned to Latin ballplayers is in part a recognition that making proper Japanese ballplayers out of North Americans is a trying proposition.)

The lights are out in San Pedro, just as they were in Santo Domingo. Yet when the lights do come on, they reveal the possible rebirth of Dominican baseball in the making.

Baseball in San Pedro is closer to the game as it was once played in the United States during its sandlot seasons, with less distance separating players and fans. The atmosphere is even looser than usual when the lights come on, with four boys playing a pickup game not fifteen feet from where pitchers loosen up. They throw errant balls back to each other as if both have equal rights to the field. Behind the San Pedro dugout, a boy pitches plastic cups, crushed flat to twirl easily, with a lazy sidearm motion to San Pedro's David Segui.

A flip game, that decidedly Latin contribution to baseball, quickly commences. This one involves the entire La Romana team as well as several San Pedro players. A losers' bracket flip game soon gets going alongside it. Batting practice does not.

There's a hungrier and more juvenile ambience in the dugouts. The players are younger and more excited than in years past. They bench jockey with relish. A few toss pebbles at their first base coach and three sitting atop the dugout steps move in synchronized fashion to the *merengue* that plays between innings.

Five years ago, San Pedro's infield included Rafael Ramírez, Nelson Norman, and Alfredo Griffin. Now it's Rafael Bornigal at third, Manny Alexander at short, and César Bernhardt at second. That Alexander, an A ball player in only his first full year of pro ball, starts at short, is indicative of the degree of change. A few years ago, several shortstops who started in the majors were not starting at short here.

Yet it is Alexander's generation, which includes infielders José Offerman, José Vizcaino, and Juan "Tito" Bell, as well as outfielders Sammy Sosa, Junior Felix, Felix José, Moises Alou, and Braulio Castillo, that offers hope for Dominican ball.

"Give these kids a chance to mature," reasons Nelson Norman, now more of a coach than a player. "These guys were born catching rocks and when they get to a decent infield, whoooo! They're the future."

As if to illustrate his point, La Romana's José Offerman goes deep in the hole, spins, and nabs the runner at first in a play that has even a few of San Pedro's players exchanging high fives. In La Romana's dugout, manager Victor Ramírez raises one hand in the air as if to give religious testimony and exclaims, "What a talent!"

Winter ball's lack of established major leaguers means that youth like Offerman are experiencing an accelerated development. In a few years, Offerman will likely be in the majors and attracting Dominican fans back to the park. The cycle of regeneration is already at work.

But that process will take a few years, years that are not guaranteed. It seems improbable that such a vibrant institution as winter ball could end, but it's on my mind as I leave the ballpark and make my way to Juan Dolio, the small strip of beach along the highway from San Pedro to Santo Domingo.

I wind up at *La Barra Sonrisa* watching three couples dancing to a mix of world beat and *merengue* on the open-air veranda. They swirl across the smooth concrete floor, their sandals and Reeboks lubricated by a film of sand. You won't see these moves on MTV, but the images of the mostly empty stands and the blacked out city are difficult to shake. Gradually, though, other memories intrude.

I think of the boys at *Batey* 59, so-named because this community of cane cutters is fifty-nine kilometers north of Santo Domingo. I had watched them playing baseball with their bats made of sticks and mitts of cardboard cartons one day several years ago. It was the dead season, the time when cane grows by its own accord and the mills and cane workers sit idle. I remember how they had come running at me when I started snapping photos, pumping the air with their fists in jubilation and mugging for the camera. Only the three Haitian boys standing in an empty cane cart failed to join in. As long as baseball captivates boys like these, I think, the sport will make it through its current malaise.

I had a more primordial memory, too. I had needed a day off from baseball on one trip and drove into the mountains near Jarabacoa. I was looking for a waterfall along the *Jimenoa* River, and finally discovered it after driving high into the evergreen forest outside the small town. The pastel painted shacks and corn fields ascending the hillsides reminded me of the Guatemalan countryside.

I found the path to the waterfalls, which descended in a series of steep switchbacks through a tropical forest of spiked plants and vines. At the bottom was a basin constantly replenished by the hundred-foot cascade of water falling from above.

I was the only person there, and by the time I climbed back up the hillside, I had pretty much gotten baseball off my brain. My shirt was damp and I was feeling light-headed as I reached the meadow at the top of the ravine.

And then I begin to think I was hallucinating. At the end of the meadow, five young boys were playing bat and ball, a children's version of cricket that I had been hearing about for years, but had never actually seen. They had made their cricket wickets out of license plates bent at the edges and their ball out of some object wrapped in a nylon stocking. Their pitch was part of the meadow, with the vegetation scrubbed away so that they could bowl, bat, and run without interference.

I stood there feeling like I was in a time warp. Had cricket somehow managed to survive here in the mountains when it had perished everywhere else on the island? I went over to a light-skinned boy with a blond afro after he was done batting. I asked him to explain why they were playing bat and ball. The most I could get out of him or anyone else there was that they always had and likely always would.

I never did track down the origins of this particular game, and I guess I'm glad that I didn't.

A power outage cuts the lights and the music ceases, interrupting my reveries. Candles stuck in *Presidente* beer bottles quickly appear, but the dancing is over. I tell one of the dancers that she dances the way Alfredo Griffin plays short. She tugs her tee-shirt down over her swimsuit, smiles, and replies that "Here, the boys play baseball, but the girls dance."

And in my mind's eye, down on the beach, a young boy lofts another chunk of coral into the air and lines it into the Caribbean.

Afterword: May 1998

The pungent fragrance of cane being ground into sugar hangs over Guachupita, a *barrio* not far from *Ingenio* Consuelo, just as it always does this time of the year. Haitian cutters sweat in nearby fields, filling railroad cars and oxen-driven carts with cane. But Roberto Caines, whose ability to fix the sugar mill's ancient water pumps made him indispensable during past grinding seasons, no longer finds his days tied to the rhythms of the harvest. Now seventy-one, Caines has retired. He looks younger, less tired, than he did when working for the *ingenio*. Between his millworker's pension and social security, the long-time community and sport activist receives about $165 a month. He earns a smaller sum working for the government in a program that Juan Marichal set up to help youth develop their baseball skills in the schools.

When I first met Roberto Caines over a decade ago, he told me that Franklyn, his youngest son, was the best ballplayer in the family. None of his and wife Alicia's twelve other children had displayed as much aptitude for the game. Though I knew that Roberto had worked with many of Consuelo's best ballplayers when they were young, I dismissed his talk of Franklyn's potential as fatherly pride. Then ten, Frankie Caines was a quiet boy who sometimes came along as his father took me through the dirt streets and paths of Consuelo, explaining its history.

When I visited Guachupita in December 1994, Roberto was a short distance away in San Pedro de Macoris, waiting in an office, hassling over his pension. But Franklyn, then seventeen years old and a man-child standing 6'2" and weighing 170 pounds, was at home. He had graduated from the *Liga Caines*, a neighborhood youth league that his father ran, to sign a contract with the Philadelphia Phillies. His bonus was $3,000, meager by U.S. standards, but more money than the family had ever seen at one time.

If Franklyn Caines makes it to the majors, he will join the dozen or so men from Consuelo who have put the sugar cane estate on the baseball map. If Franklyn becomes a big leaguer, the lives of his family will change for the better. The odds, though, are not in his favor. They rarely are for any one boy, despite the growing importance of baseball's Dominican outpost.

Twice as many Dominicans play major league ball than a decade ago. Felipe Alou is widely regarded as one of the game's outstanding managers; Pedro Martínez became the first Dominican to win the Cy Young award in

1997; and Sammy Sosa, Moises Alou, Raul Mondesí, Manny Ramírez, and Alex Rodriguez are among the late nineties' new contingent of Dominican stars.

Almost a tenth of all major leaguers come from this nation of eight million people. Only California, with over four times the population, sends more of its sons to the majors. On a per capita basis, the Dominican Republic is number one. It leads a Latin cohort which made up between 18 and 19 percent of all players on opening-day rosters in 1998. Latin players now outnumber African-Americans in the majors. Their presence is even greater in the minors, where they make up about 36 percent of all players; almost two-thirds of all Latin minor leaguers come from the Dominican Republic. But only a few of them will make it to the majors and join Sammy Sosa and Pedro Martínez among sport's new aristocrats. Sosa, a Consuelo native who spent most of his youth in San Pedro, first signed with the Texas Rangers for $3,500 in 1985. In 1997, the Chicago Cubs' powerful rightfielder signed a four-year, $42.5 million contract. Martínez, who originally signed with the Dodgers in 1988 for $5,000, dethroned Sosa as the highest paid Dominican big leaguer ever when he signed a six-year, $75 million contract with the Boston Red Sox not long afterward.

Baseball has become a substantial Dominican industry. Dominican major leaguers collectively earned about $70 million in 1997, a figure that will spiral higher in coming years. With over a thousand Dominicans in the Dominican Summer League (DSL), several hundred more in North America's major and minor leagues, a few dozen on Asian teams, and still more playing in the Dominican winter league or working for major league or Dominican clubs, baseball has emerged as a sizable employer. "And the money now!" says Pedro González with a whoop. "There's so much money involved right now that we are changing the game." During the mid-1980s, aspiring pros spoke in hushed tones about the $400,000 a year contracts that major league stars were signing; now they talk of salaries ten to twenty times larger.

Like most Dominican boys who sign with a major league organization, Franklyn Caines got his first taste of pro ball in the Dominican Summer League. Begun in 1985 with a handful of teams, the DSL now employs over a thousand young players. Along with the academies that a growing number of clubs have built on the island, the DSL is the most visible and important result of major league baseball's expanded Dominican presence. Affiliated with major league baseball, it allows the clubs to develop players for whom they cannot obtain visas to play in the United States. Major league clubs divide a total of only 865 visas a year for their minor league players, severely limiting the number of foreigners in any organization who are allowed into the United States. Players on the twenty-five-man roster are not included in this figure. But thirty-two clubs, each with thirty active and five reserve players on their rosters, compete in a seventy-two-game Dominican Summer

League season. An eight-team summer league has also played since 1997 in Venezuela, which now sends the most players to the majors from the Caribbean basin after the Dominican Republic.

These leagues, the lowest rungs in the minors, are the entry point into the industry for most Latin boys. Many of the players, who range in age from seventeen to nineteen, live up to ten months a year at the academies that their respective organizations run in the Dominican Republic. There, they study baseball as assiduously as seminary students read the Scriptures.

After returning to Pittsburgh, I looked for Franklyn Caines's name on the rosters of the Phillies' minor league teams in the States. When it failed to appear in both the 1995 and 1996 seasons, I concluded that, like most boys, he had been released before ever making it off the island. Then last summer, I spotted Franklyn Caines on the Phillies' Martinsville, Virginia, roster in the Appalachian League. Though the lowest of the six Philadelphia minor league affiliates in the United States, Martinsville meant that Franklyn's dreams of making it to the majors were still alive. His play had improved steadily during three seasons in the DSL, allowing him to get off the island, a major accomplishment most boys in the Dominican Summer League never achieve. Franklyn performed well for Martinsville and, though he was uncertain about his baseball future when we spoke at the end of the season, he assured me he would work as hard as he could that winter. But when I returned to Consuelo in May 1998, I was afraid that I would find him back at home, out of baseball.

"No, no, Franklyn is in the United States," Alicia Caines assured me as she showed me a picture of her youngest child in a Phillies uniform. Her son was a world away, but Alicia drew comfort in knowing that other Dominican players were with him.

"Franklyn Caines is a quality young man," his manager, Greg Legg, commented. "He can be so valuable here, not only on the field, but in the clubhouse." Legg praised Franklyn's make-up, character, and heart and called him a leader among the Dominican players, for whom he sometimes interprets. But to stay in baseball, Franklyn must have what Legg called a breakthrough year. "Franklyn needs to swing the bat, show a little pop, be an RBI guy, hit about .275–.280, and improve his defense." He's probably got through next season to show that he can.

Even before he left for the States, Franklyn Caines had entered a baseball world unimaginable during his father's youth. Nor did Pedro González and Junior Noboa, who began minor league play in the late 1950s and early 1980s, respectively, experience anything like the DSL. In their day, you had to leave the island to play in the minors. Now, you can study baseball, play minor league ball, and even end your career without ever stepping foot in the United States—all while under the control of a major league organization.

If the Dominican game that Franklyn Caines plays with all his heart has changed little since when his father played it on the streets of Consuelo, the business of baseball has. Driven by sport's escalating economics, the Dominican sector of the industry has exploded in size and now encompasses a growing infrastructure of academies. Agents, meanwhile, intervene at earlier stages in the players' careers. More than ever before, Dominican baseball is a satellite that revolves around the major league sun. But without breaking out of that orbit, some Dominicans have sought to influence its trajectory.

Pedro González knows the Caines family and has seen thousands of boys like Franklyn who want to play major league baseball. "The kids here, they're still hungry," affirmed González, the long-time Atlanta Braves Caribbean *jefe*. "Five boys showed up at my door this morning, on a Sunday! 'Pedro,' they say, 'you going to practice today?' I told them not today, but come for breakfast tomorrow and then we'll go to the park." It's like that most mornings outside González's home.

Junior Noboa witnesses the same phenomenon just as often. As the Arizona Diamondbacks' Latin American Coordinator, Noboa guides the development of about forty young Dominicans and other Latins at the academy that the team shares with the Toronto Blue Jays in Boca Chica.

Six to ten *chicos* make their way to the secluded complex daily, walking down the unpaved road from the highway. Bare-butted boys play in the dust in front of zinc-roofed shacks as motorcycles bounce by. A few older boys and a girl shoot hoops at a basket whose backboard bears a stencil of the Tasmanian Devil cartoon character.

"When I signed to play seventeen years ago," the thirty-four-year-old Noboa reflects, "we had nothing like this." He sits in the shade of a dugout by one of the complex's four beautifully manicured fields. The walls are painted in the club's teal and black colors, with a huge diamondback rattler rearing its head behind home plate. The complex, which houses upward of a hundred players, has two identical wings, each with a dorm, dining hall, classroom, exercise facility, and recreation room. A cluster of saguaro cacti designates the Arizona side. Two huge dish parabolas squatting atop the second floor, powered by the complex's own electrical generators, insure a steady stream of televised games. Batting and pitching cages stand nearby. Though spartan, the accommodations are far better than most of the players have ever known.

"Baseball is their opportunity to get a good life," Noboa concludes as he points at players practicing relay throws and cutoffs after a game against the Toronto farmhands. "They're doing what they love to do and have the opportunity to go to the U.S. and start a new life." Some will stay in the States after being released, work and save money, and then return home. A few never come back. "They are so hungry to be players," Noboa attests. "You know we love baseball. Baseball is in our blood *and* it is the opportunity to have a good life. Baseball right now is probably the best job in the world."

For Dominican boys, that's been so for most of the last twenty years. It's certainly better than working at the nearby *ingenio* or hawking Haitian paintings and carvings on the beach at Boca Chica. The free trade zones, whose presence grows yearly, pay less than these boys make in the Dominican Summer League, where salaries are $800 a month for first-year players, $950 a month for their second season. Unskilled hotel work in the tourist industry, the Caribbean's largest, can't compete either. A player who makes it to the majors and earns the minimum salary for a season has, by Dominican standards, hit the *lotería*. In major league baseball, the average salary, which passed the million dollar plateau in the 1990s, is more than the entire population of a village might earn in a year. But those who don't make it are often left with little. For many, more opportunity has meant only greater disappointment or exploitation.

Baseball columnist Stephen Bray, who recently spent six months in San Pedro, pointed out to me that, while "a few fortunate youngsters" will benefit from major league baseball's growing presence there, "it also magnifies the illusion of baseball as a means of escape from a life of poverty." It's a paradox, Bray concluded. "The dream of a major league career grows ever larger for thousands of kids, but the gap between the promise of baseball and the daily reality for most Dominicans becomes wider."

Though Noboa's charges can read and write, over half have not finished high school. They left school to play baseball. "I know they have made a mistake," Noboa sighs. He encourages them to continue their studies, and four of his players go to school at night or in the afternoon. All study English at the academy.

The Arizona Diamondbacks began working in the Dominican Republic in September 1995 and opened the academy fourteen months later. The Diamondbacks were lured here by the quality of players and the chance to maximize the impact of their investment. It costs far less to sign young Latins than prospects in the United States who are subject to the rules of the amateur draft. With many first-round draft picks now signing for over a million dollars, Latin youth are an even better bargain than they once were. But signed at a younger age and lacking the nutritional and medical advantages of their North American counterparts, they need help and time to develop their potential. "We have to make them into players," Noboa explains. Latin players mature later, he contends, and most scouts agree. Many of the Diamondback players gain twenty to twenty-five pounds before leaving the island. Exposed to better instruction than most young signees received in the past, they also have a leg up in making the tremendous cultural leap that accompanies the first plane ride from Santo Domingo to the United States. Noboa signed at the age of sixteen and left almost immediately for Batavia, New York. "I was crying every single day."

Noboa's affection for his players is evident. So is his pride in the complex, which he built. "This was a dream I had," he says, gesturing to the fields and buildings before his palm-sized cellular phone beeps for the second time. An injury in 1991 forced him to think about what he would do when his playing days were over. The Dodgers were then the only club with a state-of-the-art facility in the Dominican Republic. Noboa decided to build one himself and rent it to a club. He met with over a dozen organizations, spent the money he had saved playing ball, and with a friend, Edmundo González, borrowed still more from the banks. The complex cost over a million dollars and Noboa says it's not yet fully complete.

A boy has about one and a half to two years before he either heads north to play in the minors or is let go. So far, Noboa has sent over twenty of the sixty-five Dominicans he's signed to the States and released almost as many. Because Arizona is an expansion franchise, it has more openings in its system than most organizations. "For me," he confides, "it's hard when I have to make a decision and release a player. I was a player. I know how hard they have tried to make money for their family. I've cried with some of them."

Sensing the possible future if they make it and knowing all too well their prospects if they don't, the youth listen attentively to Noboa and the other instructors. They work out from about 8:15 in the morning until 2:00 in the afternoon, then eat, rest, study English, and lift weights or hit in the batting cages. Although the clouds make it almost bearable, they're playing ball in sweltering heat. Boys their age cut cane for about two dollars a day not far away.

This is the first privately built complex, but it probably won't be the last. Several former players are considering comparable projects, according to Noboa. These developments reflect a new level of Dominican participation in the game. No longer simply raw material or supervisors for the baseball industry, some Dominicans are becoming stakeholders, if at a lower level of involvement.

Major league baseball once had the field to itself. Then, in November 1990, the Hiroshima Toyo Carp built a first-class academy near Consuelo and began to compete for players. Several of their recruits have since played in the Japanese leagues and one, Robinson Checo, was subsequently sold to the Boston Red Sox. Now, Pedro González, Noboa, and others maintain, the level of competition for talent is simply incredible. Each of them tracks several boys whom they hope to sign as soon as they reach the minimum age to do so. Rumors abound of underage boys hidden from the competition.

The latest entrants in the Dominican talent hunt are not teams but agents from the United States who seek to represent young Dominicans before they sign their first contract. Representation can boost a legitimate prospect's signing bonus, although it might cause clubs to lose interest in marginal talent. Judging a young boy's potential is more of an art than a science, notes González.

For decades, clubs have taken advantage of young players' naiveté, poverty, and lack of bargaining clout to sign them for extremely low bonuses. In a recent and historic reversal, two players won their release from contracts they had initially signed when they were underage and then reaped huge bonuses upon signing legal ones. Both had agents. One player, Josephang Bernhardt, is a shortstop from San Pedro; the other, Ricardo Aramboles, is a pitcher from Sabana Perdida, a *barrio* in Santo Domingo. Both signed for relatively small amounts before they were seventeen, the legal minimum age. But when the estimation of their abilities soared, they were able to have their initial contracts invalidated. After their agents auctioned them off, Bernhardt signed for $1.1 million with the Bluejays, while Aramboles, who was fourteen when first signed, accepted a $1.52 million bonus from the Yankees. Though the clubs have become more diligent about verifying birth certificates, they are wary of being deceived and realize they have lost some of their leverage.

A sixteen-year-old can sign if he will turn seventeen during the DSL season; if he becomes seventeen after the season, he can sign on July 2 but cannot play until the following year. Most signing bonuses are still $5,000 and below, few surpass $35,000. But the bonuses that Bernhardt and Aramboles received had an impact. Increasingly sophisticated Dominican families are seeking fair market value for their sons, too. They would like them to make as much as those drafted in the United States.

Not only U.S. agents but a few Dominicans are seeking to represent players before they sign. Sammy Sosa is the latest to make his presence known. Sosa, who has emerged as one of the game's consistent sluggers, has been active in San Pedro, where he owns a commercial strip called the "30-30 Plaza" to celebrate his feat of hitting thirty home runs and stealing thirty bases in the same season. Like many Dominican stars, Sosa returns home in the off-season and is well-regarded for his community involvement. Pedro Martínez built a church in his hometown, Manoguayabo, and gave his Cy Young Award trophy to Juan Marichal, who graciously returned it. Sosa sends computers to Dominican schools and persuaded Michael Jordan to visit the country. He's also started his own baseball academy in *Barrio* Mexico.

Twenty or so boys wearing uniforms with an "S" on their caps run laps in the early morning sun as a handful of instructors sit in the shade. Across the street is a prison for women and juveniles; the *Ingenio* Colon's smokestack is visible over right field. The boys, aged sixteen to eighteen, live in a nearby dorm. Their daily regimen is similar to that at a major league club's academy. David de la Cruz, a boyhood teammate of Sosa who directs the less-than-a-year-old-Sosa Academy, says it will better prepare youth for a baseball future. But some scouts question the level of instruction the players receive; others believe the academy is trying to position itself to sell players to major league teams. Just as street agents attach themselves to prospective college basketball players in the States, agents are drawn to potential clients, even if they are underaged. They want a piece of the action, too.

Winter league play, which hit a low ebb a decade ago because of the impact of escalating salaries in the States and the Dominican's general socio-economic malaise, has recovered somewhat but remains precarious. In coming years, it will depend more than ever on minor leaguers on the cusp than on major league veterans. The government subsidizes stadium rents and insures that electricity will be available, but teams struggle to pay salaries attractive enough to lure players making millions in the majors. "I don't see any real advances for the winter league," Pedro González states frankly. "I don't see any progress in facilities, but the quality of play is fine."

Though globalization will continue to transform baseball here, an informal band of men who have played, managed, and cared for the game insures that it is still grounded in Dominican sensibilities. Pedro González is one of them. After over forty years in baseball, he remains consumed by the game. His mornings are spent teaching at the ballpark, afternoons watching kids play. "I'm not going to find a Sammy Sosa, a Moises Alou at home," he laughs. At night, he watches major league games on television, featuring many of the boys he's helped. His peers, Rafael Avila, Luis Silverio, Nelson Norman, César Geronimo, Mateo Alou, and dozens more like them, guarantee that many boys receive the best of instruction and advice.

Their ranks are refreshed by former stars like Alfredo Griffin and Tony Peña. Once opponents on the ballfield, they continue their rivalries as managers for their old teams. Griffin no longer performs his magic in the infield; he now guides the *Estrellas Orientales* in San Pedro. The irrepressible Peña retired from the majors in 1997, after eighteen seasons, fourth among all catchers in the number of games behind home plate. He became player-manager for *Aguilas* in Santiago for the 1997–98 season. In what was probably his last at-bat ever in the Dominican Republic, Peña drove in the winning run to send *Aguilas* to the Caribbean Championships. "It was a very emotional moment," explains Winston Llenas, Peña's friend and former winter league manager. *Aguilas*, reinforced by other Dominican players, then won the Caribbean Championships, their second title in a row.

Llenas is another of the men who have molded Dominican baseball in recent decades. One of the winter league's all-time hitting leaders, Llenas managed *Aguilas* during the 1980s before becoming their general manager. Since 1989, Llenas has also directed international scouting for the Cleveland Indians. "Baseball here is the same," he reflects in Santiago, "but the people are different. We have been invaded by the networks. We've gone global and the money changes people." With ballplayers now making far more money, contracts and endorsements take precedence over playing. "It's been very hard on the fans," Llenas concludes, "knowing that baseball players don't take the game as seriously. Somehow, we're ruining the love of the game for them and the fans. It's sad. How can they enjoy it as much as we once did?"

Perhaps they cannot, but men like Llenas, Roberto Caines, and Juan Marichal help renew baseball at its grassroots. Caines and Rico Carty are among those working in a program run by Juan Marichal, the Hall-of-Fame pitcher and now Minister of Sport, who has promoted baseball instruction in the schools. That effort might persuade some to pursue sport without forsaking their education.

Professor Manuel Joaquín Báez Vargas, one of the most distinguished men I met in my Dominican travels, would have appreciated that. This stalwart, who did so much to build Dominican sport, has passed on. Luis Alfau, a founder of *Escogido*, and the incomparable Horacio Martínez are gone, too. So are Luis Carty and the Rev. Joseph Ainslie, better known as *Padre* José, who helped make Consuelo one of the most incredible stories in baseball history, and a number of the other men and women who shared their thoughts with me.

Their deaths make the connections with the past more fragile. But there are those—like Professor Báez Vargas's dear friend, Pedro Julio Santana; the indefatigable Cuqui Cordova; and Renaissance man Bernardo Vega, now ambassador to the United States—who still remember and convey their passion and knowledge to younger Dominicans.

I've been back to the Dominican Republic six times since this book was first published in 1991, most recently in May 1998. Although much of the country seems suspended in time, the Dominican Republic has hardly stood still. A widened highway connects Santo Domingo with Santiago, making the once harrowing trip shorter and safer. A phalanx of U.S. fast food franchises has taken up position at key downtown intersections. Cell phones are *de rigeur* for the growing middle class and vendors hawk telecommunications peripherals, along with mangos and limes, to passing motorists. The Dominican Republic, which had the western hemisphere's highest increase in GNP in 1997, is also the most wired nation in the Caribbean. Optimism about the future is more apparent than it has been in the past. Though poverty and underdevelopment remain grave problems, this nation might yet escape the depressing cycles that have plagued other third world countries.

What could these changes mean for baseball? As a sector of the economy, the sport will grow larger and stronger. But as the Dominican Republic becomes less insular, as it shucks an authoritarian past and refashions its national identity from elements other than baseball, the game will no longer need to fill the cultural and political roles it has for much of the last century.

If the Dominican Republic does break free of the past, the 1996 presidential election will likely be seen as a watershed. Widely regarded as the fairest election in Dominican history, it catapulted Leonel Fernández into office. Basketball—not baseball—is Leonel's game and that says something about where Dominican culture is heading.

I first met Leonel in the late 1980s when he sat in on an interview with Juan Bosch, the nation's former president. I found Leonel perceptive and *simpático* and made a point of spending time with him on subsequent visits. He was especially interested in the democratic transition gaining momentum throughout Latin America.

Leonel was tired but remarkably calm when I caught up with him during the 1996 campaign. The people, however, were even more excited than at the ballpark. Usually when I go for a run in Santo Domingo, it's a solitary jog along the *malecón*, the palm-fringed promendade by the sea. But that June evening, I was surrounded by over a thousand Dominicans chanting *Ruge! Ruge! El León!* (Roar! Roar! The Lion!) and chasing Leonel's motorcade through the streets of the capital. Leonel sat atop a van at the head of the parade, preceded by a soundtruck blaring his campaign's *merengue*.

Tiny girls, their mothers in curlers, and grandmothers danced on rooftops as the caravan passed below them. They were still jubilant after the results made Fernández their next president a few weeks later. The election was the Dominican Republic's best opportunity yet to turn the page on a twisted past that reads like a novel by Gabriel García Márquez.

Leonel observed that the people "see the potential president as a personal friend who will transform their personal despair into hope." Those expectations can become enormous in a country with such difficult problems. Frustration over his administration's inability to resolve them quickly—especially constant electric power outages—led protesters into the streets in the fall of 1997. Baseball helped stabilize a volatile situation. Jubilation over Pedro Martínez winning the Cy Young award, followed by the young pitcher's appearance at the site of an angry confrontation, did much to ease tensions.

During my May 1998 visit, the election of a new congress marked the halfway point of Leonel's term in office. A day after Mark Cohen and I arrived, José Francisco Peña Gómez, Leonel's opponent in the 1996 election, succumbed to cancer. His party, the *Partido Revolucionario Dominicano*, swept to victory in the emotional outpouring that followed its gallant warrior's death. Political power will be divided during the next two years, perhaps paralyzing Fernández's initiatives, but democracy seems more firmly in place.

Peña Gómez, the charismatic former mayor of Santo Domingo, was a fervent baseball fan who once worked as a broadcaster. Leonel, too, has baseball in his blood. During the years he lived in Manhattan during the 1960s, other boys called him Marichal. When he became president, Leonel appointed his hero as the Minister of Sport. But in his campaign, Leonel highlighted basketball instead of baseball.

Leonel's first television spot featured him shooting jump shots and dunking the ball (on a lowered hoop, he confessed). The ad underscored Leonel's youth and the passing of the old guard. It also reflected how much the Dominican Republic has been affected by global hip hop culture.

The *nueva gente* I had met playing basketball a decade ago in Santiago are now out in full force. They can be found not only in the Dominican Republic, but across the Caribbean basin. I've even seen them in my classes at the University of Pittsburgh, which have included several Dominican Yorks there on basketball scholarships. Each time I return to the Dominican Republic, more and better basketball is played and even more basketball apparel is worn.

Boys bounce basketballs in the dirt of *Barrio La Loma* near the *Rio Higuamo* in Consuelo. They practice finger rolls at baskets lacking nets and backboards while Dominican rap music rocks nearby houses. Pedro González laughs as he tells me "You'd be surprised how many boys I invite to the ball park who say 'No, no, Pedro, I want to play basketball.' They're 6′6″, 6′7″ and I say let me make a pitcher out of you but no, basketball's their game."

The ascendancy of basketball, the most popular sport among teenagers worldwide, suggests how much traditional Dominican culture is changing. The nation's insularity, like its authoritarian political heritage, is disappearing rapidly.

Most Dominican boys still turn to baseball first; the tangible rewards of such a career choice are much more evident. The question is not whether baseball will continue to grow in the foreseeable future. History, momentum, and money insure that. The question, I think, is whether the Dominican Republic can hold on to a sense of baseball's rich past and redefine the sport's complex array of meanings as it rushes pell-mell toward the next century.

Index